ging lives

ResultsPlusRevision

Edexcel GCSE

History A

The Making of the Modern World

Units 1–3

With diagnostic tests on CD-ROM

A PEARSON COMPANY

How to use the book and CD-ROM

Welcome to the ResultsPlus Revision guide for Edexcel's Modern World History.

This book will help you prepare for your exams with more confidence. It contains the key information you need to know, along with plenty of practice questions and tips from the people that write and mark your exams.

But before you start revising, why not take a diagnostic test? This will help you to identify what you already know and where you need to improve.

Insert the CD-ROM and follow the easy installation instructions. Then choose a test from the Tests menu. You can take each diagnostic test as many times as you want! Your latest results will be saved on your computer.

After taking a test, click on the Results tab. The Analysis screen shows your scores, question-by-question. Test review lets you look back at your answers and compare them with the correct answers. And your personalised skills map shows you how you performed in each area of your course. By copying across the red, amber and green symbols to the revision tracker at the front of your book, you can see where to spend more time revising...

The book is divided into the units and topics from your specification.

Each section explains what you need to know about that topic. We've also included some helpful ResultsPlus features.

There are 12 tests on the CD. You need to take 5 of them:

Tests 1-6 cover the topics in Unit 1. You need to check which three Sections of Unit 1 you are doing in the exam, before you do the test. Tests 7-9 cover the three options in Unit 2, and Tests 10-12 those in Unit 3. You only take the test for the exam you are doing in each case.

SuperFacts and Answering questions

There are two types of pages in this book. SuperFacts pages tell you what you need to learn. Answering questions pages help you practice the skills you need to do well.

SuperFacts all you need to learn, broken down into 20–25 'SuperFacts'.

Section summary gives you a quick overview of the topic.

Edexcel key terms words and phrases that you need to recall and use in your exams.

What you need to do ***tells*** you how to answer each question and get top marks.

How you do it ***shows*** you how to do it.

Unit 2 Modern World Depth Study

Answering questions: Question 1 (c)

Question 1 (c) will always ask you to '**explain the effects**' of something.

What you need to do
The best answers will:

- state not one, but **two** effects
- **support** each effect with extra factual **detail** to write a developed statement
- use this detail to **explain how** each effect happened
- and show **links** or connections between the effects.

How you do it
Take this question as an example:

Explain the effects of the Treaty of Versailles on Germany 1918–23.

The SuperFacts on pages 56–57 will provide us with the information to answer thi
question. The titles of the relevant SuperFacts have been listed on this page to hel

The SuperFacts suggest the following **effect** and **supporting detail**.

Effect	Supporting detail
One effect on Germany of the Treaty of Versailles was economic problems.	For example, reparations were set at £6,600m This damaged German industry and government finances.

Notice how we have made it very clear to the examiner how we are answering the question. We have:

- use **two** sentences, one for the **effect** and one for the **supporting detail**.
- started each sentence with 'signposts' to show what we are doing, but saying '**effect was ...**' and '**For example ...**'

Use this approach when you write answers.

Now test yourself
The SuperFacts suggest another effect was **political problems**. Using this second
write in the boxes below to show that you can set out the **effect** and **supporting d**
[You can check your answer in the top box on page 67.]

Effect	Supporting detail
(i)	(ii)

SuperFacts

The Treaty of Versailles The new Weimar government had to accept the Treaty. But this caused unrest. Germans called it a diktat because they were not part of the negotiations. They said that, by accepting it, the new government had given Germany a 'stab in the back' (*dolchstoss*) – and called them 'the November Criminals'.

Political problems The new Weimar government was blamed for Versailles and the economic problems. Many German workers supported left-wing parties, like the communists (KPD). Many ex-soldiers and landowners supported right-wing parties.

Political unrest over Versailles and the economic problems led to frequent strikes and protests. Between 1919 and 1922, there were 376 political murders.

The Spartacists, a communist group, led uprisings all over Germany in 1919. They thought the Weimar Republic was run by the middle-class. They wanted workers' councils to run the country. The government ended the revolt violently, using the *Freikorps* (anti-communist private armies formed after the war by ex-officers).

The Kapp Putsch (1920), led by Wolfgang Kapp, was a right-wing revolt to get the Kaiser back into power: 5,000 rebels took control of Berlin. The government promoted a general strike by workers. The city was paralysed and the revolt failed.

66

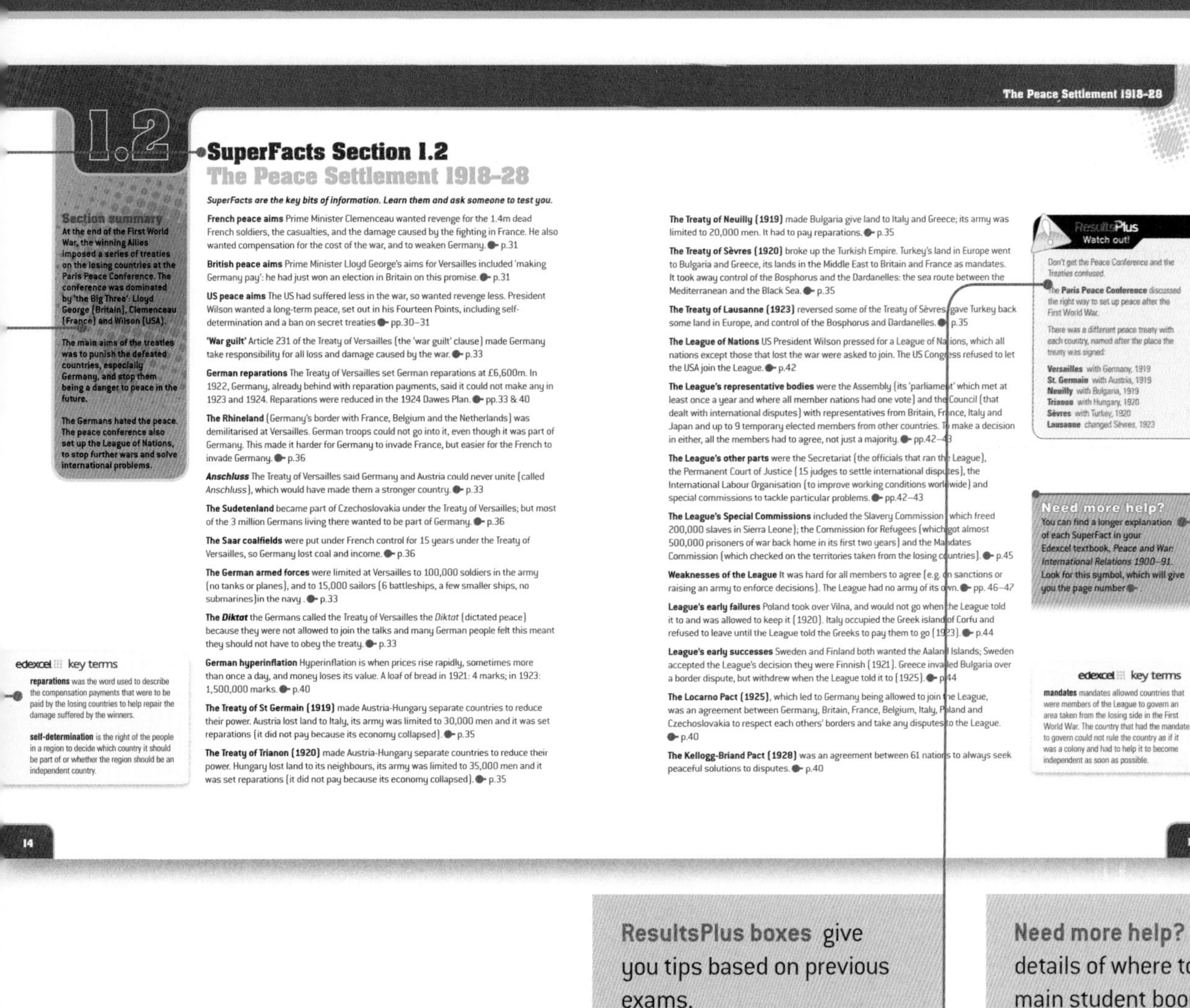

1.2

SuperFacts Section 1.2

The Peace Settlement 1918–28

SuperFacts are the key bits of information. Learn them and ask someone to test you.

Section summary

At the end of the First World War, the winning Allies imposed a series of treaties on the losing countries at the Paris Peace Conference. The conference was dominated by 'the Big Three': Lloyd George (Britain), Clemenceau (France) and Wilson (USA).

The main aims of the treaties was to punish the defeated countries, especially Germany, and stop them being a danger to peace in the future.

The Germans hated the peace. The peace conference also set up the League of Nations, to stop further wars and solve international problems.

French peace aims Prime Minister Clemenceau wanted revenge for the 1.4m dead French soldiers, the casualties, and the damage caused by the fighting in France. He also wanted compensation for the cost of the war, and to weaken Germany. p.31

British peace aims Prime Minister Lloyd George's aims for Versailles included 'making Germany pay': he had just won an election in Britain on this promise. p.31

US peace aims The US had suffered less in the war, so wanted revenge less. President Wilson wanted a long-term peace, set out in his Fourteen Points, including self-determination and a ban on secret treaties pp.30–31

'War guilt' Article 231 of the Treaty of Versailles (the 'war guilt' clause) made Germany take responsibility for all loss and damage caused by the war. p.33

German reparations The Treaty of Versailles set German reparations at £6,600m. In 1922, Germany, already behind with reparation payments, said it could not make any in 1923 and 1924. Reparations were reduced in the 1924 Dawes Plan. pp.33 & 40

The Rhineland (Germany's border with France, Belgium and the Netherlands) was demilitarised at Versailles. German troops could not go into it, even though it was part of Germany. This made it harder for Germany to invade France, but easier for the French to invade Germany. p.36

Anschluss The Treaty of Versailles said Germany and Austria could never unite (called *Anschluss*), which would have made them a stronger country. p.33

The Sudetenland became part of Czechoslovakia under the Treaty of Versailles; but most of the 3 million Germans living there wanted to be part of Germany. p.36

The Saar coalfields were put under French control for 15 years under the Treaty of Versailles, so Germany lost coal and income. p.36

The German armed forces were limited at Versailles to 100,000 soldiers in the army (no tanks or planes), and to 15,000 sailors (6 battleships, a few smaller ships, no submarines)in the navy . p.33

The *Diktat* the Germans called the Treaty of Versailles the *Diktat* (dictated peace) because they were not allowed to join the talks and many German people felt this meant they should not have to obey the treaty. p.33

German hyperinflation Hyperinflation is when prices rise rapidly, sometimes more than once a day, and money loses its value. A loaf of bread in 1921: 4 marks; in 1923: 1,500,000 marks. p.40

The Treaty of St Germain (1919) made Austria-Hungary separate countries to reduce their power. Austria lost land to Italy, its army was limited to 30,000 men and it was set reparations (it did not pay because its economy collapsed). p.35

The Treaty of Trianon (1920) made Austria-Hungary separate countries to reduce their power. Hungary lost land to its neighbours, its army was limited to 35,000 men and it was set reparations (it did not pay because its economy collapsed). p.35

The Treaty of Neuilly (1919) made Bulgaria give land to Italy and Greece; its army was limited to 20,000 men. It had to pay reparations. p.35

The Treaty of Sèvres (1920) broke up the Turkish Empire. Turkey's land in Europe went to Bulgaria and Greece, its lands in the Middle East to Britain and France as mandates. It took away control of the Bosphorus and the Dardanelles: the sea route between the Mediterranean and the Black Sea. p.35

The Treaty of Lausanne (1923) reversed some of the Treaty of Sèvres, gave Turkey back some land in Europe, and control of the Bosphorus and Dardanelles. p.35

The League of Nations US President Wilson pressed for a League of Nations, which all nations except those that lost the war were asked to join. The US Congress refused to let the USA join the League. p.42

The League's representative bodies were the Assembly (its 'parliament' which met at least once a year and where all member nations had one vote) and the Council (that dealt with international disputes) with representatives from Britain, France, Italy and Japan and up to 9 temporary elected members from other countries. To make a decision in either, all the members had to agree, not just a majority. pp.42–43

The League's other parts were the Secretariat (the officials that ran the League), the Permanent Court of Justice (15 judges to settle international disputes), the International Labour Organisation (to improve working conditions worldwide) and special commissions to tackle particular problems. pp.42–43

The League's Special Commissions included the Slavery Commission (which freed 200,000 slaves in Sierra Leone); the Commission for Refugees (which got almost 500,000 prisoners of war back home in its first two years) and the Mandates Commission (which checked on the territories taken from the losing countries). p.45

Weaknesses of the League It was hard for all members to agree (e.g. on sanctions or raising an army to enforce decisions). The League had no army of its own. pp. 46–47

League's early failures Poland took over Vilna, and would not go when the League told it to and was allowed to keep it (1920). Italy occupied the Greek island of Corfu and refused to leave until the League told the Greeks to pay them to go (1923). p.44

League's early successes Sweden and Finland both wanted the Aaland Islands; Sweden accepted the League's decision they were Finnish (1921). Greece invaded Bulgaria over a border dispute, but withdrew when the League told it to (1925). p.44

The Locarno Pact (1925), which led to Germany being allowed to join the League, was an agreement between Germany, Britain, France, Belgium, Italy, Poland and Czechoslovakia to respect each others' borders and take any disputes to the League. p.40

The Kellogg-Briand Pact (1928) was an agreement between 61 nations to always seek peaceful solutions to disputes. p.40

ResultsPlus Watch out!

Don't get the Peace Conference and the Treaties confused.

The **Paris Peace Conference** discussed the right way to set up peace after the First World War.

There was a different peace treaty with each country, named after the place the treaty was signed:

Versailles with Germany, 1919
St. Germain with Austria, 1919
Neuilly with Bulgaria, 1919
Trianon with Hungary, 1920
Sèvres with Turkey, 1920
Lausanne changed Sèvres, 1923

Need more help?
You can find a longer explanation of each SuperFact in your Edexcel textbook, *Peace and War: International Relations 1900–91*. Look for this symbol, which will give you the page number.

edexcel key terms

reparations was the word used to describe the compensation payments that were to be paid by the losing countries to help repair the damage suffered by the winners.

self-determination is the right of the people in a region to decide which country it should be part of or whether the region should be an independent country.

edexcel key terms

mandates mandates allowed countries that were members of the League to govern an area taken from the losing side in the First World War. The country that had the mandate to govern could not rule the country as if it was a colony and had to help it to become independent as soon as possible.

ResultsPlus boxes give you tips based on previous exams.

Need more help? gives details of where to look in the main student book for more information.

king the answer better
this is not enough. The best answers will **explain how** the effect happened.
e is an example of how you can use supporting detail to explain how the effect
opened. This time, we have used **political problems** as our example.

fect and supporting detail	Explanation of how the effect happened
ne effect on Germany of the eaty of Versailles was political oblems. The new Weimar overnment had to accept the eaty. But this caused unrest.	People said the new government had given Germany a 'stab in the back'; they called them 'the November Criminals'. The Treaty caused political problems because it made many German workers support left-wing parties, like the KPD, while many soldiers and landowners supported right-wing parties. Some people felt so strongly that they supported uprisings like the Spartacist revolt in 1919 and the Kapp Putsch in 1920.

w test yourself
Write in the box to show that you can explain how the effect happened.

fect and supporting detail	Explanation of how the effect happened
ne effect on Germany the Treaty of Versailles as economic problems. For ample, reparations were set £6,600m. This damaged erman industry and overnment finances.	(iii)

u can check your answer on page 74.)

final touch
very best answers show links between effects. So, now try this.
Write a paragraph to show:
ow the economic problems caused by the Treaty of Versailles
made the political problems worse.
ou find this hard, there is a **[Hint for (iv)]** on page 74. You can also check the answer
e.)
)

SuperFacts

German reparations were set at £6,600 million by the Treaty of Versailles. This damaged German industry and government finances.

German land was taken by the Treaty of Versailles. Around 13% of German land was given to its neighbours, including Alsace and Lorraine, Eupen and Malmedy, Danzig, West Prussia, and Posen. Germany also lost 50% of its iron and 15% of its coal reserves and 11 colonies in Africa. Accepting all this made the Weimar Republic unpopular.

Economic problems The Weimar government was bankrupt: Germany's gold reserves had been spent on the war. Its income was drained by reparation payments. It had also lost the land with its richest coal and iron reserves. Later it faced serious inflation.

The French occupied the Ruhr (1923) when Germany could not pay its reparations. They took raw materials, industrial machines and manufactured goods. The Ruhr had many factories and 80% of Germany's coal production, so Germany's economic problems were made worse.

Hyperinflation meant German money became almost worthless. A loaf of bread in 1919 cost 1 mark; in 1922, 200 marks; and in 1923, 100,000 million marks. In 1918, you could exchange 20 marks for £1. By 1923, you needed 20 billion marks for £1.

All Germans suffered as vital goods were hard to purchase. Many workers became unemployed. The pensions and savings of the middle-classes became worthless. This made the government even more unpopular.

Selected SuperFacts are repeated on the questions page to help you learn how to use them to support your answers – this is what many of the marks are for in the exam.

Test yourself gives you ***practice*** so you can be sure you know how to do it. The answers are on another page.

Unit 1 Peace and War: International Relations 1900–91

Unit 2 Modern World Depth Study

Option 2A Germany 1918–39

Option 2B: Russia 1917–39

Option 2C: The USA 1919–41

Unit 3 Modern World Source Enquiry

Section summary

In 1900, the Great Powers (especially Germany, France and Britain) were rivals over trade, colonies and military strength.

European countries formed alliances (both open alliances and secret ones) that led to increasing suspicion and tension between rival nations. This led to an arms race that both sides justified as preparing for defence.

By 1914, this rivalry had produced considerable tensions, especially in the Balkans. When the heir to the Austrian Empire was assassinated in the Balkans, Europe was tipped into a war.

SuperFacts Section 1.1
Why did war break out 1900–14?

SuperFacts are the key bits of information. Learn them and ask someone to test you.

The Triple Alliance (1882) between Germany, Austria-Hungary, and Italy, said these countries would help each other in time of war. It left France isolated and nervous. p.8

The Entente Cordiale (1904) was an agreement between France and Britain not to quarrel over colonies. It strengthened them against the growing power of Germany. p.9

The Triple Entente (1907) was between France, Britain and Russia. It gave them security against the Triple Alliance. Europe split into two powerful, rival groups. p.9

Economic competition In 1913, Britain made about £1.2 million from trade, just ahead of Germany, with £1 million. But by 1914, Germany was producing more iron, more steel, and more cars than Britain. This rivalry caused tension. p.14

Colonial competition Britain and France gained cheap raw materials and export markets in their colonies. These things made them more powerful. Britain took £1000 million in tax and goods just from India from 1750 to 1900. Germany had few colonies and wanted more. This caused tension. p.10

The Algeciras Conference was held in 1906 to discuss Morocco. The Kaiser said it should be independent. He knew France wanted it as a colony. Britain backed France and the conference agreed. Britain also promised troops to help France if it was attacked by Germany. p.11

The Agadir Crisis In 1911, after a rebellion in Morocco, France took over. A German gunboat, the *Panther*, sailed to Agadir and threatened the French. Britain said it would go to war if Germany kept bullying France. Germany had to back down again. p.11

Morocco The two crises in Morocco (Algeciras and Agadir) made war more likely. Twice the Kaiser tested the Entente Cordiale, but the Alliance held and he just made Britain and France keener to resist him. p.11

Naval rivalry Germany began to threaten Britain's naval superiority. In 1898, the Kaiser announced that Germany would build 41 battleships and 61 cruisers. In 1906, Britain responded with the Dreadnought, a much more powerful battleship. From 1906 to 1914 Britain built 29 dreadnoughts and Germany built 17. p.12

The Arms Race As tensions rose, all the Great Powers, except Britain, introduced conscription. By 1914, the German army numbered 1.5 million. Large armies, in rival alliances committed to defend each other, were a dangerous development. p.13

Ottoman weakness in the Balkans The Balkans were divided among surrounding powers, mostly the Ottoman Empire. But the Ottoman Empire was now weak and started to break up. In 1878, Serbia and Bulgaria split from the Ottoman Empire. p.16

edexcel key terms

the Great Powers were Britain, Germany, France, Austria-Hungary, Russia and Italy.

Balkan nationalism Encouraged by Serbia, Slav people in the Balkans demanded that they should be independent. This also threatened Austria-Hungary, where there were millions of Slavs, Czechs, and Croats. p.16

The Great Powers split over the Balkans The Ottoman Empire and Austria-Hungary actively opposed Balkan nationalism. Russia, a Slav country, encouraged it. Britain and France did all they could to protect their Balkan trade routes. p.16 & 18

Bosnian Crisis In 1908, Austria-Hungary ran Bosnia-Herzegovina. The new Turkish government threatened to take Bosnia-Herzegovina back into the Ottoman Empire. So, in September 1908, Austria-Hungary formally annexed Bosnia-Herzegovina. This angered Russia and Balkan nationalists. p.18

The Balkan League In 1911 the Turkish government fell. Balkan states took advantage. Serbia, Greece, Montenegro, and Bulgaria set up the Balkan League. This was a clear threat to the Ottoman and Austrian empires. p.19

The First Balkan War (1912–13) In 1912, the Balkan League attacked the Ottoman Empire and forced it out of Europe. This worried Austria-Hungary. At a conference in London, Austria-Hungary, Britain, and France put pressure on both sides to make peace in 1913. p.19

The Second Balkan War (1913) broke out a month after the first war ended. Balkan states fought each other for land; the Turks joined in too. When fighting stopped, no one was content. Serbia had grown in power, but still wanted more land. p.19

Franz Ferdinand was heir to the throne of Austria. In June 1914 he went to Sarajevo, the capital of Bosnia-Herzegovina. Balkan nationalists resented him being there. Gavrilo Princip, a Serbian nationalist from Bosnia, assassinated him. p.20

Franz Ferdinand's assassination was an attack on Austria-Hungary by nationalists. Austria-Hungary said Serbia had organised the killing. On 23 July, they sent Serbia a list of unreasonable demands, which Serbia rejected. Austria declared war on 28 July. p.21

The Alliance System now turned a local conflict into a world war. To help Serbia, Russia prepared for war against Austria-Hungary, so Germany declared war on Russia on 1 August. To support Russia, France joined the war on 2 August. When Germany invaded France through Belgium, Britain joined the war on 4 August. p.22

The Schlieffen Plan speeded up the start of war. This was because if Germany was to fight Russia, it needed to attack and defeat France quickly to avoid a war on two fronts. p.24

The names 'Ottoman Empire' and 'Turkish Empire' are often used interchangeably. 'Ottoman' is more correct, but political writings and cartoons from the 1900s often refer to 'Turkey' and 'the Turk'.

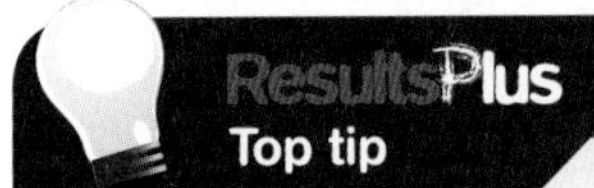

When using SuperFacts to support a statement, make sure you do not just produce a list of facts. Always say **how** the detail supports the statement.

Need more help?

You can find a longer explanation of each SuperFact in your Edexcel textbook, *Peace and War: International Relations 1900–91*. Look for this symbol, which will give you the page number.

SuperFacts

Naval rivalry Germany began to threaten Britain's naval superiority. In 1898 the Kaiser announced that Germany would build 41 battleships and 61 cruisers. In 1906, Britain responded with the Dreadnought, a much more powerful battleship. From 1906 to 1914, Britain built 29 dreadnoughts and Germany built 17.

SuperFacts

Colonial competition Britain and France gained cheap raw materials and export markets in their colonies. These things made them more powerful. Britain took £1,000 million in tax and goods just from India from 1750 to 1900. Germany had few colonies and wanted more. This caused tension.

The Arms Race As tensions rose, all the Great Powers, except Britain, introduced conscription. By 1914, the German army numbered 1.5 million. Large armies, in rival alliances committed to defend each other, were a dangerous development.

The Schlieffen Plan speeded up the start of war. This was because if Germany was to fight Russia, it needed to attack and defeat France quickly to avoid a war on two fronts.

Need more help?

See page 26 in the textbook for another example of how to write the best kind of answer to this type of question.

The answer

The best answer to this question appears on page 13.

Answering questions: Section 1 Part (a)

The Part (a) question will always ask you to '**describe one**' piece of information from this section of the course. It may ask you to:

- **describe one** action taken by ...
- **describe one** decision made by ...
- **describe one** cause of ...
- etc.

What you need to do

The best answers will always:

- **state** one relevant action, decision, reaction, cause, etc.
- AND also **describe** it with extra information or an explanation.

How you do it

Take this question as an example:

Describe one reaction to the Kaiser's 1898 announcement of 41 new battleships.

If you know your SuperFacts, you'll have no trouble answering the question.

The relevant SuperFact, about **naval rivalry**, is on this page.

You need to **select** and **describe** one reaction. A good reaction to select would be:

Britain responded with the Dreadnought.

But this isn't enough. The question asks you to 'describe' the reaction.

You can describe it by adding an explanation like this:

They did this because the Dreadnought was a much more powerful battleship than Germany's.

Or you can describe it by adding supporting **detail** like this:

From 1906 to 1914, Britain built 29 new dreadnoughts.

Now test yourself

Here are three possible Part (a) questions.

- ***Describe one benefit that Britain and France gained from having colonies.***
- ***Describe one aspect of the Arms Race.***
- ***Describe one effect of the Schlieffen Plan.***

Using the SuperFacts printed on the left:

- Highlight the benefit or aspect or effect you would **select**.
- Underline the words you would use to **describe** (i.e. explain or support) it.

Answering questions: Section 1 Part (b)

Part (b) questions will always ask you to '**briefly explain**' something.

What you need to do

The best answers will always:

- identify not one, or two, but **three** key features
- give extra information or an explanation for each key feature.

How you do it

Take this question as an example:

Briefly explain the key features of military rivalry before the First World War.

If you know your SuperFacts, you'll have no trouble answering the question. You need to **select** and **support** three key features. So, a good feature is:

Europe split into two powerful rival groups.

This isn't enough. You need to support this statement, to show the examiner you know what you are talking about. Something like this:

Germany, Austria-Hungary and Italy formed the Triple Alliance to help each other in time of war. The Triple Entente was formed between Britain, France, and Russia to give them security against the Triple Alliance.

Before you look at the answer below, write in the support column of the table what you think would be good support for each of the next two key features.

Key Feature	Support
A second feature of the military rivalry was powers trying to get the strongest navy.	
A third feature of the military rivalry was competition to have the biggest army.	

You can see that we point out to the examiner each time we introduce another key feature. You are giving **three** key features, so tell the examiner when you start each new one.

One *key feature of the military rivalry before the First World War was that Europe split into two powerful rival groups. Germany, Austria-Hungary, and Italy formed the Triple Alliance to help each other in times of war. The Triple Entente was formed between Britain, France, and Russia to give them security against the Triple Alliance.* ***A second*** *feature of military rivalry was powers wanting the strongest navy. In 1898 the Kaiser ordered 41 extra battleships; Britain replied by building 29 new dreadnoughts.* ***A third*** *feature of rivalry was competition for the biggest army. For example, by 1914 all the Great Powers except Britain introduced conscription.*

An answer like this, with three key features, each explained with detail, will get full marks. Check your support in the table against the version here. How well did you do?

SuperFacts

The Triple Alliance (1882) between Germany, Austria-Hungary, and Italy, said these countries would help each other in time of war. It left France isolated and nervous.

The Entente Cordiale (1904) was an agreement between France and Britain not to quarrel over colonies. It strengthened them against the growing power of Germany.

The Triple Entente (1907) was between France, Britain, and Russia. It gave them security against the Triple Alliance. Europe split into two powerful, rival groups.

Naval rivalry Germany began to threaten Britain's naval superiority. In1898, the Kaiser announced that Germany would build 41 battleships and 61 cruisers. In 1906, Britain responded with the Dreadnought, a much more powerful battleship. From 1906 to 1914, Britain built 29 dreadnoughts and Germany built 17.

The Arms Race As tensions rose, all the Great Powers, except Britain, introduced conscription. By 1914, the German army numbered 1.5 million. Large armies, in rival alliances committed to defend each other, were a dangerous development.

Need more help?

See page 27 in the textbook for another example of how to write the best kind of answer to this type of question.

SuperFacts

Colonial competition Britain and France gained cheap raw materials and export markets in their colonies. Britain took £1,000 million in tax and goods just from India from 1750 to 1900. Germany had few colonies and wanted more. This caused tension.

The Algeciras Conference was held in 1906 to discuss Morocco. The Kaiser said Morocco should be independent. He knew France wanted it as a colony. Britain backed France and the conference agreed. Britain also promised troops to help France if it was attacked by Germany.

The Agadir Crisis In 1911, after a rebellion in Morocco, France took over. A German gunboat, the *Panther*, sailed to Agadir and threatened the French. Britain said it would go to war if Germany kept bullying France. Germany had to back down again.

Morocco The two crises in Morocco (Algeciras and Agadir) made war more likely. Twice the Kaiser tested the Entente Cordiale, but the alliance held and he just made Britain and France keener to resist him.

Naval rivalry Germany began to threaten Britain's naval superiority. In 1898, the Kaiser announced that Germany was going to build 41 battleships and 61 cruisers. In 1906, Britain responded with the Dreadnought, a much more powerful battleship. From 1906 to 1914, Britain built 29 dreadnoughts and Germany built 17.

Test yourself

Briefly explain the key features of tensions over Morocco before 1914.

Tackle the question like this.

First, read the SuperFacts provided on the left.

Next, consider the following statements, based on the five SuperFacts.

One key feature of the tensions over Morocco was that ...

A ... the Kaiser said that Morocco should be independent.
B ... Germany had few colonies and was keen to seize more.
C ... in 1911, a German gunboat sailed to Morocco and threatened France.
D ... Germany was beginning to threaten Britain's navy.
E ... twice the Kaiser tested the Entente Cordiale.

Choose the three statements which best answer the question about the key features of the *tensions over Morocco*. Then write them in the answer box below.

Finally, choose extra information or explanation from the SuperFacts and add this to each of your key features in the answer box below.

Answer box

One key feature of the tensions over Morocco before 1914 was that...
Further details of this feature are that...
A second feature of the tensions over Morocco before 1914 was that...
Further details of this feature are that...
A third feature of the tensions over Morocco before 1914 was that...
Further details of this feature are that...

The answer

The best answer to this question appears on page 13.

Answering questions: Section 1 Part (c)

Part (c) questions will always ask you to '**explain why**' something happened.

What you need to do

The best answers will always:

- identify not one, or two, but **three** causes
- use **detailed information** to explain **how** each cause made something happen
- make a judgement about the three causes to show:
  - which of the three was **most important**
  - and how the three causes are **linked** or connected.

How you do it

Take this question as an example:

Explain why British and French relations with Germany got worse before 1914.

The SuperFacts on p.6–7 show several reasons why Britain and France's relations with Germany worsened before 1914. The SuperFact headings are listed on this page.

These SuperFacts could be organised into **three causes**:

The Alliance System	Rivalries	Incidents

with three sets of detailed information from the SuperFacts:

The Triple Alliance 1882 The Entente Cordiale 1904 The Triple Entente 1907	Economic competition Colonial competition Arms and naval rivalry	The Algeciras Conference 1905 The Agadir crisis 1911

Let's start with **one** cause. Using the SuperFacts, **write a paragraph** explaining how the Alliance System made relations with Germany worse. Remember, we need to:

- **state the first cause**
- then **give detailed information about it**
- and **then explain how it made relations worse**.

So the paragraph will look like this:

One cause making British and French relations with Germany worse was the Alliance System.

The Alliance System was... **[give details from the SuperFacts].**

The Alliance System made relations worse because... **[using the SuperFacts, explain how the Triple Alliance made France isolated and nervous, etc].**

SuperFacts

The SuperFacts on p.6–7 show many factors which made the British and French relationship with Germany worse before 1914.

You will find it useful to refer to the full SuperFacts on p.6–7, but the titles of the relevant SuperFacts are printed for you here.

The Triple Alliance (1882)
The Entente Cordiale (1904)
The Triple Entente (1907)
Economic competition
Colonial competition
The Algeciras Conference
The Agadir Crisis
Morocco
Naval rivalry
The Arms Race

Need more help?

See page 137 in the textbook for another example of how to write a good answer to this type of question.

A model answer with **three** fully developed causes might look like the one below.

- First, compare the opening paragraph with your answer. How did you do?
- Next, read the whole answer. Which extracts fill the gaps best?

One cause which made Britain's and France's relations with Germany worse was the Alliance System. The Alliance System started in 1882 with the Triple Alliance, when Germany, Italy, and Austria-Hungary said they would help each other in times of war. It grew with the Entente Cordiale (1904) and then the Triple Entente (1907), when Britain and France and then Russia allied to give each other security against the Triple Alliance. The Alliance System made British and French relations with Germany worse because the Triple Alliance made France isolated and nervous and because, by 1907, Europe was split into two powerful, rival groups.

A second cause which made Britain and French relations with Germany worse was the rivalries between them. The three countries were economic, colonial and military rivals. For example,...

Option A: *... from 1906 to 1914, Britain built 29 dreadnoughts and Germany built 17. The German army reached 1.5 million, but by 1914, Germany was producing more iron, more steel, and more cars than Britain.*

Option B: *...the Schlieffen Plan said that Germany needed to attack and defeat France quickly to avoid a war on two fronts.*

i) Which text box fills this gap better, Option A or Option B? Circle your answer.

These rivalries made relations worse because Germany had few colonies and wanted more. This caused tension. The arms rivalry made relations worse because large military alliances, committed to defend each other, were a dangerous development.

A third cause which made relations worse was colonial rivalry. Morocco was one place which Britain and France argued with Germany about. In 1905, the Kaiser meddled in French affairs by saying Morocco should be independent from France. This caused a confrontation at the Algeciras Conference. Then in 1911, the Kaiser tested the Entente Cordiale again by sending a German gunboat, the Panther, to Morocco to support a rebellion against France. Incidents like these made relations worse because...

Option C: *...Britain and France gained cheap raw materials and export markets in their colonies.*

Option D: *...Germany was bullying France, so Britain stood up for its ally. In 1911, Britain said it would go to war to support France.*

ii) Which text box fills this gap better, Option C or Option D? Circle your answer.

There is one final thing the best answers will do now: they will **prioritise** the causes and show the **links** between them.

iii) Circle 'Option E' or 'Option F' to show which paragraph you think does this better.

Option E: *The Alliance System made relations much worse. When Germany went into the Triple Alliance, France was so isolated and nervous that it looked for allies too. So France and Britain formed the Entente Cordiale and, later, joined with Russia in the Triple Entente. This meant that, when a crisis occurred in the Balkans, all the powers of Europe were quickly dragged into a war to defend their allies in the Alliance System.*

Option F: *The Alliance System was the most important problem with relations with Germany. This was because it made the other two causes worse. In the Alliance System, the Triple Alliance and Triple Entente were opposed to each other, so when Britain increased its navy, Germany had to compete. So the Alliances and naval rivalry were linked. Also, because Britain was allied to France, when Germany bullied France in Morocco, the Alliance System made the incident worse because Britain had to defend France and threaten Germany in return.*

The answer

The best answer to this question appears on page 13.

Answers: Section 1 Parts (a–c)

Part (a)

The highlighted parts of the SuperFacts below **state** the:

- one benefit,
- one aspect,
- and one effect

you were asked for.

The underlined parts of the SuperFacts below are the words which best **describe** (explain or support) the highlighted statement.

Colonial competition Britain and France gained cheap raw materials and export markets in their colonies. Britain took £1,000 million in tax and goods just from India from 1750 to 1900. Germany had few colonies and wanted more. This caused tension.

The Arms Race As tensions rose all the Great Powers, except Britain, introduced conscription. By 1914, the German army numbered 1.5 million. Large armies, in rival alliances committed to defend each other, were a dangerous development.

The Schlieffen Plan speeded up the start of war. This was because if Germany was to fight Russia, it needed to attack and defeat France quickly to avoid a war on two fronts.

Part (b)

The best picture of the **key features** of the tensions over Morocco would be provided by the following **statements** and **further details**.

- Statement A with ...
  ... He knew France wanted it as a colony.
- Statement C with ...
  ...Britain said it would go to war if Germany kept bullying France.
- Statement E with ...
  ... but the alliance held and he just made Britain and France keener to resist him.

Part (c)

The most appropriate text-box choices are:

i) Option A

Option B is not a good choice.

- It does not give information about British and French rivalry with Germany.

ii) Option D

Option C is not a good choice.

- It gives information that is factually correct.
- But it does not explain why the arguments over Morocco made the British and French relationship with Germany worse.

iii) Option F

Option E is not a good summary.

- It only discusses one cause.
- It does not discuss all three causes and weigh them against each other.
- Neither does it explain any links between the three causes.

1.2

SuperFacts Section 1.2
The Peace Settlement 1918–28

Section summary

At the end of the First World War, the winning Allies imposed a series of treaties on the losing countries at the Paris Peace Conference. The conference was dominated by 'the Big Three': Lloyd George (Britain), Clemenceau (France) and Wilson (USA).

The main aims of the treaties were to punish the defeated countries, especially Germany, and stop them being a danger to peace in the future.

The Germans hated the peace. The peace conference also set up the League of Nations, to stop further wars and solve international problems.

SuperFacts are the key bits of information. Learn them and ask someone to test you.

French peace aims Prime Minister Clemenceau wanted revenge for the 1.4 million dead French soldiers, the casualties, and the damage caused by the fighting in France. He also wanted compensation for the cost of the war, and to weaken Germany. p.31

British peace aims Prime Minister Lloyd George's aims for Versailles included 'making Germany pay': he had just won an election in Britain on this promise. p.31

US peace aims The US had suffered less in the war, so wanted revenge less. President Wilson wanted a long-term peace, set out in his Fourteen Points, including self-determination and a ban on secret treaties. pp.30–31

'War guilt' Article 231 of the Treaty of Versailles (the 'war guilt' clause) made Germany take responsibility for all loss and damage caused by the war. p.33

German reparations The Treaty of Versailles set German reparations at £6,600 million. In 1922, Germany, already behind with reparation payments, said it could not make any in 1923 and 1924. Reparations were reduced in the 1924 Dawes Plan. pp.33 & 40

The Rhineland (Germany's border with France, Belgium and the Netherlands) was demilitarised at Versailles. German troops could not go into it, even though it was part of Germany. This made it harder for Germany to invade France, but easier for the French to invade Germany. p.36

Anschluss The Treaty of Versailles said Germany and Austria could never unite (called *Anschluss*), which would have made them a stronger country. p.33

The Sudetenland became part of Czechoslovakia under the Treaty of Versailles; but most of the 3 million Germans living there wanted to be part of Germany. p.36

The Saar coalfields were put under French control for 15 years under the Treaty of Versailles, so Germany lost coal and income. p.36

The German armed forces were limited at Versailles to 100,000 soldiers in the army (no tanks or planes), and to 15,000 sailors (6 battleships, a few smaller ships, no submarines) in the navy. p.33

The *Diktat* the Germans called the Treaty of Versailles the *Diktat* (dictated peace) because they were not allowed to join the talks and many German people felt this meant they should not have to obey the treaty. p.33

German hyperinflation Hyperinflation is when prices rise rapidly, sometimes more than once a day, and money loses its value. A loaf of bread in 1921: 4 marks; in 1923: 1,500,000 marks. p.40

The Treaty of St Germain (1919) made Austria-Hungary separate countries to reduce their power. Austria lost land to Italy, its army was limited to 30,000 men and it was set reparations (it did not pay because its economy collapsed). p.35

The Treaty of Trianon (1920) made Austria-Hungary separate countries to reduce their power. Hungary lost land to its neighbours, its army was limited to 35,000 men and it was set reparations (it did not pay because its economy collapsed). p.35

edexcel key terms

reparations was the word used to describe the compensation payments that were to be paid by the losing countries to help repair the damage suffered by the winners.

self-determination is the right of the people in a region to decide which country it should be part of or whether the region should be an independent country.

The Treaty of Neuilly (1919) made Bulgaria give land to Italy and Greece; its army was limited to 20,000 men. It had to pay reparations. p.35

The Treaty of Sèvres (1920) broke up the Turkish Empire. Turkey's land in Europe went to Bulgaria and Greece, its lands in the Middle East to Britain and France as mandates. It took away control of the Bosphorus and the Dardanelles: the sea route between the Mediterranean and the Black Sea. p.35

The Treaty of Lausanne (1923) reversed some of the Treaty of Sèvres, gave Turkey back some land in Europe, and control of the Bosphorus and Dardanelles. p.35

The League of Nations US President Wilson pressed for a League of Nations, which all nations except those that lost the war were asked to join. The US Congress refused to let the USA join the League. p.42

The League's representative bodies were the Assembly (its 'parliament' which met at least once a year and where all member nations had one vote) and the Council (that dealt with international disputes) with representatives from Britain, France, Italy and Japan and up to 9 temporary elected members from other countries. To make a decision in either, all the members had to agree, not just a majority. pp.42–43

The League's other parts were the Secretariat (the officials that ran the League), the Permanent Court of Justice (15 judges to settle international disputes), the International Labour Organisation (to improve working conditions worldwide) and special commissions to tackle particular problems. pp.42–43

The League's Special Commissions included the Slavery Commission (which freed 200,000 slaves in Sierra Leone); the Commission for Refugees (which got almost 500,000 prisoners of war back home in its first two years) and the Mandates Commission (which checked on the territories taken from the losing countries). p.45

Weaknesses of the League It was hard for all members to agree (e.g. on sanctions or raising an army to enforce decisions). The League had no army of its own. pp. 46–47

League's early failures Poland took over Vilna, and would not go when the League told it to and was allowed to keep it (1920). Italy occupied the Greek island of Corfu and refused to leave until the League told the Greeks to pay them to go (1923). p.44

League's early successes Sweden and Finland both wanted the Aaland Islands; Sweden accepted the League's decision they were Finnish (1921). Greece invaded Bulgaria over a border dispute, but withdrew when the League told it to (1925). p.44

The Locarno Pact (1925), which led to Germany being allowed to join the League, was an agreement between Germany, Britain, France, Belgium, Italy, Poland and Czechoslovakia to respect each others' borders and take any disputes to the League. p.40

The Kellogg-Briand Pact (1928) was an agreement between 61 nations to always seek peaceful solutions to disputes. p.40

Don't get the Peace Conference and the Treaties confused.

The **Paris Peace Conference** discussed the right way to set up peace after the First World War.

There was a different peace treaty with each country, named after the place the treaty was signed:

Versailles with Germany, 1919
St. Germain with Austria, 1919
Neuilly with Bulgaria, 1919
Trianon with Hungary, 1920
Sèvres with Turkey, 1920
Lausanne changed Sèvres, 1923

Need more help?

You can find a longer explanation of each SuperFact in your Edexcel textbook, *Peace and War: International Relations 1900–91*. Look for this symbol, which will give you the page number.

edexcel key terms

mandates allowed countries that were members of the League to govern an area taken from the losing side in the First World War. The country that had the mandate to govern could not rule the country as if it was a colony and had to help it to become independent as soon as possible.

SuperFacts

French peace aims Prime Minister Clemenceau wanted revenge for the 1.4 million dead French soldiers, the casualties, and the damage caused by the fighting in France. He also wanted compensation for the cost of the war, and to weaken Germany.

SuperFacts

The Treaty of Trianon (1920) made Austria-Hungary into separate countries to reduce their power. Hungary lost land to its neighbours, its army was limited to 35,000 men and it was set reparations (it did not pay because its economy collapsed).

The League's Special Commissions included the Slavery Commission (which freed 200,000 slaves in Sierra Leone), the Commission for Refugees (which got almost 500,000 prisoners of war back home in its first two years), and the Mandates Commission (which checked on the territories taken from the losing countries).

League's early successes Sweden and Finland both wanted the Aaland Islands; Sweden accepted the League's decision they were Finnish (1921). Greece invaded Bulgaria over a border dispute, but withdrew when the League told it to (1925).

Need more help?

See page 26 in the textbook for another example of how to write the best kind of answer to this type of question.

The answer

The best answer to this question appears on page 21.

Answering questions: Section 2 Part (a)

The Part (a) question will always ask you to '**describe one**' piece of information from this section of the course. It may ask you to:

- **describe one action** taken by ...
- **describe one decision** made by ...
- **describe one cause** of ...
- etc.

What you need to do

The best answers will always:

- **state** one relevant action, decision, reaction, cause, etc.
- AND also **describe** it with extra information or an explanation.

How you do it

Take this question as an example:

Describe one of the aims of France at the 1918 Versailles peace conference.

If you know your SuperFacts, you'll have no trouble answering the question.

The relevant SuperFact, about French peace aims, is printed on this page.

You need to select and describe one aim. A good aim to select would be:

Clemenceau wanted revenge.

But this isn't enough. The question says '**describe**' the aim.

You can describe it by adding supporting **detail** like this:

The French wanted revenge in the form of compensation for the cost of the war.

Or you can describe it by adding an **explanation** like this:

He wanted revenge because 1.4 million French soldiers had died during the war.

Now test yourself

Here are three possible Part (a) questions.

- ***Describe one change made by the Treaty of Trianon (1920).***
- ***Describe one special commission of the League of Nations.***
- ***Describe one early success of the League of Nations.***

Using the SuperFacts printed alongside these questions:

- Highlight the change, special commission or success you would **select**.
- Underline the words you would use to **describe** (i.e. explain or support it).

Answering questions: Section 2 Part (b)

Part (b) questions will always ask you to 'briefly explain' something.

What you need to do

The best answers will always:

- identify not one, or two, but **three** key features
- give extra information or an explanation for each key feature.

How you do it

Take this question as an example:

Briefly explain the key features of the organisation of the League of Nations.

If you know your SuperFacts you'll have no trouble answering the question. You need to **select** and **support** three key features.

So, a good feature is:

The League of Nations had an Assembly.

This isn't enough, You need to support this statement – to show the examiner you know what you are talking about. Something like this:

This was the 'parliament' of the League; it met once a year, and all members of the League had one vote.

Before you look at the answer below, write in the support column of the table what you think good support for each of the next two key features would be.

Key Feature	Support
A second feature of the League was its Council	
A third feature of the League was its commissions.	

You can see that we point out to the examiner each time we introduce another key feature. You are giving **three** key features, so tell the examiner when you start each new one.

__One__ key feature of the organisation of the League was the Assembly. This was the 'parliament' of the League; all members had one vote. __A second__ feature of the League's organisation was its Council. The Council took the major decisions; it met five times a year, and had some permanent members – Britain, France, Italy, Japan, and some temporary members. __A third__ feature of the League's organisation was the commissions. The commissions carried out specialist work; for example, there was a Refugees Commission and also a Slavery Commission which freed 200,000 slaves in Sierra Leone.

An answer like this, with three key features, each one explained with detail, will get top marks. Check your support in the table against the version here. How well did you do?

SuperFacts

The League's representative bodies were the Assembly (its 'parliament' which met at least once a year and where all member nations had one vote) and the Council (that dealt with international disputes) with representatives from Britain, France, Italy and Japan and up to 9 temporary elected members from other countries. To make a decision in either, all the members had to agree, not just a majority.

The League's other parts were the Secretariat (the officials that ran the League), the Permanent Court of Justice (15 judges to settle international disputes), the International Labour Organisation (to improve working conditions worldwide) and special commissions to tackle particular problems.

The League's Special Commissions included the Slavery Commission (which freed 200,000 slaves in Sierra Leone); the Commission for Refugees (which got almost 500,000 prisoners of war back home in its first two years) and the Mandates Commission (which checked on the territories taken from the losing countries).

Need more help?

See page 48 in the textbook for another example of how to write a top answer to this question.

SuperFacts

The Rhineland (Germany's border with France, Belgium and the Netherlands) was demilitarised at Versailles. German troops could not go into it, even though it was part of Germany. This made it harder for Germany to invade France, but easier for the French to invade Germany.

The *Diktat* the Germans called the Treaty of Versailles the *Diktat* (dictated peace) because they were not allowed to join the talks and many people felt this meant they should not have to obey the treaty.

The German armed forces were limited at Versailles to 100,000 soldiers in the army (no tanks or planes), and to 15,000 sailors (6 battleships, a few smaller ships, no submarines) in the navy.

German reparations The Treaty of Versailles set German reparations at £6,600 million. In 1922, Germany, already behind with reparation payments, said it could not make any in 1923 and 1924. Reparations were reduced in the 1924 Dawes Plan.

The answer

The best answer to this question appears on page 21.

Test yourself

Describe the key features of the military clauses of the Treaty of Versailles in 1919.

Tackle the question like this.

First, read the SuperFacts on the left.

Next, consider the following statements, based on the four SuperFacts.

One key feature of the military clauses of the Treaty of Versailles was that ...

A … it was made harder for Germany to attack its neighbours.
B … the Treaty was a diktat; Germany was not consulted.
C … a limit was placed on the strength of the German army.
D … a limit was placed on the strength of the German navy.
E … Germany was made to pay reparations to pay for damage caused by the war.

Choose the 3 statements which best answer the question about the key features of the *military* clauses of the Treaty of Versailles. Then write them in the Answer Box below.

Finally, choose extra information or explanation from the SuperFacts and add this to each of your key features in the Answer Box below.

Answer box

One key feature of the military clauses in the Treaty of Versailles was that…
An example of this feature was that…
A second feature of the military clauses of Versailles was that…
An example of this feature was that…
A third feature of the military clauses of Versailles was that…
An example of this feature was that…

Answering questions: Section 2 Part (c)

Part (c) questions will always ask you to '**explain why**' something happened.

What you need to do

The best answers will always:

- identify not **one**, or **two**, but **three** causes
- use **detailed information** to explain how each cause made something happen
- make a judgement about the three causes to show:
  - how the three causes are **linked** or connected
  - which of the three was **most important**.

How you do it

The four boxes below show you how to do this, all as if you were answering this question:

Explain why the Germans were hostile to the Treaty of Versailles.

A What is a cause with detailed information?

This is the skill you have just been practising in questions Part (a) and Part (c).

A good SuperFact to use is '***War guilt***'.

But just saying 'war guilt' is not enough – you need to give the examiner enough detail to show that you really know what you are talking about. So you need to say:

Article 231 of the Treaty of Versailles (the 'war guilt' clause) made Germany take responsibility for all loss and damage caused by the war.

B Explaining how causes make things happen

So far you've shown that you know what 'war guilt' was – now you have to show how it was a cause of hostility to the Treaty of Versailles. Something like this:

... The Germans thought this was unfair. They had lost the war, but that didn't mean they were the only country responsible for starting it. The unfairness of it made them very hostile to the treaty.

C Explaining how causes link together

Obviously, you now need to be talking about more than one cause. To keep the example short, we will just use one more: that the Treaty of Versailles forced Germany to pay reparations to compensate for the losses Britain, France, and the USA suffered. (Backed up with detail, and how it was a cause.)

What you need to do is show the examiner you know that these causes were linked. For example:

Because the Allies said that Germany was responsible for the war, they thought it was right to fine Germany, so they imposed the reparations.

D Which cause is the most important?

Think about the causes you have chosen. They will not all be equally important. Work out which was the most important, then tell the examiner, giving the reasons for your choice.

'War guilt' is the most important of these causes. The Germans hated being told they were 'guilty' and that it was all their fault. Even worse, the Allies could impose the reparations on Germany because the treaty said that Germany was responsible for the war. So without 'war guilt' there could not have been reparations.

Test yourself

Explain why the League of Nations was not a success up to 1928.

Now it's time to practise all four of the skills you need to answer this question.

i) Select three causes (use the SuperFacts box for clues).
1
2
3

ii) Give some detail about each cause (use pages 14–15 if you need some help).
1

2

3

iii) Explain how these causes made things happen.
1

2

3

iv) Explain how these causes link together.
First link

Second link

v) Explain which was the most important

Chosen cause

Reasons

SuperFacts

1 'War guilt'
2 German hyperinflation
3 The League of Nations
4 The League's representative bodies
5 Weaknesses of the League
6 League's early failures
7 League's early successes.

Need more help?

For more detail on each of these SuperFacts, see pages 14–15.

Answers: Section 2 Part (a)–(c)

Part (a)

The Treaty of Trianon (1920) made Austria-Hungary separate countries to reduce their power.

or

Hungary lost land to its neighbours, its army was limited to 35,000 men, and it was set reparations (it did not pay because its economy collapsed).

The League's Special Commissions included the Slavery Commission (which freed 200,000 slaves in Sierra Leone).

or

The Commission for Refugees (which got almost 500,000 prisoners of war back home in its first two years).

or

The Mandates Commission (which checked on the territories taken from the losing countries).

League's early successes: Sweden and Finland both wanted the Aaland Islands; the League decided they were Finnish and Sweden accepted (1921).

or

Greece invaded Bulgaria over a border dispute, but withdrew when the League told it to (1925).

Part (b)

The best picture of the **key features** of the military clauses of the Treaty of Versailles would be provided by the following **statements** and **further details**:

- Statement A with ...

  The Rhineland was demilitarised at Versailles. German troops could not go into it, even though it was part of Germany. This made it hard for Germany to invade France.

- Statement C with ...

  The German armed forces were limited to 100,000 soldiers in the army and they were allowed no tanks.

- Statement D with ...

  The German navy was limited to 15,000 sailors; they were allowed only six battleships, a few smaller ships and no submarines.

Part (c)

i)

1 *Membership.* (**SuperFact 3**)

2 *Hard to make decisions.* (**SuperFacts 4** and **5**)

3 *Could not enforce its decisions.* (**SuperFacts 5** and **6**)

ii)

1 Important countries were not members – Germany (because defeated countries could not join) and USA which refused to join.

2 All members of the Assembly or Council had to agree before the League could act.

3 *It had no army of its own.*

iii)

1 *This made it hard for the League to be a success because some of the most powerful nations were not members, which meant the League was less of a threat.*

2 *This made it hard for the League to come to a quick decision and act on it.*

3 *Not having an army of its own meant it could be ignored. For example, Poland invaded Vilna, and would not leave when the League told it to. The League could do nothing and Poland stayed. Italy occupied Corfu and would not leave when the League told it to.*

iv)

First link

Because every country that was a member of the League had one vote in the Assembly, any country could block or slow down a decision by voting against it.

Second link

Because some of the most powerful countries were not members, when the League did make a decision it was easier for some countries to ignore it, like Poland over Vilna.

v) You can choose any cause, as long as you can give sensible reasons for it. A good answer would be:

Membership, because:

a) if the USA had been a member with all its power and money it would have been harder to ignore.

b) If Germany had been a member, it would not have just been the winners of the First World War.

1.3

SuperFacts Section 1.3

Why did war break out 1929–39?

SuperFacts are the key bits of information. Learn them and ask someone to test you.

The Wall Street Crash in the USA, in October 1929, helped to set off a worldwide depression. Many countries suffered unemployment and economic problems. This strained international relations; some countries chose authoritarian governments in the hope of solving the problems. p.51

Japan's population was over 65 million by 1929; it needed more land for its people to live and grow food. This led some Japanese leaders to seek new land abroad. p.52

Manchuria was a province of China in which the Japanese owned a railway. A bomb blew up part of this railway at Mukden in 1931. Japan used this as an excuse to send troops into Manchuria, take over, and rule it under the new name of Manchukuo. p.52

The Lytton Inquiry was set up by the League of Nations to investigate the invasion of Manchuria. It took a whole year and decided that Japan had acted illegally, so the League told Japan to withdraw. Japan refused, left the League and, in 1933, invaded Jehol, another Chinese province. p.53

Italy invaded Abyssinia in October 1935, using bomber planes and tanks against Abyssinian spears. Mussolini wanted an Italian empire in Africa. The Abyssinian leader, Haile Selassie, asked the League of Nations for help. p.54

The League failed to save Abyssinia It imposed some economic sanctions on Italy. However, Britain and France, leading League members, did not want to annoy Mussolini and force him into an alliance with Hitler. They even let Italy use the Suez Canal for ships going to Abyssinia. p.55

Secret treaty The League banned secret treaties between members. But in 1935, Britain and France made the secret Hoare-Laval Pact, allowing Italy to divide Abyssinia and keep most of it. p.55

The League seemed weak Powerful members like France and Britain followed their own political or economic needs rather than support the League in all disputes. p.55

The Rome-Berlin Axis (1936) was an agreement between Italy and Germany to work more closely together. It dismayed Britain and France because it gave Hitler a powerful ally. p.55

Hitler's aims Hitler wanted to take land from neighbouring countries to make a 'Greater Germany' (*Grossdeutschland*) and more 'living space' (*lebensraum*) for Germans. Doing this would break the Treaty of Versailles. p.58

Undoing Versailles Hitler said he wanted an army of 600,000. He introduced conscription in 1935. He also started building an air force. In 1936, he sent German troops into the Rhineland. All this broke the Treaty of Versailles. p.58

Section summary

The Great Depression of 1929 created huge economic problems worldwide. Many countries reacted by choosing authoritarian governments.

Germany elected the Nazi Party, led by Adolf Hitler. Hitler wanted to reverse the terms of the Versailles treaty and create a Greater Germany by taking land from neighbouring countries. From 1933 onwards, he took more and more extreme steps to achieve his aims.

Europe, led by Britain, followed a policy of appeasement – accepting each step in the hope of avoiding war. But, as the League of Nations failed to deal with aggression by Germany, Italy, and Japan, the world went to war again in 1939.

edexcel key terms

the Wall Street Crash of October 1929 was when the prices of US shares collapsed. It got this name because the New York Stock Exchange, on Wall Street, was where most US shares were bought and sold. So many banks, companies and individuals had been buying and selling shares, that the Crash affected huge numbers of people. Everyone who had savings in the banks that collapsed lost their money.

appeasement is the policy of giving in to demands, or allowing someone to do something, in order to keep the peace.

Hitler's aims for Austria Austria was German-speaking. Hitler wanted it in his 'Greater Germany'. He held meetings with Schuschnigg (the Austrian chancellor), who accepted some Austrian Nazis in government but not a German takeover. p.60

Anschluss In 1938, German troops took over Austria; this broke the Treaty of Versailles. Hitler succeeded; Italy supported him. Britain and France did nothing to prevent it. p.60–61

Appeasement and the Allies The Treaty of Versailles seemed unfair on Germany. Britain did not want to risk war to keep it intact in far away countries. Appeasement also gave Britain and France more time to rearm. But to Hitler it made them seem weak. p.61

Appeasement and Hitler Appeasement gave Hitler time to increase Germany's military strength and the confidence to go on invading neighbouring countries. p.60-61

The Sudetenland was part of Czechoslovakia. It had valuable coal deposits, the Skoda armaments factory, and 3 million German speakers, so Hitler demanded it as part of his 'Greater Germany'. This would be a breach of the Treaty of Versailles. p.62

The Munich Conference (September 1938) gave part of the Sudetenland to Hitler. Britain and France were not prepared to go to war to protect it – an example of appeasement. Hitler had to promise to leave the rest of Czechoslovakia alone, but the Munich agreement convinced him that Britain and France would not go to war against him. p.62

Czechoslovakia In March 1939, Hitler invaded the rest of Czechoslovakia – to expand German 'living space' and advance his aims for a 'Greater Germany'. This was a breach of the Treaty of Versailles and the Munich Agreement. p.64

Protecting Poland Hitler's invasion of Czechoslovakia ended appeasement for Britain and France. They decided that Hitler could be given no more. In March 1939, they promised Poland military aid if it was invaded. p.64

The Pact of Steel Hitler knew that he needed strong allies; this could persuade Britain and France not to fight him. If they did fight, strong allies would help him. So, in 1939, he formed a **military** alliance with Italy. p.65

The Nazi-Soviet Pact was between the USSR and Germany in August 1939. It meant that Hitler would not have to divide his troops fighting Europe in the west and the USSR in the east. Britain and France feared Hitler was preparing for war. p.64

War breaks out Germany invaded Poland on 1 September 1939 – to expand German 'living space' and 'Greater Germany'. It was a breach of Versailles. Britain and France no longer saw Hitler's aims as reasonable. They declared war on 3 September. p.65

ResultsPlus
Top tip

When choosing SuperFacts to support a statement, read the question carefully and consider the limits it puts on the information you use. If you are asked for one cause, action, or decision, give just one, explained. Do not give more than one: you will get no more marks.

Need more help?
You can find a longer explanation of each SuperFact in your Edexcel textbook, *Peace and War: International Relations 1900–91*. Look for this symbol, which will give you the page number.

Answering questions: Section 3 Part (a)

The Part (a) question will always ask you to '**describe one**' piece of information from this section of the course. It may ask you to:

- **describe one action** taken by ...
- **describe one decision** made by ...
- **describe one cause** of ...
- etc.

What you need to do

The best answers will always:

- **state** one relevant action, decision, reaction, cause, etc.
- AND also **describe** it with extra information or an explanation.

How you do it

Take this question as an example:

Describe one challenge faced by the League of Nations in the 1930s.

If you know your SuperFacts, you'll have no trouble answering the question.

One relevant SuperFact is about Abyssinia. It is printed on this page.

You need to use it to **select** and **describe** one challenge to the League.

A good challenge to select would be:

Italy invaded Abyssinia.

But this isn't enough. The question says '**describe**' one challenge.

You can describe it by adding supporting **detail** like this:

They invaded in October 1935, using planes and tanks against Abyssinian spears.

Or you can describe it by adding an **explanation** like this:

Mussolini ordered the invasion because he wanted an Italian empire in Africa.

Now test yourself

Here are three possible Part (a) questions.

- ***Describe one effect of the Wall Street Crash of 1929.***
- ***Describe one way Hitler broke the military terms of the Treaty of Versailles.***
- ***Describe one example of appeasement in the 1930s.***

Using the SuperFacts printed alongside these questions:

- Highlight the effect, way or example you would **select**.
- Underline the words you would use to **describe** (i.e. explain or support it).

SuperFacts

Italy invaded Abyssinia in October 1935, using bomber planes and tanks against Abyssinian spears. Mussolini wanted an Italian empire in Africa. The Abyssinian leader, Haile Selassie, asked the League of Nations for help.

The Wall Street Crash in the USA in October 1929, helped to set off a worldwide depression. Many countries suffered unemployment and economic problems. This strained international relations; some countries chose authoritarian governments in the hopes of solving the problems.

Undoing Versailles Hitler said he wanted an army of 600,000. He introduced conscription in 1935. He also started building an air force. In 1936, he sent German troops into the Rhineland. All this broke the Treaty of Versailles.

The Munich Conference (September 1938) gave part of the Sudetenland to Hitler. Britain and France were not prepared to go to war to protect it – an example of appeasement. Hitler had to promise to leave the rest of Czechoslovakia alone.

Need more help?

See page 26 in the textbook for another example of how to write the best kind of answer to this type of question. An example of the question on the next page can be found on page 114 of the textbook.

The answer

The best answer to this question appears on page 29.

Answering questions: Section 3 Part (b)

Part (b) questions will always ask you to '**briefly explain**' something.

What you need to do

The best answers will always:

- identify not one, or two, but **three** key features
- give extra information or an explanation for each key feature.

How you do it

Take this question as an example:

Briefly explain the key features of appeasement in the 1930s.

If you know your SuperFacts, you'll have no trouble answering the question. You need to **select** and **support** three key features. So, a good feature is:

The Allies agreed to reasonable German demands.

This isn't enough. You need to support this statement, to show the examiner you know what you are talking about. Something like this:

For example, when Hitler sent troops into Austria, Britain and France did nothing to oppose him. They felt the Treaty of Versailles had been unfair not allowing *Anschluss*. Austria was German-speaking.

Before you look at the answer below, write in the 'Support' column of the table what you think would provide good support for each of the next two key features.

Key Feature	Support
A second feature of appeasement was that the Allies did not want war to save far-off countries.	An example of this was...
A third feature of appeasement was that it made Hitler think France and Britain were too weak to stop him.	Evidence of this was when...

You can see that we point out to the examiner each time we introduce another key feature. You are giving **three** key features, so tell the examiner when you start each new one.

One key feature of appeasement was that the Allies agreed to reasonable German demands. For example, when Hitler invaded Austria, Britain and France did nothing to oppose him. They felt the Treaty of Versailles had been unfair not allowing Anschluss. Austria was German-speaking. **A second** feature was that the Allies did not want war to save far-off countries. An example of this was the Sudetenland. Britain and France were not prepared to go to war to protect it. **A third** feature was that appeasement made Britain and France look weak. The Munich talks convinced Hitler that they would not go to war against him. This is why he invaded Czechoslovakia and Poland in 1939.

An answer like this, with three key features, each explained with detail, will get full marks. Check your support in the table against the version here. How well did you do?

SuperFacts

Appeasement and the Allies The Treaty of Versailles seemed unfair on Germany. Britain did not want to risk war to keep it intact in far away countries. Appeasement also gave Britain and France more time to rearm. But to Hitler it made them seem weak.

Appeasement and Hitler Appeasement gave Hitler time to increase Germany's military strength and the confidence to go on invading neighbouring countries.

Hitler's aims for Austria Austria was German-speaking; Hitler wanted it in his 'Greater Germany'. He held meetings with Schuschnigg (the Austrian chancellor) who accepted some Austrian Nazis in government but not a German takeover.

Anschluss In 1938, German troops took over Austria; this broke the Treaty of Versailles. Hitler succeeded; Italy supported him. Britain and France did nothing to prevent it.

The Sudetenland was part of Czechoslovakia. It had valuable coal deposits, the Skoda armaments factory, and 3 million German speakers, so Hitler demanded it as part of his 'Greater Germany'. This would be a breach of the Treaty of Versailles.

The Munich Conference (September 1938) gave part of the Sudetenland to Hitler. Britain and France were not prepared to go to war to protect it – an example of appeasement. But Hitler had to promise to leave the rest of Czechoslovakia alone.

Czechoslovakia In March 1939, Hitler invaded the rest of Czechoslovakia – to expand German 'living space' and 'Greater Germany'. This was a breach of the Treaty of Versailles and the Munich Agreement. He considered Britain and France too weak to stop him.

SuperFacts

Italy invaded Abyssinia in October 1935, using bomber planes and tanks against Abyssinian spears. Mussolini wanted an Italian empire in Africa. The Abyssinian leader, Haile Selassie, asked the League of Nations for help.

The League failed to save Abyssinia It imposed some economic sanctions on Italy. But Britain and France, leading League members, did not want to annoy Mussolini and force him into an alliance with Hitler. They even let Italy use the Suez Canal for ships going to Abyssinia.

Secret treaty The League banned secret treaties between members. But in1935, Britain and France made the secret Hoare-Laval Pact, allowing Italy to divide Abyssinia and keep most of it.

The League seemed weak Powerful members, like France and Britain, followed their own political or economic needs rather than support the League in all disputes.

The Rome-Berlin Axis (1936) was an agreement between Italy and Germany to work more closely together. It dismayed Britain and France because it gave Hitler a powerful ally.

The answer

The best answer to this question appears on page 29.

Test yourself

Briefly explain the key features of the Abyssinian Crisis (1935).

Tackle the question like this.

First, read the SuperFacts provided on the left.

Next, consider the following statements, based on the five SuperFacts.

One key feature of the Abyssinian Crisis was that ...

A ...the Wall Street Crash strained international relations.
B ...Italy invaded Abyssinia.
C ...Italy and Germany agreed to work more closely together.
D ...Britain and France did not want to annoy Mussolini.
E ...it made the League of Nations seem weak.

Choose the three statements which best answer the question about the key features of the Abyssinian Crisis. Write them in the answer box below.

Finally, choose extra information or explanation from the SuperFacts and add this to each of your key features in the answer box below.

Answer box

One key feature of the Abyssinian Crisis was that...

Further details of this feature are that...

A second feature of the Abyssinian Crisis was that...

Further details of this feature are that...

A third feature of the Abyssinian Crisis was that...

Further details of this feature are that...

Answering questions: Section 3 Part (c)

Part (c) questions will always ask you to '**explain why**' something happened.

What you need to do

The best answers will always:

- identify not one, or two, but **three** causes
- use **detailed information** to explain **how** each cause made something happen
- make a judgement about the three causes to show:
  - which of the three was **most important**
  - how the three causes are **linked** or connected.

How you do it

Take this question as an example:

Explain why war broke out in 1939.

The SuperFacts on pages 22–23 show several reasons why war broke out. The relevant SuperFact headings are listed on this page.

These SuperFacts could be organised into **three causes**:

Weakness of League of Nations	Hitler's demands	Appeasement

with three sets of detailed information from the SuperFacts:

Manchuria Abyssinia	Undoing Versailles Austria/ Czechoslovakia Poland	Treaty of Versailles Austria Czechoslovakia

Let's start with one cause. Using the SuperFacts, **write a paragraph** explaining how a weak League of Nations contributed to the outbreak of war. Remember, we need to

- **state the first cause**
- then **give detailed information about it**
- then **explain how it made relations worse.**

So the paragraph will look like this:

One cause which helps to explain why war broke out was the weakness of the League of Nations.

The League was shown to be weak when... **[give details, using the SuperFacts]**.

A weak League of Nations helped to cause war because... **[use the SuperFacts to show how the League failed to solve problems and allowed aggression]**.

SuperFacts

The SuperFacts on p.22–23 show many factors that helped to cause the outbreak of war in 1939.

You will find it useful to refer to the full SuperFacts on p.22–23, but the titles of the relevant SuperFacts are printed for you here.

Manchuria

The Lytton Inquiry

Italy invaded Abyssinia

The League failed to save Abyssinia

The League seemed weak

Undoing Versailles

Anschluss

The Sudetenland

The Munich Conference

Czechoslovakia

Appeasement and the Allies

Appeasement and Hitler

Need more help?

See page 71 in the textbook for another example of how to write a top answer to this question.

A model answer with **three** fully developed causes might look like the one below.

- First, compare the opening paragraph with your answer. How did you do?
- Next, read the whole answer. Which extracts fill the gaps best?

One cause of war breaking out in 1939 was the weakness of the League of Nations. The League set up the Lytton Inquiry into the invasion of Manchuria and then told Japan to withdraw. But Japan just ignored this; in 1933, it left the League and invaded Jehol, another province of China. Another example is Abyssinia. When Italy invaded there, the League only imposed some economic sanctions. The League failed to save Abyssinia. This weakness of the League made war more likely, because it showed that powerful members like Britain and France followed their own needs rather than support the League. So the League could not solve disputes or stop aggression.

A second cause of war breaking out was Hitler's demands. These involved...

i) Which text box fills this gap better, Option A or Option B? Circle your answer.

Hitler's demands helped to cause the outbreak of war because when he invaded Poland, Britain and France declared war.

A third cause which helped cause the war to break out was appeasement. The Treaty of Versailles seemed unfair to Britain and France by the 1930s and they would not go to war to save far-off countries. This policy helped the outbreak of war because...

ii) Which text box fills this gap better, Option C or Option D? Circle your answer.

There is one final thing that the best answers will do now. They will **prioritise** the causes and show the **links** between them.

iii) Circle 'Option E' or 'Option F' to show which paragraph you think does this best.

Option E: *The weakness of League of Nations was the main cause of war breaking out in 1939. If the League had been strong, Hitler would not have been able to achieve his demands by force. If the League had been strong, Chamberlain would not have had to go to Munich and appease Hitler. All nations would have decided if Hitler's demands were reasonable. The League's weakness allowed Hitler's aggressive demands and caused appeasement. It was the main cause.*

Option F: *Hitler's demands were the main cause of the outbreak of war in 1939. Hitler thought that the Treaty of Versailles was unfair. He introduced conscription, went into the Rhineland, merged with Austria, and took over the Sudetenland. He even broke his promise and took the rest of Czechoslovakia. Invading Poland was the direct cause of war. It was the main cause.*

Option A: *... creating the Rome-Berlin Axis, the Pact of Steel and the Nazi-Soviet Pact, so he did not have to divide his troops fighting Europe in the west and other enemies in the east.*

Option B: *... unpicking the restrictions of the Treaty of Versailles and expanding German territory into areas like Austria, Czechoslovakia and Poland to get 'living space' for Germans and create a 'Greater Germany'.*

Option C: *... appeasement gave Hitler time to increase Germany's military strength and the confidence to go on invading neighbouring countries. It made him think that Britain and France were too weak to stop him.*

Option D: *...appeasement allowed Hitler to gain new allies, like Italy, Japan and the USSR.*

The answer

The best answer to this question appears on page 29.

Answers: Section 3 Parts (a)–(c)

Part (a)

The Wall Street Crash in the USA in October 1929 helped to set off a worldwide depression. Many countries suffered unemployment and economic problems. This strained international relations; some countries chose authoritarian governments in the hope of solving the problems.

Undoing Versailles: Hitler said he wanted an army of 600,000. He introduced conscription in 1935. He also started to build an air force. In 1936, he sent German troops to occupy the Rhineland. All this broke the Treaty of Versailles.

The Munich Conference (September 1938) gave the Sudetenland to Hitler. Britain and France were not prepared to go to war to protect it – an example of appeasement. But Hitler had to promise to leave the rest of Czechoslovakia alone.

Part (b)

The best picture of the **key features** of the Abyssinian crisis would be provided by the following **statements** and **further details:**

- Statement B with ...
  ...using bomber planes and tanks against Abyssinian spears. Mussolini wanted an Italian empire in Africa.
- Statement D with ...
  ...They even let Italy use the Suez Canal.
- Statement E with ...
  ...Powerful members, like France and Britain, followed their own political or economic needs rather than support the League in far-off countries.

Part (c)

The most appropriate text-box choices are:

i) Option B

Option A is not a good choice.

- It gives information about Hitler's foreign policy, which is factually correct.
- But this information is not about Hitler's demands.

ii) Option C

Option D is not a good choice.

- Hitler did make allies of Italy, Japan and the USSR.
- But this did not happen because of appeasement.

iii) Option E

Option F is not a good summing up.

- It only talks about one cause.
- It does not weigh up the importance of all three causes.
- It does not show the links between the three causes.

1.4

SuperFacts Section 1.4
How did the Cold War develop? 1943–56

Section summary

After the Second World War, the alliance between the communist USSR and the democratic/capitalist West fell apart and the Cold War began.

Both sides felt that other countries in the world should choose one side or the other in the Cold War, and both sides felt that the other side was out to destroy them. They worked hard to spread their influence and stop the influence of the other side.

The Cold War included an 'arms race' and a 'space race' to become the most powerful superpower. The actions of the superpowers in other countries, for example the influence of the USSR in Hungary, could be violent and destructive.

SuperFacts are the key bits of information. Learn them and ask someone to test you.

The Grand Alliance (1941) of Britain, the USA and USSR only formed to defeat Hitler. With him gone, different ideologies and disputes at conferences made it crumble. Also, once the USA had atomic bombs (after 1945) it didn't need the support of the USSR. p.74

Communism v. democracy/capitalism The USSR believed in communism where the Communist Party dominated government and the government controlled all aspects of the economy. The West believed in democracy, with free elections, and capitalism, with a free-market economy. This split weakened the Grand Alliance. p.74

At the Tehran Conference (1943) the Big Three discussed what to do when Hitler was defeated. They agreed on a Soviet 'sphere of influence' in Eastern Europe and a capitalist one in Western Europe. They could not agree on what to do in Germany. p.74

At the Yalta Conference (1945) the Big Three agreed that Poland would be communist, the USSR would help the war against Japan, and the United Nations would be set up. They also agreed to work for democracy; but what this meant was unclear. p.74

At the Potsdam Conference (1945) the Big Three agreed to ban the Nazi Party and punish surviving Nazis as war criminals. They agreed to temporarily divide Germany, and its capital Berlin, into four zones run by the USSR, USA, Britain and France. p.76

The 'Long' and Novikov Telegrams (1946) An American diplomat in Moscow and the Soviet ambassador in the USA both sent telegrams home in 1946, warning about military build-ups. The telegrams contributed to the build-up of the Cold War. p.78

Cold War The break-up of the Grand Alliance and the telegrams made the Big Three suspicious of each other. From 1947, the USA and USSR waged a 'Cold War'; a war of propaganda, military pacts, an 'arms race', and a 'space race'. p.78

The Truman Doctrine (1947) resulted from political differences between the Great Powers (see above). US President Truman worried that communism would spread in Europe; so, his Doctrine said the USA would use military and economic means to stop it spreading. It led to the Marshall Plan (see below) and fed the Cold War. p.80

The Marshall Plan (1947) aimed to reduce poverty to stop the spread of communism. The USA offered $13 billion to rebuild Europe. Britain, France and 14 other nations took the help offered. This helped their economies and boosted their trade with the USA. p.80

Satellite states The Marshall Plan was a threat to the USSR. Stalin was worried it would buy US influence in Eastern European states. To prevent this, he increased Soviet control over countries like Bulgaria, Czechoslovakia, Hungary and Poland. They became satellite states – supposedly independent, but really controlled by the USSR. p.82

edexcel key terms

the Cold War (1945–90) was the period when the USA and the USSR were enemies, and trying to force other countries to take sides. They took part in conflicts in various parts of the world, without actually going to war with each other.

containment is the policy of using political, economic and diplomatic strategies to stop the spread of ideas that you are opposed to.

Cominform (1947) was an organisation which represented communist parties all over Europe. For example, in 1947, it encouraged 2 million French workers to go on strike in protest against Marshall Aid. Stalin used Cominform to control the satellite states. p.82

Comecon (1949) was another way Stalin controlled his satellite states. It was a rival to the Marshall Plan. It encouraged trade and industry in Eastern Europe and discouraged trade with the West. This contributed to the Cold War. p.83

Bizonia (US and British zones of Germany) was run almost as one unit. It had good relations with the French Zone. In 1948, the Western Allies started to make the three zones (Trizonia) a democratic, capitalist state, increasing tension with the USSR. p.84

The Berlin Blockade (1948–49) was Stalin's retaliation against events in Trizonia. The USSR tried to get all parts of Berlin to vote to become communist. When they refused, it cut off all supply routes except from the USSR. The aim was to prevent the new state, set up by the Western Allies, from being run from Berlin. p.85

The Berlin Airlift (1948–49) started with 70 US cargo planes carrying about 700 tonnes of food and supplies a day. The British also flew in supplies. During January 1949, the Airlift provided over 170,000 tonnes of supplies. Lack of trust meant that any dispute after this simply increased existing tension and suspicion. p.85

Divided Germany In 1949, Germany was formally divided in two. In September, western Germany became the Federal Republic of Germany (FDR). In October, eastern Germany became the German Democratic Republic (GDR). p.85

NATO (the North Atlantic Treaty Organisation) was set up in1949. It was made up of the USA and its allies. Its members promised to defend each other if attacked. The communist version of NATO was the **Warsaw Pact**, set up in 1955. p.86

Arms Race The USA had the atomic bomb by 1945; the USSR had its own by 1949. By 1953, both had more powerful 'hydrogen' bombs. They each raced to get more bombs than the other. p.86

Hungary was a satellite state of the USSR. It became communist, lost land and its coal and oil were shipped to Russia. In 1949, Cominform made Matyas Rakosi dictator there. Under Rakosi, 387,000 Hungarians were gaoled and 2,000 executed. p.88

Khrushchev was Soviet leader after Stalin died in 1953. His 'Secret Speech' (1956) promised to change Stalin's policy and relax Soviet control of satellite states. p.87

Nagy became leader of Hungary in 1956. The 'Secret Speech' had made Hungarians riot for change. Nagy proposed reforms such as leaving the Warsaw Pact and ending communism in Hungary. The USA offered $20 million of aid to Nagy's government. p.87

Crushing Hungary (1956) Fearing Hungary would set a trend, 200,000 Soviet troops invaded. The USA and UN disapproved, but sent no military aid. 20,000 Hungarians died in the Soviet takeover. Nagy was found guilty of treason and hanged. pp.87–88

When choosing SuperFacts to support a statement, don't use all the SuperFacts you know on the topic. Choose the most relevant. So, in a question about why relations between the USA and the USSR worsened between certain dates, focus on those dates and the **reasons** for the deterioration.

Need more help?
You can find a longer explanation of each SuperFact in your Edexcel textbook, *Peace and War: International Relations 1900–91*. Look for this symbol, which will give you the page number.

Answering questions: Section 4 Part (a)

The Part (a) question will always ask you to '**describe one**' piece of information from this section of the course. It may ask you to:

- **describe one action** taken by ...
- **describe one decision** made by ...
- **describe one cause** of ...
- etc.

What you need to do

The best answers will always:

- **state** one relevant action, decision, reaction, cause, etc.
- AND also **describe** it with extra information or an explanation.

How you do it

Take this question as an example:

Describe one way Stalin controlled communism outside the USSR.

If you know your SuperFacts, you'll have no trouble answering the question.

One relevant SuperFact is about the **Cominform**. It is printed on this page.

We can use it to **select** and **describe** one way in which Stalin controlled communism in Europe. A good selection to make would be:

Stalin controlled communism outside the USSR using the Cominform.

But this isn't enough. The question says '**describe**' one way.

You can describe it by adding an *explanation* like this:

Cominform was an organisation which represented communist parties across Europe.

Or you can describe it by adding supporting detail like this:

For example, in 1947, it encouraged 2 million French workers to protest against Marshall Aid.

Now test yourself

Here are three possible Part (a) questions.

- ***Describe one issue discussed at the Tehran Conference (1943).***
- ***Describe one decision about governing Germany taken at Potsdam in 1945.***
- ***Describe one way the Marshall Plan helped Europe after 1947.***

Using the SuperFacts printed alongside these questions:

- Highlight the issue, decision or way you would **select**.
- Underline the words you would use to **describe** (i.e. explain or support it).

SuperFacts

Cominform (1947) was an organisation which represented communist parties all over Europe. For example, in 1947, it encouraged 2 million French workers to go on strike in protest against Marshall Aid. Stalin used Cominform to control the satellite states.

SuperFacts

At the Tehran Conference (1943), the Big Three discussed what to do when Hitler was defeated. They agreed on a Soviet 'sphere of influence' in Eastern Europe and a capitalist one in Western Europe. They could not agree on what to do in Germany.

At the Potsdam Conference (1945), the Big Three agreed to ban the Nazi Party and punish surviving Nazis as war criminals. They agreed to temporarily divide Germany, and its capital Berlin, into four zones run by the USSR, USA, Britain and France.

The Marshall Plan (1947) aimed to reduce poverty to stop the spread of communism. The USA offered $13 billion to rebuild Europe. Britain, France and 14 other nations took the help offered. This helped their economies and boosted their trade with the USA.

The answer

The best answer to this question appears on page 37.

Need more help?

See page 26 in the textbook for another example of how to write the best kind of answer to this type of question.

Answering questions: Section 4 Part (b)

Part (b) questions will always ask you to '**briefly explain**' something.

What you need to do

The best answers will always:

- identify not one, or two, but **three** key features
- give extra information or an explanation for each key feature.

How you do it

Take this question as an example:

Briefly explain how the Grand Alliance broke up after the Second World War.

If you know your SuperFacts, you'll have no trouble answering the question. You need to **select** and **support** three key features. So, a good feature is:

The Grand Alliance was only formed to beat Hitler.

This isn't enough. You need to support this statement, to show the examiner you know what you are talking about. Something like this:

With him gone, it began to break up. Anyway, armed with atomic bombs, the USA didn't need the support of the USSR any more.

Before you look at the answer below, write in the support column of the table what you think good support for each of the next two key features would be.

Key Feature	Support
A second feature of the break-up was ideological differences.	
A third feature of the break-up was that disagreements led to growing suspicion.	

You can see that we point out to the examiner each time we introduce another key feature. You are giving **three** key features, so tell the examiner when you start each new one.

***One** key feature of the break-up of the Grand Alliance was that it was only formed to beat Hitler. Once Hitler was defeated it began to break up. Anyway, armed with atomic bombs, the USA didn't need the USSR any more. **A second** feature of the break-up was ideological differences. The USSR believed in communism where the Communist Party dominated government and all aspects of the economy. The West believed in democracy, with free elections, and capitalism, with a free market. **A third** feature was disagreements over practical issues. There were several things which the Big Three could not agree on at Tehran and Yalta. By 1946, the 'Long' and Novikov Telegrams showed that they were both very suspicious of each other.*

An answer like this, with three key features, each explained with detail, will get full marks. Check your support in the table against the version here. How well did you do?

SuperFacts

The Grand Alliance (1941) of Britain, the USA, and USSR only formed to beat Hitler. With him gone, different ideologies and disputes at conferences made it crumble. Also, once the USA had atomic bombs (after 1945) it didn't need the support of the USSR.

Communism v. democracy/ capitalism The USSR believed in communism where the Communist Party dominated government and the government controlled all aspects of the economy. The West believed in democracy, with free elections, and capitalism, with a free-market economy. This split weakened the Grand Alliance.

At the Tehran Conference (1943) the Big Three discussed what to do when Hitler was defeated. They agreed on a Soviet 'sphere of influence' in Eastern Europe and a capitalist one in Western Europe. They could not agree on what to do in Germany.

At the Yalta Conference (1945) the Big Three agreed Poland would be communist, the USSR would help the war against Japan and the United Nations would be set up. They also agreed to work for democracy; but were unclear what this meant.

The 'Long' and Novikov Telegrams (1946) An American diplomat in Moscow and the Soviet ambassador in the USA both sent telegrams home in 1946, warning about military build-ups. The telegrams contributed to the build-up of the Cold War.

Need more help?

See page 48 in the textbook for another example of how to write a top answer to this question.

SuperFacts

At the Potsdam Conference (1945), the Big Three agreed to ban the Nazi Party and punish surviving Nazis as war criminals. They agreed to temporarily divide Germany, and its capital, Berlin, into four zones run by the USSR, USA, Britain and France.

Bizonia (US and British zones of Germany) was run almost as one unit. It had good relations with the French zone. In 1948, the Western Allies started to make the three zones (Trizonia) a democratic, capitalist state, increasing tension with the USSR.

The Berlin Blockade (1948–49) was Stalin's retaliation against events in Trizonia. The USSR tried to get all parts of Berlin to vote to become communist. When they refused, it cut off all supply routes except from the USSR. The aim was to prevent the new state, set up by the Western Allies, from being run from Berlin.

The Berlin Airlift (1948–49) started with 70 US cargo planes carrying about 700 tonnes of food and supplies a day. The British also flew in supplies. During January 1949, the Airlift provided over 170,000 tonnes of supplies. Lack of trust meant that any dispute after this increased tension and suspicion.

Divided Germany In 1949, Germany was formally divided in two. In September, western Germany became the Federal Republic of Germany (FDR). In October, eastern Germany became the German Democratic Republic (GDR).

The answer

The best answer to this question appears on page 37.

Test yourself

Briefly explain how Germany was governed after the Second World War.

Tackle the question like this.

First, read the SuperFacts provided on the left.

Next, consider the following statements, based on the five SuperFacts.

One key feature of the way Germany was governed was that ...

A ...in 1945, at Potsdam, the 'Big Three' agreed to divide Germany up.
B ...the US and British zones were run as one unit with good links to the French zone.
C ...in 1948, the USSR cut off all supply routes to Berlin, except from the USSR.
D ...the USA and British carried out an airlift into Berlin.
E ...in 1949, Germany was formally divided into two countries.

Choose the three statements which best answer the question about how Germany was governed. Write them in the answer box below.

Finally, choose extra information or explanation from the SuperFacts and add this to each of your key features in the answer box below.

Answer box

One key feature of the way Germany was governed after the Second World War was...
Further details of this feature are that...
A second feature of the way Germany was governed was...
Further details of this feature are that...
A third feature of the way Germany was governed was...
Further details of this feature are that...

Answering questions: Section 4 Part (c)

Part (c) questions will always ask you to '**explain why**' something happened.

What you need to do

The best answers will always:

- identify not one, or two, but **three** causes
- use **detailed information** to explain **how** each cause made something happen
- make a judgement about the three causes to show:
  - how the three causes are **linked** or connected
  - and which of the three was **most important.**

How you do it

The four boxes below show you how to do this, if you were answering this question:

Explain why relations between the USSR and USA got worse 1943–49.

A What is a cause with detailed information?

One cause of worsening relations was the break-up of the Grand Alliance.

But this is not enough – you need detail, so you need to say:

One cause was the break-up of the Grand Alliance. This was an alliance made in 1943 between Britain, the USA and the USSR to defeat Hitler.

B Explaining how causes make things happen

So far you've shown you know what the break-up of the Grand Alliance was – now you have to show how it caused the relationship to worsen. Something like this:

When the war ended, the threat of Hitler no longer kept the USA and USSR together. And, with atomic bombs (after 1945), the USA no longer needed the support of the USSR. So their relationship got worse.

C Explaining how causes link together

You need at least three causes, and detail, and how each one caused change. Your causes could be:

- the break-up of the Grand Alliance
- different ideologies (communism/capitalism)
- arguments over Berlin.

You now need to show how these causes were linked or connected. For example:

The break-up of the Grand Alliance was linked to the Berlin crisis. The Allies never agreed how Germany should be governed before the Alliance broke up, so the problem of Berlin could not be solved.

D Which cause is the most important?

The examiner wants to know which cause you think is most important. He or she doesn't have to agree. You only need to choose a sensible reason and make a case for it, supported by the events. For example:

'Different ideologies were the most important reason for worsening relations. They helped to break up the Grand Alliance. And, because the USSR wanted to spread communism and Truman wanted to stop it, there was never any trust between them. This meant the disputes could never be solved.

SuperFacts

You may want to refer the SuperFacts on p.30–31 when you do this activity.

To help you, the titles of the relevant SuperFacts are listed here:

Communism v. democracy/capitalism

The Truman Doctrine (1947)

The Marshall Plan (1947)

Satellite states

Cominform (1947)

Comecon (1949)

Bizonia

The Berlin Blockade (1948–49)

The Berlin Airlift (1948–49)

NATO

Arms Race

Need more help?

If you need more help with Part (c) questions like this one, you can refer to page 93 of the textbook.

Test yourself

Here is a new **question** and **three causes** for you to practise.

Explain why there was a Cold War between the USA and USSR 1947–56.

Cause 1 – arguments about the spread of communism in Eastern Europe

Cause 2 – arguments about governing Germany and Berlin

Cause 3 – suspicion created by the Arms Race, NATO and Warsaw Pact.

i) Give some detail about each cause (use p.30–31 if you need some help).

1

2

3

ii) Explain how these causes helped to make the Cold War happen.

1

2

3

iii) Explain how these causes link together.

iv) Explain which was the most important.

Chosen cause with reasons:

Answers: Section 4 Parts (a)–(c)

Part (a)

At the Tehran Conference (1943), the Big Three discussed what to do when Hitler was defeated. They agreed on a Soviet 'sphere of influence' in Eastern Europe and a capitalist one in Western Europe. They could not agree on what to do in Germany.

At the Potsdam Conference (1945), the Big Three agreed to ban the Nazi Party and punish surviving Nazis as war criminals. They agreed to temporarily divide Germany, and its capital Berlin, into four zones run by the USSR, USA, Britain, and France.

The Marshall Plan (1947) aimed to reduce poverty to stop the spread of communism. The USA offered $13 billion to rebuild Europe. Britain, France and 14 other nations took the help offered. This helped their economies and boosted their trade with the USA.

Part (b)

The best picture of the **key features** of how Germany was governed would be provided by the following **statements** and **further details**.

- Statement A with ...

... *Germany, and its capital, Berlin, [were divided] into four zones run by the USSR, USA, Britain, and France.*

- Statement B with ...

... *The three western zones were called Trizonia. In 1948, the Western Allies started to turn Trizonia into a democratic, capitalist state.*

- Statement E with ...

... *In September, western Germany became the Federal Republic of Germany (FDR). In October, eastern Germany became the German Democratic Republic (GDR).*

Part (c)

i)

1. Any details about the Truman Doctrine, Marshall Plan, Soviet satellite states, Cominform or Comecon:
   e.g. *US President Truman was worried that communism would spread in Europe, so he set out his Truman Doctrine.*
2. Any details about the government of Bizonia, Trizonia, the Berlin Blockade or the Berlin Airlift:
   e.g. *In 1948, the Western Allies started to make the three zones (Trizonia) a democratic, capitalist state.*
3. Any details about NATO, the Warsaw Pact or the Arms Race:
   e.g. *The North Atlantic Treaty Organisation was set up in 1949. It was made up of the USA and its allies. They promised to defend each other if attacked.*

ii)

1. Any explanation about how tensions were caused by the Truman Doctrine, Marshall Plan, Soviet satellite states, Cominform or Comecon:
   e.g. *Truman's Doctrine said the USA would use military and economic means to stop communism spreading.*
2. Any details about how tensions were caused by Bizonia, Trizonia, the Berlin Blockade or the Berlin Airlift:
   e.g. *When the Western Allies started to make Trizonia a democratic, capitalist state, this increased tension with the USSR.*
3. Any details about how tensions were caused by NATO, the Warsaw Pact or the Arms Race:
   e.g. *They each raced to get more bombs than the other.*

iii)

Any reasonable link, such as:

- *Rivalry in Eastern Europe made disputes in Berlin harder to solve.*
- *Suspicions caused by the Berlin crisis persuaded them to form armed alliances.*
- *Nuclear arms increased tensions between the USA and the USSR making disputes harder to solve.*

iv)

Any reasonable opinion, such as:

- *The arguments about communism were most important because it made trust impossible.*
- *Berlin was the most important because it was an ongoing argument souring relations from 1943 to 1949.*
- *Arms race was the most important because it caused tension and the threat of nuclear destruction.*

1.5

Section summary

Berlin, Cuba and Czechoslovakia were all crises in the Cold War between 1957 and 1969. The drain of refugees from East to West Berlin led to Khrushchev ordering the building of the Berlin Wall in 1961. It soon became a worldwide symbol of the Cold War divide.

The Cuban Missile Crisis of 1962 is often said to have been the point when the Cold War came closest to turning into an actual nuclear war, which would have caused appalling devastation.

The 'Prague Spring' of 1968 and the Soviet occupation that followed showed just how determined the USSR was to keep control of the satellite states that were a buffer between the USSR and the West.

SuperFacts Section 1.5
Three Cold War crises

SuperFacts are the key bits of information. Learn them and ask someone to test you.

Berlin refugees Almost 3 million East Germans fled to West Germany 1949–61. Most went from East to West Berlin. One reason was that the East German government was very unpopular. Another was that people wanted western freedom and wealth. p.95

Berlin ultimatum (1958) It embarrassed the East that refugees preferred the West and they were losing skilled people. So Khrushchev said all Berlin belonged to East Germany. To humiliate the Western powers, he gave their troops 6 months to leave Berlin. p.95

Eisenhower's Berlin talks (1959) Khrushchev and President Eisenhower agreed to discuss Berlin. Khrushchev withdrew his ultimatum. In 1959, they met in Geneva and then at Camp David in the USA. They met again in Paris in 1960, but could not agree what to do about Berlin. Before the talks a US spy plane was shot down over the USSR. When Eisenhower refused to apologise for the incident, Krushchev walked out. p.96

Kennedy's Berlin talks (1960–61) Krushchev met the new president, Kennedy, in Geneva. Hoping to take advantage of the new president's inexperience, Krushchev again told the USA they had 6 months to leave Berlin. p.96

Kennedy plans for war The USA refused to leave Berlin. In case of war, Kennedy put $3.2 billion more into military funds, and spent $270 million on nuclear fall-out shelters. p.97

The Arms Race By 1961, the USA had 20 times more nuclear weapons than the USSR and, unlike them, had B52 planes that carried nuclear bombs. p.100

The Berlin Wall (1961) Khrushchev could not force US troops to leave Berlin, but he had to save face. So overnight on 12 August, East Germany sealed off West Berlin with barbed wire, then gradually built the Berlin Wall. p.98

Berlin Wall's effects The Wall stopped people leaving East Germany. Khrushchev also avoided war – and it made him look like a decisive leader. p.98

Castro and Cuba Cuba is only 145 km from the USA and had been its ally. In 1959, Fidel Castro led a revolution there, taking over all American property in Cuba. The USSR offered Cuba aid and experts to industrialise. All this worried the USA. p.102

The Bay of Pigs In 1961, the CIA trained Cuban refugees from the revolution who invaded Cuba at the Bay of Pigs to overthrow Castro. The invasion failed. p.102

The Cuban Missile Crisis Worried about the US threat, Castro asked the USSR to defend Cuba; 114 Soviet ships set off for Cuba, carrying nuclear missiles. This would put the USA within range of Soviet nuclear missiles for the first time. For 'Thirteen Days' in 1962, US and Soviet forces were both ready to go to war. pp.103–105

edexcel key terms

Prague Spring is the name given to the reforms introduced in Czechoslovakia in 1968 by Alexander Dubcek when he came to power there.

The Soviet ships turned around Neither side wanted nuclear war. Kennedy and Khrushchev agreed that the USA would not invade Cuba, the USSR would not base missiles there and the USA would withdraw its missiles from Turkey. p.104

Cuban Missile Crisis – results The USA and USSR wanted to avoid a similar crisis. In 1963, they agreed to a policy of building better relations. They set up the 'hotline' between Washington and Moscow and agreed to limit further nuclear testing. p.106

Mutually Assured Destruction (MAD) By the 1960s, the USA and the USSR both had so many weapons that any nuclear war would cause crippling damage to both sides. This brought a little more stability to their relationship. p.107

Czechoslovakia and the USSR Communist rule was unpopular in Czechoslovakia, a satellite state of the USSR. The secret police crushed all political opposition and the economy suffered under the rule of the communist leader, Novotny. p.108

Alexander Dubcek, the popular secretary of the Czech Communist party, became leader there in 1968. His reforms (including making political opposition groups legal and allowing some 'capitalist' profit-making) are called the 'Prague Spring'. p.109

The Soviet Response Brezhnev repeatedly warned Dubcek about his actions, but Dubcek failed to take the hint. As a result, in August 1968, Soviet troops invaded Czechoslovakia. p110

Dubcek's reaction Dubcek told Czechs not to fight the invading troops. Students stood in the way of tanks holding anti-invasion banners. But Dubcek was forced to reverse his reforms. p.110

International reaction Western powers condemned the USSR, but gave no military help. Communists outside Russia were angry at the Soviet action; some turned to China for leadership; others set up a rival form of communism: Eurocommunism. p.112

The Brezhnev Doctrine Dubcek's reforms were not just a problem in Czechoslovakia. Brezhnev worried that they would spread to other satellite states. Therefore, his 'Brezhnev Doctrine' said the USSR would invade any satellite state that threatened the security of the Eastern Bloc. p.110

Make sure you get the right US president and leader of the USSR.

USA
1953–61 Eisenhower
1961–63 Kennedy
1963–69 Johnson

USSR
1953–64 Khrushchev
1964–82 Brezhnev

Need more help?
You can find a longer explanation of each SuperFact in your Edexcel textbook, *Peace and War: International Relations 1900–91*. Look for this symbol, which will give you the page number.

SuperFacts

Cuban Missile Crisis – results The USA and USSR wanted to avoid a similar crisis. In 1963, they agreed to a policy of building better relations. They set up the 'hotline' between Washington and Moscow and agreed to limit further nuclear testing.

SuperFacts

Mutually Assured Destruction (MAD) By the 1960s, the USA and the USSR both had so many weapons that any nuclear war would cause crippling damage to both sides. This brought a little more stability to their relationship.

Czechoslovakia and the USSR Communist rule was unpopular in Czechoslovakia, a satellite state of the USSR. The secret police crushed all political opposition and the economy suffered under the rule of the communist leader, Novotny.

International reaction Western powers condemned the USSR, but gave no military help. Communists outside Russia were angry at the Soviet action; some turned to China for leadership; others set up a rival form of communism: Eurocommunism.

The answer

The best answer to this question appears on page 45.

Need more help?

See page 70 in the textbook for another example of how to write the best kind of answer to this type of question.

Answering questions: Section 5 Part (a)

The Part (a) question will always ask you to '**describe one**' piece of information from this section of the course. It may ask you to:

- **describe one action** taken by ...
- **describe one decision** made by ...
- **describe one cause** of ...
- etc.

What you need to do

The best answers will always:

- state one relevant action, decision, reaction, cause, etc.
- AND also describe it with extra information or an explanation.

How you do it

Take this question as an example:

Describe one result of the Cuban Missile Crisis.

If you know your SuperFacts, you'll have no trouble answering the question.

The relevant SuperFact about the **Cuban Missile Crisis** is printed on this page.

You need to **select** and **describe** one result of the crisis. A good result would be:

The USA and USSR agreed to a policy of building better relations.

But this isn't enough. The question says '**describe**' one result.

You can describe it by adding an **explanation** like this:

They wanted to avoid a similar crisis happening again.

Or you can describe it by adding supporting **detail** like this:

They set up a 'hotline' and agreed to limit further nuclear testing.

Now test yourself

Here are three possible Part (a) questions.

- ***Describe one effect of MAD (Mutually Assured Destruction) in the 1960s.***
- ***Describe one effect of communist rule in Czechoslovakia in the 1960s.***
- ***Describe one international reaction to the Soviet invasion of Czechoslovakia.***

Using the SuperFacts printed alongside these questions:

- Highlight the effect or reaction you would **select**.
- Underline the words you would use to **describe** (i.e. explain or support it).

Answering questions: Section 5 Part (b)

Part (b) questions will always ask you to '**briefly explain**' something.

What you need to do

The best answers will always:

- identify not one, or two, but **three** key features
- give extra information or an explanation for each key feature.

How you do it

Take this question as an example:

Briefly explain the key features of the Cuban Missile crisis (1962).

If you know your SuperFacts, you'll have no trouble answering the question. You need to **select** and **support** three key features. So, a good feature is:

Castro asked the USSR to defend Cuba.

This isn't enough. You need to support this statement, to show the examiner you know what you are talking about. Something like this:

In response, Khrushchev sent 114 ships to Cuba, carrying nuclear missiles, which would put the USA within range of Soviet missiles.

Before you look at the answer below, write in the support column of the table what you think good support for each of the next two key features would be.

Key Feature	Support
A second feature of the crisis was the agreement which the USSR and USA reached.	
A third feature of the Cuban Missile Crisis was its long-term effects	

You can see that we point out to the examiner each time we introduce another key feature. You are giving **three** key features, so tell the examiner when you start each new one.

***One** key feature of the Cuban missile crisis was Castro asking the USSR to defend Cuba. In response, Khrushchev sent 114 ships to Cuba, carrying nuclear missiles, which would put the USA within range of Soviet missiles. **A second** feature of the crisis was the agreement which the USSR and USA reached. They agreed that the USA would not invade Cuba, the USSR would not base missiles there and that the USA would withdraw its missiles from Turkey. **A third** feature was the long-term effects of the crisis. The USSR and USA began a policy of détente, agreed further limits to nuclear testing and set up a 'hotline' between Washington and Berlin.*

An answer like this, with three key features, each explained with detail, will get full marks. Check your support in the table against the version here. How well did you do?

SuperFacts

The Cuban Missile Crisis Worried about the US threat, Castro asked the USSR to defend Cuba. 114 Soviet ships set off for Cuba, carrying nuclear missiles. This would put the USA within range of Soviet nuclear missiles for the first time. For 'Thirteen Days' in 1962, US and Soviet forces were both ready to go to war.

The Soviet ships turned around Neither side wanted nuclear war. Kennedy and Khrushchev agreed that the USA would not invade Cuba, the USSR would not base missiles there and the USA would withdraw its missiles from Turkey.

Cuban Missile Crisis – results The USA and USSR wanted to avoid a similar crisis. In 1963, they agreed to a policy of building better relations. They set up the 'hotline' between Washington and Moscow and agreed to limit further nuclear testing.

Need more help?

See page 48 of the textbook for another example of how to write the best kind of answer to this type of question.

SuperFacts

Berlin ultimatum (1958) It embarrassed the East that refugees preferred the West and they were losing skilled people. So Khrushchev said all Berlin belonged to East Germany. To humiliate the Western powers, he gave their troops 6 months to leave Berlin.

Eisenhower's Berlin talks (1959) Khrushchev and President Eisenhower agreed to discuss Berlin. Khrushchev withdrew his ultimatum. In 1959, they met in Geneva and then at Camp David in the USA. They met again in Paris in 1960, but could not agree what to do about Berlin. Before the talks a US spy plane was shot down over the USSR. When Eisenhower refused to apologise for the incident, Krushchev walked out.

Kennedy's Berlin talks (1960–61) Krushchev met the new president, Kennedy, in Geneva. Hoping to take advantage of the new president's inexperience, Krushchev again told the USA they had 6 months to leave Berlin.

Kennedy plans for war The USA refused to leave Berlin. In case of war, Kennedy put $3.2 billion more into military funds, and spent $270 million on nuclear fall-out shelters.

The Berlin Wall (1961) Khrushchev could not force US troops to leave Berlin, but he had to save face. So overnight on 12 August, East Germany sealed off West Berlin with barbed wire, then gradually built the Berlin Wall.

The answer

The best answer to this question appears on page 45.

Test yourself

Briefly explain the key features of the Berlin Crisis in 1961.

Tackle the question like this.

First, read the SuperFacts provided on the left.

Next, consider the following statements, based on the five SuperFacts.

One key feature of the Berlin Crisis of 1961 was that ...

A ... in 1958, Khrushchev gave Western troops 6 months to leave Berlin.
B ... in 1959. Khrushchev and Eisenhower could not agree what to do about Berlin.
C ... in 1961, Khrushchev became angry and ordered the USA to leave Berlin.
D ... the USA refused to leave Berlin and prepared for war.
E ... Khrushchev built the Berlin Wall.

Choose the three statements which best answer the question about the Berlin Crisis of 1961. Write them in the answer box below.

Finally, choose extra information or explanation from the SuperFacts and add this to each of your key features in the answer box below.

Answer box

One key feature of the Berlin Crisis of 1961 was...
Further details of this feature are that...
A second feature of the Berlin Crisis of 1961 was...
Further details of this feature are that...
A third feature of the Berlin Crisis of 1961 was...
Further details of this feature are that...

Answering questions: Section 5 Part (c)

Part (c) questions will always ask you to '**explain why**' something happened.

What you need to do

The best answers will always:

- identify not one, or two, but **three** causes
- use **detailed information** to explain **how** each cause made something happen
- make a judgement about the three causes to show
  - which of the three was **most important**
  - and how the three causes are **linked** or connected.

How you do it

Take this question as an example:

Explain why relations between the USA and USSR were so tense from 1957 to 1968.

The SuperFacts on pages 38–39 show several reasons why relations changed. The relevant SuperFact headings are listed on this page.

These SuperFacts could be organised into **three causes**:

Arguments over Berlin	**The Cuban Crisis**	**The invasion of Czechoslovakia**

with three sets of detailed information from the SuperFacts:

Berlin ultimatum Berlin talks The Berlin Wall	Castro and Cuba The Bay of Pigs The Missile Crisis	Alexander Dubcek The Brezhnev Doctrine Dubcek's reaction

Let's start with **one** cause. Using the SuperFacts, **write a paragraph** explaining why relations between the USA and USSR were so tense from 1957 to 1968. Remember, we need to:

- **state the first cause**
- then **give detailed information about it**
- and **then explain how it made relations worse**.

So the paragraph will look like this:

One cause which helps explain why relations were so tense was arguments over Berlin.

What happened in Berlin was... **[give details, using the SuperFacts]**.

These arguments over Berlin made relations tense because ... **[use the SuperFacts to show why the arguments caused such tension]**.

SuperFacts

The SuperFacts on p.38–39 show many factors that made relations between the USA and USSR so tense 1957–68.

You will find it useful to refer to the full SuperFacts on p.38–39, but the titles of the relevant SuperFacts are printed for you here.

Berlin ultimatum

Eisenhower's Berlin talks 1959

Kennedy's Berlin talks 1960–61

Kennedy's plans for war

The Berlin Wall

Castro and Cuba

The Bay of Pigs

The Cuban Missile Crisis

Alexander Dubcek

The Brezhnev Doctrine

Dubcek's reaction

International reaction

Mutually Assured Destruction

Need more help?

See page 137 in the textbook for another example of how to write a top answer to this question.

A model answer with three fully developed causes might look like the one below.

- First, compare the opening paragraph with your answer. How did you do?
- Next, read the whole answer. Which extracts fill the gaps best?

One cause which made relations between the USA and USSR so tense was argument over Berlin. It embarrassed the USSR that so many refugees preferred the West to life under communism and escaped from East Berlin. Khrushchev had talks with Eisenhower, then Kennedy, but they could not find a solution. These arguments over Berlin made relations tense because Khrushchev gave the Western powers 6 months to get its troops out of Berlin. Kennedy refused. It was a tense stand-off. When Kennedy refused, Khrushchev created the Berlin Wall, another cause of tension.

A second cause making relations so tense was Cuba. What happened here was...

Option A: *... Cuba was only 145 miles from the USA. In 1959, Fidel Castro led a revolution there, taking over all American property in Cuba. The USSR offered Cuba help to industrialise. This worried the USA.*

Option B: *... Cuba had been a US ally, but Castro took over and set up ties with the USSR. In 1961 the CIA tried to overthrow him so he asked for Soviet help. They sent 114 ships, with missiles, to defend Cuba from US attack.*

i) Which text box fills this gap better, Option A or Option B? Circle your answer.

Events in Cuba made relations tense because Soviet missiles in Cuba would have been in reach of US soil for the first time. For 13 days in October 1962, they were on the brink of nuclear war.

A third cause which made relations tense was Czechoslovakia. Communist rule there was not popular and Dubcek's reforms in the 'Prague Spring' changed life there. But Brezhnev said this destabilised the Eastern Bloc, so he invaded Czechoslovakia. This made relations tense because...

Option C: *... the invasion was violent. Communists outside the USSR were angry and some turned to China for leadership. Others set up a rival form of communism in Europe known as Eurocommunism.*

Option D: *... the USA liked Dubcek's reform, like making political opposition legal and capitalist profit-making. They didn't want these ideas brutally put down. The USA condemned the USSR, causing tension.*

ii) Which text box fills this gap better, Option C or Option D? Circle your answer.

There is one final thing which the best answers will do. They will **prioritise** the causes and show the **links** between them.

iii) Circle 'Option E' or 'Option F' to show which paragraph you think does this best.

Option E: *The Cuban Crisis was the main cause of tension between the USA and USSR. The USA were already worried about losing American property in Cuba and Soviet experts helping Cuba industrialise. When 114 ships carrying nuclear weapons sailed for Cuba, for 13 days in October 1962 the world was on the brink of nuclear war. So this was the most important cause.*

Option F: *The link between the causes of tension was the threat of nuclear war. In the Berlin Crisis, Kennedy spent $270 million on nuclear shelters. The USA and USSR had enough nuclear arms to destroy each other's cities. So arguments like Berlin and Cuba were very tense. Czechoslovakia caused the least tension because by then nuclear testing was limited and the USA did not threaten war. So the Arms Race was the main cause and the link between causes.*

The answer

The best answer to this question appears on page 45.

Answers: Section 5 Parts (a)–(c)

Part (a)

Mutually Assured Destruction (MAD) By the 1960s, the USA and the USSR both had so many weapons that any nuclear war would cause unacceptable damage to both sides. This brought a little more stability to their relationship.

Czechoslovakia and the USSR Communist rule was unpopular in Czechoslovakia, a satellite state of the USSR. The secret police crushed all political opposition and the economy suffered under the rule of the communist leader, Novotny.

International reaction Western powers condemned the USSR, but gave no military help. Communists outside Russia were angry at the Soviet action; some turned to China for leadership; others set up a rival form of communism: Eurocommunism.

Part (b)

The best picture of the **key features** of the Berlin Crisis would be provided by the following **statements** and **further details**.

- Statement C with ...
  . . . he told the USA they had 6 months to get their troops out of Berlin.
- Statement D with ...
  ...Kennedy put $3.2 billion more into military funds, and spent $270 million on nuclear fall-out shelters.
- Statement E with ...
  Overnight on 12 August, East Germany sealed off West Berlin with barbed wire, then gradually built the Berlin Wall.

Part (c)

The most appropriate text box choices are:

i) **Option B**

Option A is not a good choice.
- It gives background information about Cuba...
- but it leaves out the events leading up to the crisis.

ii) **Option D**

Option C is not a good choice.
- It gives the response of communists to the invasion...
- but it does not include any information about the US response.
- So doesn't explain why Soviet relations with the USA were affected.

iii) **Option F**

Option E is not a good summing up.
- It only talks about one cause.
- It does not weigh the importance of this cause against the other two.
- It does not show any links between the three causes.

1.6

SuperFacts Section 1.6
Why did the Cold War end?

Section summary

The Cuban Missile Crisis had scared the superpowers so much that they had tried a policy of détente – an easing of the tensions between them.

Détente flourished in the 1970s, but began to collapse after the Soviet invasion of Afghanistan in 1979, which the USA fiercely opposed.

During the 1980s and 1990s relations between the USA and the USSR shifted, as the USA became the wealthier, more advanced superpower. At the same time, the USSR's hold on its satellite states was badly weakened, and the 1985 policies of *glasnost* and *perestroika* introduced by Gorbachev speeded up the collapse of the USSR.

SuperFacts are the key bits of information. Learn them and ask someone to test you.

Détente flourished by the 1970s. The USA and USSR wanted to reduce the chance of nuclear war; they also wanted to compete less; they co-operated more. p.117

Détente in space 1967 Outer Space Treaty – USA and USSR ban nuclear arms in space; 1975: first joint space mission. p.117

Détente and arms limitations 1972 Strategic Arms Limitations Treaty (SALT 1) – limited numbers of nuclear weapons on both sides; 1975 Helsinki Conference – superpowers and allies agree areas of co-operation, e.g. respecting human rights. p.117

The Kabul Revolution in Afghanistan in 1978 overthrew the government. Mohammed Taraki became the new, communist, leader and an ally of the USSR. But his communist government was not stable. Civil war broke out. p.118

The USSR invaded Afghanistan in 1979. It wanted to support communism and to stop the growth of Islamic or Western control. Its war against Afghan rebels lasted 10 years; about 1.5 million people died, including 15,000 Soviet troops. p.118

Détente was damaged by the invasion of Afghanistan. The USA feared Soviet expansion into the oil-rich Middle East. President Carter imposed economic sanctions. He ended the SALT 2 talks. He also joined China in supporting Afghan rebels. p.120

Olympic boycotts In protest against the Soviet invasion, the USA and around 60 other countries boycotted the 1980 Olympics in Moscow. The USA ran an alternative Olympic Boycott Games in Philadelphia. In retaliation, in 1984, the USSR and 14 other communist countries boycotted the Olympics in Los Angeles. p.121

The 'Second Cold War' (1979–85) was caused by the invasion of Afghanistan and a new US president – Ronald Reagan. He believed détente had strengthened the USSR. He called it 'the Evil Empire'. He believed that the USA should stop it growing. p.122

The Strategic Defence Initiative (SDI – 'Star Wars') was a US plan for satellites that could destroy Soviet nuclear weapons from space. It was planned to give the US arms superiority. It reversed arms détente. It also broke the Outer Space Treaty. p.124

Soviet response to SDI By the 1980s, the USSR was behind the USA in computer technology and was too poor to keep up with SDI, the arms race or space race. p.125

Mikhail Gorbachev became Soviet leader in 1985, when communism was becoming increasingly inefficient and unpopular there. He proposed *glasnost* (openness, cutting censorship; détente) and *perestroika* (economic reform to increase efficiency). He was very slow to allow democratic elections. He felt his reforms would help communism. p.127

edexcel key terms

détente is the policy of working to ease tensions between two groups or countries that have been enemies or fiercely opposed.

glasnost is the term used for Gorbachev's policy of greater openness, the allowing of public discussion of issues, and détente.

perestroika is the term used for Gorbachev's policy of economic reform to increase efficiency, cutting back state control and bureaucracy and allowing more foreign trade.

The Second Cold War ended after 1985 because the West liked Gorbachev's new approach, because Gorbachev knew the space and arms races were harming the Soviet economy, and because he wanted trade with the West. p.128

At the Geneva Summit (1985), Gorbachev hoped to get Reagan to drop SDI. He replaced the anti-détente foreign minister Andrei Gromyko with pro-détente Eduard Shevardnadze. They did not reach agreement, but agreed to meet again. p.128

At Reykjavik (1986), Reagan would not drop SDI but offered to scrap ballistic nuclear missiles. Gorbachev refused, but talks went on. Gorbachev saw the cost of nuclear weapons was draining the Soviet economy and did not make the USSR safer. He also saw that Reagan could not afford to back down on SDI and that accepting this would help détente. p.128

Intermediate-Range Nuclear Forces (INF) Treaty At Washington (1987), both sides signed this treaty. They agreed to ban all nuclear weapons with a range of 500–5,000 km, while SDI was left in place. p.129

Gorbachev and the satellite states Gorbachev did not want to limit Soviet trade only to satellite states. He also did not want the expense of having Soviet bases there. He wanted communism to benefit from *perestroika* and *glasnost* there too. p.130

Berlin Wall crumbles Once some Eastern Bloc countries became free, it was not possible to stop East Germans getting to the West. So, in November 1989, travel was allowed from East to West Germany and from East to West Berlin. p.131

Communism crumbles Freed from Soviet control, elections were announced and by 1990, communists lost power in Poland, Czechoslovakia, Hungary and East Germany. As the Warsaw Pact was an alliance of communist powers, this collapsed too. p.130

Gorbachev falls Gorbachev was liked in the West for *glasnost*, for *perestroika*, and for freeing satellite states. But some Russians felt his policies had weakened communism. In 1991, the 'Gang of Eight', senior communists, removed him from power. p.132

The Soviet Union falls The new Soviet government lasted only three days. Gorbachev returned. He tried to rewrite the constitution of the USSR, giving Soviet republics more freedom. But his overthrow had hurt his authority. The republics demanded freedom. In December 1991, Gorbachev dissolved the Soviet Union and resigned. pp.133–134

Need more help?

You can find a longer explanation of each SuperFact in your Edexcel textbook, *Peace and War: International Relations 1900–91*. Look for this symbol, which will give you the page number.

SuperFacts

Olympic boycotts In protest against the Soviet invasion, the USA and around 60 other countries boycotted the 1980 Olympics in Moscow. The USA ran an alternative Olympic Boycott Games in Philadelphia. In retaliation, in 1984, the USSR and 14 other communist countries boycotted the Olympics in Los Angeles.

SuperFacts

Détente in space 1967: Outer Space Treaty – USA and USSR ban nuclear arms in space; 1975: First joint space mission.

The Kabul Revolution in Afghanistan in 1978 overthrew the goverment. Mohammed Taraki became the new, communist, leader and an ally of the USSR, but his communist government was not stable. Civil war broke out.

INF Treaty at Washington (1987), both sides signed the Intermediate-Range Nuclear Forces (INF) Treaty. They agreed to ban all nuclear weapons with a range of 500–5,000 km, while SDI was left in place.

Need more help?

See page 26 in the textbook for another example of how to write the best kind of answer to this type of question.

The answer

The best answer to this question appears on page 53.

Answering questions: Section 6 Part (a)

The Part (a) question will always ask you to '**describe one**' piece of information from this section of the course. It may ask you to:

- **describe one action** taken by ...
- **describe one decision** made by ...
- **describe one cause** of ...
- etc.

What you need to do

The best answers will always:

- **state** one relevant action, decision, reaction, cause, etc.
- AND also **describe** it with extra information or an explanation.

How you do it

Take this question as an example:

Describe one feature of the Olympic boycotts of the 1980s.

If you know your SuperFacts, you'll have no trouble answering the question.

The relevant SuperFact about **Olympic boycotts** is printed on this page.

We need to **select** and **describe** one feature of the boycotts. A good feature would be:

The USA boycotted the 1980 Olympics.

But this isn't enough. The question says '**describe**' one feature.

You can describe it by adding an explanation like this:

They did this as a protest against the Soviet invasion of Afghanistan.

Or you can describe it by adding supporting detail like this:

The 1980 Olympics were in Moscow. Around 60 other nations joined the US boycott.

Now test yourself

Here are three possible Part (a) questions.

- ***Describe one example of détente in space in the 1960s.***
- ***Describe one outcome of the Kabul Revolution in 1978.***
- ***Describe one decision made at the Washington Conference in 1987.***

Using the SuperFacts printed alongside these questions:

- Highlight the example, outcome or decision you would **select**.
- Underline the words you would use to **describe** (i.e. explain or support it).

Answering questions: Section 6 Part (b)

Part (b) questions will always ask you to '**briefly explain**' something.

What you need to do

The best answers will always:

- identify not one, or two, but **three** key features
- give extra information or an explanation for each key feature.

How you do it

Take this question as an example:

Briefly explain the key features of détente between the USA and USSR in the 1970s.

If you know your SuperFacts, you'll have no trouble answering the question. You need to **select** and **support** three key features. So, a good feature is:

Co-operation in space.

This isn't enough. You need to support this statement, to show the examiner you know what you are talking about. Something like this:

In 1975, the USA and USSR co-operated to run their first joint space mission.

Before you look at the answer below, write in the support column of the table what you think would be good support for each of the next two key features.

Key Feature	Support
A second feature of détente was co-operation about arms	
A third feature of détente was other areas of co-operation	

You can see that we point out to the examiner each time we introduce another key feature. You are giving **three** key features, so tell the examiner when you start each new one.

__One__ key feature of détente between the USA and USSR in the 1970s was co-operation in space. An example of this was that, in 1975, they co-operated to run their first joint space mission. __A second__ feature of détente was co-operation about arms. For example, the 1967 Outer Space Treaty banned nuclear arms in space and the 1972 SALT 1 treaty limited the number of nuclear weapons on both sides. __A third__ feature of détente was co-operation in other areas. For example, at the 1975 Helsinki Conference they agreed to co-operate over trade and respect human rights.

An answer like this, with three key features, each one explained with detail, will get full marks. Check your support in the table against the version here. How well did you do?

SuperFacts

Détente flourished by the 1970s. The USA and USSR wanted to reduce the chance of nuclear war; they also wanted to compete less; they co-operated more.

Détente in space 1967 Outer Space Treaty – USA and USSR ban nuclear arms in space; 1975: First joint space mission.

Détente and arms limitations 1972 Strategic Arms Limitations Treaty (SALT 1) – limited numbers of nuclear weapons on both sides; 1975 Helsinki Conference – superpowers and allies agree areas of co-operation, e.g. respecting human rights.

Need more help?

See page 136 in the textbook for another example of how to write a top answer to this question.

SuperFacts

The Kabul Revolution in Afghanistan in 1978 overthrew the government. Mohammed Taraki became the new, communist, leader and an ally of the USSR, but his communist government was not stable. Civil war broke out.

The USSR invaded Afghanistan in 1979. It wanted to support communism and to stop the growth of Islamic or Western control. Its war against Afghan rebels lasted 10 years; about 1.5 million people died, including 15,000 Soviet troops.

Détente was damaged by the invasion of Afghanistan. The USA feared Soviet expansion into the oil-rich Middle East. US President Carter imposed economic sanctions. He ended the SALT 2 talks. He also joined China in supporting Afghan rebels.

Olympic boycotts As a protest against the invasion, the USA and around 60 other countries boycotted the 1980 Olympics in Moscow. The USA ran an alternative Olympic Boycott Games in Philadelphia. In retaliation, in 1984, the USSR and 14 other communist countries boycotted the Olympics in Los Angeles.

The 'Second Cold War' (1979–85) was caused by the invasion of Afghanistan and a new US president – Ronald Reagan. He believed détente had strengthened the USSR. He called it 'the Evil Empire'. He believed that the USA should stop it growing.

The answer

The best answer to this question appears on page 53.

Test yourself

Describe the key features of the US response to the Soviet invasion of Afghanistan in 1979.

Tackle the question like this.

First, read the SuperFacts provided on the left.

Next, consider the following statements, based on the five SuperFacts.

One key feature of the US response to the Soviet invasion of Afghanistan in 1979 was…

A … the government of Afghanistan was overthrown.
B … the Soviet war against the Afghan rebels lasted over ten years.
C … détente was damaged.
D … there was a boycott of the 1980 Olympic Games in Moscow.
E … the Second Cold War started.

Choose the three statements which best answer the question about the key features of the US response to the Soviet invasion of Afghanistan in 1979. Write them in the answer box below.

Finally, choose extra information or explanation from the SuperFacts and add this to each of your key features in the answer box below.

Answer box

One key feature of the US response to the Soviet invasion of Afghanistan in 1979 was that …
Further details of this feature are that …
A second feature of the US response to the Soviet invasion of Afghanistan in 1979 was that …
Further details of this feature are that …
A third feature of the US response to the Soviet invasion of Afghanistan in 1979 was that …
Further details of this feature are that …

Answering questions: Section 6 Part (c)

Part (c) questions will always ask you to '**explain why**' something happened.

What you need to do

The best answers will always:

- identify not one, or two, but **three** causes
- use **detailed information** to explain **how** each cause made something happen
- make a judgement about the three causes to show:
  - which of the three was **most important**
  - and how the three causes are **linked** or connected.

How you do it

The four boxes below show you how to do this, if you were answering this question:

Explain why relations between the USSR and USA changed 1979–91.

A What is a cause with detailed information?

One cause of changing US / USSR relations was the Soviet invasion of Afghanistan.

But this is not enough – you need detail.

So you need to say:

One cause of changing US / USSR relations was the Soviet invasion of Afghanistan. Its war against Afghan rebels lasted 10 years and 1.5m people died.

B Explaining how causes make things happen

So far, you've shown you know what the Soviet invasion of Afghanistan was – now you have to show how it caused relations to change. Something like this:

The invasion made the USA fear Soviet expansion into the oil-rich Middle East. So relations got worse. US President Carter imposed economic sanctions, ended the SALT 2 talks and supported the rebels.

C Explaining how causes link together

You need at least three causes, and detail, and how each one caused change. Your causes could be:

- the Soviet invasion of Afghanistan
- President Reagan's 'Second Cold War'
- President Gorbachev's reforms .

You need to show the links between the causes.

Invading Afghanistan told Reagan that the USSR was 'the Evil Empire', prompting his SDI project. SDI, in turn, told Gorbachev that he couldn't compete with the US and made him adopt reform instead. The three causes were a linked chain of events.

D Which cause is the most important?

The examiner wants to know which cause you think is most important. He or she doesn't have to agree. You only need to choose a sensible reason and make a case for it, supported by the events. For example:

The Strategic Defence Initiative (SDI) was the most important cause of changing relations. At first, it frightened the USSR and made them very suspicious and mistrusting of the USA. But later, SDI convinced Gorbachev that glasnost (friendship and détente) was the only way forward.

SuperFacts

You may want to refer the SuperFacts on p.46–47 when you do this activity.

To help you, the titles of the relevant SuperFacts are listed here:

The USSR invaded Afghanistan

Détente was damaged

Olympic boycotts

The Second Cold War 1979–85

The Strategic Defence Initiative

Test yourself

Here is a new question and three causes with which you can practise.

Explain why there was a 'Second Cold War between the USA and USSR 1979–85.

Cause 1 – the Soviet invasion of Afghanistan

Cause 2 – President Reagan's opinions about the USSR

Cause 3 – the Strategic Defence Initiative (SDI).

i) Give some detail about each cause (use pages 46–47 if you need some help).

1

2

3

ii) Explain how these causes helped to make the 'Second Cold War' happen.

1

2

3

iii) Explain how these causes link together.

iv) Explain which was the most important.

Chosen cause with reasons:

Need more help?

If you need more help with Part (c) questions like this one, you can refer to page 93 of the textbook.

Answers: Section 6 Parts (a)–(c)

Part (a)

Détente in space 1967: Outer Space Treaty – USA and USSR ban nuclear arms in space; 1975: First joint space mission.

The Kabul Revolution in Afghanistan in 1978 overthrew the government. Mohammed Taraki became the new, communist, leader and an ally of the USSR. But his communist government was not stable. Civil war broke out.

At Washington (1987), both sides signed the Intermediate-Range Nuclear Forces (INF) Treaty. They agreed to ban all nuclear weapons with a range of 500–5,000 km, while SDI was left in place.

Part (b)

The best picture of the **key features** of the US response to the Soviet invasion of Afghanistan would be provided by the following **statements** and **further details**.

- Statement C with.
  The USA feared Soviet expansion into the oil-rich Middle East. President Carter imposed economic sanctions. He ended the SALT 2 talks. He also joined China in supporting Afghan rebels.
- Statement D with ...
  the USA and around 60 other countries joined the boycott. The USA ran an alternative Olympic Boycott Games in Philadelphia.
- Statement E with ...
  Ronald Reagan called the USSR 'the Evil Empire'. He believed that the USA should halt this evil.

Part (c)

i)

1 Any details about the invasion of Afghanistan:

e.g. *The Soviet war in Afghanistan lasted 10 years and about 1.5 million people were killed.*

2 Any details about Reagan's opinions about the USSR:

e.g. *He called it 'the Evil Empire'.*

3 Any details about SDI:

e.g. *It was a US plan for satellites that could destroy Soviet nuclear weapons from space.*

ii)

1 Any explanation about how the invasion helped cause a Second Cold War:

e.g. *The USA feared Soviet expansion into the oil-rich Middle East. US President Carter imposed economic sanctions. He ended the SALT 2 talks. He also joined China in supporting Afghan rebels.*

2 Any details about how Reagan's opinions helped cause a Second Cold War:

e.g. *He believed détente had strengthened the USSR. He believed that the USA should halt the Evil Empire.*

3 Any details about how SDI helped cause a Second Cold War:

e.g. *It was planned to give the USA arms superiority. It reversed arms détente. It also broke the Outer Space Treaty.*

iii)

Any reasonable link, such as:

- *The Afghan invasion convinced Reagan that the USSR was evil.*
- *Reagan's opinion that the USSR was evil led him to abandon détente and adopt SDI.*

iv)

Any reasonable opinion, such as:

- *The invasion of Afghanistan was the most important because it ended détente and convinced Reagan he needed to destroy the USSR.*
- *Reagan's opinions were most important because they shaped his view of the USSR and made him adopt SDI.*
- *SDI was the most important. It showed the USSR they could not keep up with the USA in space or computers. This made them very wary of the USA and cooled relations.*

Where to find help

The Unit 2 Exam: A Depth Study

The Depth Study is a chance to study a short period (about 20 years) of the history of a major power. You will have chosen ONE of the following:

either:	Unit 2A	Germany	1918–39
or	Unit 2B	Russia	1917–39
or	Unit 2C	USA	1919–41

The **structure** of the **examination** is the same for each. You will always have:

- **One paper** on Unit 2. It will last **1hr 15mins**. You will answer **6 questions**.

The questions will always follow the pattern below.

- The number of **marks** you can score for each question is given below.
- So is the **time** the examiners recommend you spend on each question.

Qn 1(a)

4 marks 6 minutes	Question 1 (a) will always give you a source to read. Then it will ask: **What does Source A tell us about** ... [something to do with the source]

Qn 1(b)

6 marks 8 minutes	Question 1 (b) will always ask you to: **Describe** ... [something]

Qn 1(c)

8 marks 12 minutes	Question 1 (c) will always ask you to: **Explain the effects of** ... [something]

Qn 1(d)

8 marks 12 minutes	Question 1 (d) will always ask you to : **Explain why** ... [something happened]

Qn 2 (a) or (b)

8 marks 12 minutes	You choose Question 2 (a) **OR** Question 2 (b). Both questions will always ask you to: **Explain how** ... [something happened]

Qn 3 (a) or (b)

16 marks 25 minutes	You choose Question 3 (a) **OR** Question 3 (b). Both questions expect you to use your judgement to answer questions such as: Was [a specified thing] the **main cause**/the **worst effect** of [a specified thing]?

To help you prepare for this examination, this book gives three kinds of help.

First, we help you with **content**:

- a **one-page overview** of the content of your Unit
- the **SuperFacts** for each part of the Unit (SuperFacts are the key bits of information you need to answer the questions).

Secondly, we help you with **questions** – explaining what you have to do to answer every type of question you will be asked and giving you a chance to test yourself.

Thirdly, we provide **model answers** to all the questions, so you can see how you did.

Overview: Germany 1918–39

1918

Germany loses the First World War.
The Treaty of Versailles

Hitler leaves the army and joins DAP.

The new Weimar Republic

NSDAP formed
- Hitler leader
- membership up
- SS.

Munich Putsch

Early problems
- constitutional weakness
- economic problems
- political turmoil.

Attempted coups
- Spartacists
- Kapp Putsch.

1923

NSDAP re-launched
- clearer ideas
- better organisation

but support falls.

Stresemann
- economic recovery
- political stability
- international status.

1929

The Great Depression
- Bruning's government falters → Hindenburg wavers → Hitler becomes chancellor.

1933

Nazi dictatorship
- Reichstag fire
- Enabling Act
- Night of the Long Knives.

Nazi domestic issues
- control of education
- youth groups (such as Hitler Youth)
- the position of women: seen as wives and mothers, not workers
- 'Aryanisation': the persecution of Jews and other minority groups.

Nazi control consolidated
- the police state
- censorship
- propaganda.

1939

Key Topic summary

Germany was blamed for the First World War (1914–18). The new Weimar Republic had to sign the Treaty of Versailles (ending the war with Germany) that took away much German land and set high reparation payments. The Weimar government was blamed by many Germans for accepting this harsh peace, when the German army had not been defeated in the war.

The German economy, already weak from war, was hard hit by the repayments, the loss of land with raw materials and factories and the shortages of food and other essentials (such as fuel).

The Weimar Republic, facing opposition from many political parties, worked to restore the economy and re-negotiate reparations. They seemed to be succeeding when the 1929 Great Depression caused widespread economic collapse.

edexcel key terms

reparations was the word used to describe the compensation that was to be paid by the countries on the losing side in the First World War.

demilitarisation means forbidding the army to enter an area. The Rhineland became demilitarised as a way of weakening Germany and making France feel safer from attack.

SuperFacts Key Topic 1
The Weimar Republic 1918–33

SuperFacts are the key bits of information. Learn them and ask someone to test you.

At the end of the First World War, the Kaiser abdicated. A new government was set up, led by Chancellor Ebert. This government created the Weimar Republic. p.6

The Treaty of Versailles The new Weimar government had to accept the Treaty. But this caused unrest. Germans called it a *diktat* because they were not part of the negotiations. They said that, by accepting it, the new government had given Germany a 'stab in the back' (*dolchstoss*) – and called them 'the November Criminals'. p.7 & 9

German reparations were set at £6,600 million by the Treaty of Versailles. This damaged German industry and government finances. p.8

German armed forces, although not defeated in the war, were limited at Versailles to 100,000 soldiers (with no tanks or planes). The navy was limited to 6 battleships, 6 cruisers, 24 smaller ships and no submarines. This was very unpopular. p.8

The Rhineland (Germany's border with France, Belgium and the Netherlands) was demilitarised at Versailles. It became a 'buffer' zone to protect those countries: German troops could not go into it, even though it was part of Germany. p.8

German land was taken by the Treaty of Versailles. About 13% of German land was given to its neighbours, including Alsace and Lorraine, Eupen and Malmedy, Danzig, West Prussia, and Posen. Germany also lost 50% of its iron and 15% of its coal reserves and 11 colonies in Africa. Accepting all this made the Weimar Republic unpopular. p.8

The Weimar Constitution allowed everyone over 20 to vote by secret ballot for members of the Reichstag, which passed the laws. The chancellor led the government. He chose ministers and proposed laws. The president was head of state. He chose the chancellor and, under Article 48, could pass laws by decree in a crisis. p.10

The Weimar government was weak The constitution shared out power. But this made chancellors weak. They had to rely on coalitions of small parties to get a majority in the Reichstag. The second house, the Reichsrat, could delay legislation. p.10

Economic problems The Weimar government was bankrupt: Germany's gold reserves had been spent on the war. Its income was drained by reparation payments. It had also lost the land with its richest coal and iron reserves. Later it faced serious inflation. p.12

The French occupied the Ruhr (1923) when Germany could not pay its reparations. They took raw materials, industrial machines and manufactured goods. The Ruhr contained many factories and around 80% of Germany's coal, iron and steel production, so Germany's economic problems were made worse. p.12

Hyperinflation meant German money became almost worthless. A loaf of bread in 1919 cost 1 mark; in 1922, 200 marks; and in 1923, 100,000 million marks. By November 1923, it cost 200,000 million marks. In 1918, you could exchange 20 marks for £1. By 1923, you needed 20 billion marks for £1. p.13

All Germans suffered as vital goods were hard to purchase. Many workers became unemployed. The pensions and savings of the middle-classes became worthless. This made the government even more unpopular. p13

Gustav Stresemann, chancellor in 1923, solved the economic problems. He negotiated a French withdrawal from the Ruhr and the Dawes Plan (1924) which cut reparations; he dealt with inflation by replacing the mark with a new currency, the rentenmark. p.18

Political problems The new Weimar government was blamed for Versailles and the economic problems. Many German workers supported left-wing parties, like the communists (KPD). Many ex-soldiers and landowners supported right-wing parties. p.14

Political unrest over Versailles and the economic problems led to frequent strikes and protests. Between 1919 and 1922, there were 376 political murders. p.15

The Spartacists, a communist group, led a huge uprising in Berlin in 1919. They thought the Weimar Republic was run by the middle-class. They wanted workers' councils to run the country. The government ended the revolt violently, using the *Freikorps* (anti-communist private armies formed after the war by ex-officers). p.16

The Kapp Putsch (1920), led by Wolfgang Kapp, was a right-wing revolt to get the Kaiser back into power: 5,000 rebels took control of Berlin. The government promoted a general strike by workers. The city was paralysed and the revolt failed. p.17

The Dawes Plan (1924) agreed by Stresemann and Dawes, a US banker, reduced Germany's reparation payments and arranged for US banks to invest in German industry. So government finances improved and German industry recovered. p.18

The Young Plan (1929) further reduced reparations from £6.6 billion to £2 billion and gave Germany 59 more years to pay them off. This made the Weimar government popular with some Germans – but not all, as repayments were still £50 million per year. p.19

In the Locarno Pact (1925), Germany accepted the borders agreed at the Treaty of Versailles. Allied troops began to leave the Rhineland, and France promised not to invade as it had done in the Ruhr. This helped improve the popularity of the Weimar Republic. p.19

Germany was allowed to join the League of Nations in 1926; it was even given a seat on the Council. This boosted the reputation of the Weimar Republic. p.20

In the Kellogg–Briand Pact (1928), 61 nations promised not to go to war to resolve disputes. Germany was part of this pact. This showed the German people that the Weimar Republic was now a respected part of the international community. p.20

The Wall Street Crash (1929) set off a worldwide Great Depression. Sales of German exports fell, causing bankruptcies. Unemployment rose from 1 million to 5 million by 1932. This caused political unrest. Voters turned against the Weimar Republic again. p.21

ResultsPlus
Top tip

When choosing SuperFacts to support a statement, read the question carefully and consider the limits it puts on the information you use. Question 1a) asks, 'What can you learn from the source about...?' This is the one question where you should not use SuperFacts at all. It is asking what you can learn from the source, not what you know.

Need more help?
You can find a longer explanation of each SuperFact in your Edexcel textbook, *Germany 1918–39*. Look for this symbol, which will give you the page number.

SuperFacts Key Topic 2
Hitler and the growth of the Nazi Party 1918–33

SuperFacts are the key bits of information. Learn them and ask someone to test you.

Hitler and the First World War Hitler was in the German army during the First World War. He won the Iron Cross for bravery. He worked for the army after the war. p.27

Hitler hated the Treaty of Versailles He saw it as a 'stab in the back' for Germany. He believed Germany had been betrayed by socialists and Jews. p.27

Hitler joined the German Workers' Party (DAP) in 1919 (when it had only about 40 members). It was a right-wing group, angry about Versailles and economic problems. It was anti-communist, anti-socialist, anti-Jewish and regarded democracy as weak. p.27

Hitler helped the DAP grow He and Anton Drexler (the DAP leader) drew up a 25-Point Programme – it included scrapping the Versailles treaty, expanding Germany, and removing citizenship from Jews. By 1920, membership was 3,000. p.28

The Nazi Party In 1920 the DAP changed its name to the National Socialist German Workers' Party (NSDAP in German, Nazi for short). Hitler became the party leader (Führer) in 1921. His rousing speeches began to attract even more members. p.29

The first Nazi newspaper was called *Völkischer Beobachter*. Newspapers were an important way of spreading Nazi propaganda. p.29

The Sturmabteilung (SA), set up in 1921 and led by Ernst Röhm, was the Nazi private army. They wore brown uniforms and were called 'brownshirts'. They helped the party grow by scaring rivals, protecting Nazi leaders and disrupting rival meetings. p.29

Reasons for the Munich Putsch (1923) Hitler wanted to exploit discontent about hyperinflation and the French occupation of the Ruhr. He wanted to act before Stresemann improved the economy and cracked down on right-wing groups. p.30

Events of the Munich Putsch Hitler and 600 SA stormed a meeting of Bavarian state leaders and forced them to accept a Nazi takeover. Next day, the state leaders, no longer being physically threatened, called out the local police and army. The Nazis tried to take over the city; but state troops defeated them. Goering was wounded, 16 Nazis were killed, and Hitler was captured. p.30–31

The Munich Putsch failed Firstly, this was because Hitler did not have the support of local Bavarian leaders. Secondly, the Nazis were too weak: they had only 2,000 rifles and they were outnumbered by Bavarian troops. p.31

Results of the Munich Putsch Hitler was given 5 years in prison. But his trial gave the Nazis publicity and he used his time in prison to write *Mein Kampf (My Struggle)* – which also gave him publicity – and he was released after only 9 months. p.31

Key Topic summary

Adolf Hitler was the leader and driving force behind the Nazi Party, which came to dominate German politics from 1933, when Hitler became chancellor.

The Nazis despised the Weimar government and the Versailles treaty and first tried to seize power by force in the Munich Putsch of 1923. The Putsch failed, and Hitler decided the Nazis had to be elected to power.

The Nazis became a powerful political force because of Hitler's leadership and abilities as a speaker; the economic problems caused by the Great Depression; skilful use of propaganda; use of violence to intimidate opposition; and the appeal of such clear and simple messages as 'Work and Bread'.

edexcel key terms

the Nazi Party was the National Socialist German Workers' Party. In German, this was **N**ational**s**ozialistische **D**eutsche **A**rbeiterpartei (NSDAP). German pronunciation means it became 'Nazi' for short.

putsch means an attempt to overthrow the government by violence.

Nazi Party aims Hitler renewed Nazism on his release in 1923. It wanted a stronger Germany (e.g. expanding its borders); state control of society and the economy (e.g. treating workers fairly); traditional German values (e.g. encouraging families); and keeping German blood 'pure' (e.g. not allowing marriage with 'inferior' races). p.32

Nazi Party Organisation was improved after 1923. Hitler created *gauleiters* for each region, boosted party funds, employed more SA and started the SS. Goebbels improved party propaganda. The NSDAP had 100,000 members by 1929. p.34

The NSDAP remained weak in the Reichstag however. By 1928, they had only 12 seats. This was because the Weimar government improved the economy and did well in foreign affairs. Hindenburg, a popular ex-army leader, was president. p.35

The Great Depression (began 1929) changed German politics. From 1929, the economy worsened, unemployment and unrest grew. Chancellor Brüning's government could not cope. He tried raising taxes and banning protests. Both failed. This boosted support for extreme parties: by September 1930, the Nazis had 107 Reichstag seats. p.36

The Nazis gained support, more than other parties, because Hitler was an excellent speaker who impressed people at spectacular rallies; Nazi propaganda used simple messages like 'Work and Bread'; the SA made the Nazis seem strong and organised and broke up rival meetings. The NSDAP had 400,000 members by 1930. p.37

The Nazis appealed to workers by promising work and bread; to the middle-class as a strong, moral, party; to farmers and businesses as protection against communism. Nazi propaganda targeted groups like women and young people. p.37–39

In the 1932 presidential election Hindenburg was re-elected, with 19 million votes. But Hitler came second with 13 million votes. He was now a national political figure. p.40

In May 1932, the chancellor, Brüning, was sacked, his government could not deal with the problems caused by the Depression. Von Papen, the new chancellor, needed Nazi votes in the Reichstag, so he made Hitler one of his cabinet. p.40

In July 1932, the Nazis became the biggest party in the Reichstag (230 seats). Hitler withdrew his support and von Papen could not continue as chancellor. Hindenburg didn't want Hitler and appointed von Schleicher as chancellor. p.41

By January 1933, von Schleicher could not rule without Nazi support. Hindenburg had little choice but to appoint Hitler, the leader of the biggest party in the Reichstag, as the new chancellor of Germany. p.41

ResultsPlus
Top tip

Remember the powers of the chancellor and the president in the Weimar Republic.

The chancellor chose ministers and ran the country, but he needed the support of a majority in the Reichstag to pass laws.

The president chose the chancellor and could dismiss the Reichstag and rule by decree.

Hitler could not become chancellor unless the president chose him. But, by 1932, a chancellor could not pass laws without Nazi support – they could stop him getting a majority.

Need more help?
You can find a longer explanation of each SuperFact in your Edexcel textbook, *Germany 1918–39*. Look for this symbol, which will give you the page number.

Key Topic summary
From 1933 to 1939, Hitler tightened his hold on Germany. He did this by a combination of careful planning, manipulation of the legal system, and intimidation.

In 1933, Hitler was chancellor of a government elected from many political parties with local and national representatives and two powerful heads of government.

By 1939, Hitler was sole leader of a single-party state with no independent local government.

SuperFacts Key Topic 3
The Nazi dictatorship 1933–39

SuperFacts are the key bits of information. Learn them and ask someone to test you.

The Reichstag fire (February 1933) was blamed on a young Dutch communist, Marinus van der Lubbe. Hitler used the Reichstag fire to make Hindenburg declare a state of emergency, so Hitler, as chancellor, could pass laws by decree. p.45

The Decree for the Protection of the People and the State was passed by Hitler before the 1933 elections. It suspended civil rights, which meant he could imprison his election rivals. It also banned communist newspapers. p.45

The March 1933 election campaign was violent. 70 people died in clashes between the SA and Nazi opponents. The Nazis won 288 seats, the communists only 81. p.45

Hitler banned the communists from taking their 81 seats by using his emergency powers. This meant Hitler, with the aid of the Nationalists, had two thirds of the votes in the Reichstag he needed to change the constitution. p.46

The Enabling Act (March 1933) was passed by 444 votes to 94, the SA and SS filled the Kroll Opera House where the voting was held. The Act said Hitler could make laws without the consent of the Reichstag. He got this extra power for four years. p.46

Hitler banned trade unions in 1933 and made strikes illegal. He did this because strikes could undermine his power. It removed a possible source of opposition. p.46

Hitler banned all political parties except the Nazi Party in 1933. He did this to remove organised opposition to his government. It made the Nazis stronger. p.47

Hitler banned the Länder (local parliaments) in 1934. He did this because the Nazis did not control them. It removed another possible source of opposition to the Nazis. p.47

Ernst Röhm was the leader of the SA. He disagreed with some of Hitler's policies. By 1934, the SA numbered 3 million. This made Röhm a threat to Hitler. p.48

The Night of the Long Knives was Hitler's purge of the SA in 1934. About 400 people were shot, including the SA leader, Ernst Röhm. This removed a threat to Hitler. pp.48–49

President Hindenburg died in August 1934; Hitler declared himself Führer – with the powers of both chancellor and president. In a plebiscite to confirm this, 90% of voters agreed. This change, combined with earlier ones, made Hitler a dictator. p.49

Hitler set up the SS in 1925 as his 'protection squad'. From 1929, Himmler ran it and expanded it to 50,000 men. The SS controlled all the security forces in the Nazi police state. The Death's Head Units of the SS ran concentration camps. p.50

The Gestapo (Hitler's secret police) was part of the Nazi police state; it was led by Heydrich. It had no uniform, so it could easily spy on everyone. By 1939, the Gestapo had arrested 150,000 people for political opposition. pp.50–51

edexcel key terms

the Enabling Act (March 1933) was the act that allowed Hitler to pass laws without the consent of the Reichstag. It was this law that gave him the power to change the constitution to make the Nazi Party the only political party in Germany and himself its only leader.

decrees (in the sense the word is used in this book) are laws made by the leaders of an elected government in an emergency. They can be passed without the approval of the elected representatives.

German Law courts were controlled by Hitler as part of his police state. He could sack any judges who displeased him or change sentences they set. Hitler set up the People's Court, with handpicked judges, to hear 'crimes against the state'. p.51

Concentration camps were another part of the Nazi police state. The first one, Dachau, opened in 1933. The camps were set up to punish political opponents; then they took those the Nazis called 'undesirables' such as Jews, homosexuals and gypsies. By 1939, there were six camps with about 20,000 prisoners. p.51

The Concordat (1933) was an agreement between Hitler and the Pope. It said Hitler would allow Catholics to worship and the Catholic Church would not interfere in politics. Hitler hoped it would reduce opposition to Nazi rule. p.52

The Concordat failed Hitler wanted more control of the Catholic Church. He made its schools teach his curriculum; he banned Catholic youth groups; he arrested priests. In 1937, the Pope criticised the Nazis in a statement called 'With Burning Anxiety'. p.53

Some Protestants accepted the Nazis and even put Nazi flags in church. But the Pastors' Emergency League (PEL) campaigned against the Nazis. The PEL leader, Pastor Martin Niemöller, was arrested in 1937 and sent to a concentration camp. This was one of many ways in which Hitler suppressed opposition. p.53

Joseph Goebbels ran the Ministry of People's Enlightenment and Propaganda. It controlled newspapers, magazines, films, plays and radio broadcasts. It censored information it didn't like and put in propaganda to give out Nazi messages. p.54

Propaganda was used to persuade people to support the Nazis and their ideas. It was spread in many clever ways. Goebbels made radio broadcasts, films and plays support Nazi ideas, then made radios, and film and theatre tickets, cheap. He also used massive, spectacular rallies to boost the image of Hitler and the Nazi Party. p.56

Books were vetted Banned books were regularly collected up and publicly burned. In just one book-burning in Munich, 20,000 books were destroyed. Authors of these books included Freud and Einstein. p.55

Academic ideas were controlled by the Nazis too. Between 1933 and 1938, 3,000 university teachers were sacked. The Nazis controlled what research could be done, and results were expected to confirm Nazi views. p.55

Music, art and sport were also controlled 'German' music, like Beethoven's, was encouraged; 'foreign' music, like jazz, was banned. The Nazis approved of sport. They used the Olympics as a chance to show off Nazi success. p.55 & 57

Be clear about the distinction between the SA and the SS.

The SA were the brownshirts, the Nazi Party's original private army. Hitler reduced their numbers and power greatly in the Night of the Long Knives (1934).

The SS started as Hitler's black-shirted personal guard and became the Nazi Party's political police. They took over many of the roles of the SA after the Night of the Long Knives.

Need more help?

You can find a longer explanation of each SuperFact in your Edexcel textbook, *Germany 1918–39*. Look for this symbol, which will give you the page number.

SuperFacts Key Topic 4
Nazi domestic policies 1933–39

SuperFacts are the key bits of information. Learn them and ask someone to test you.

Nazi education was planned to make Germany strong. Hitler wanted children to grow fit and healthy; girls to be good wives and mothers; boys to be workers and soldiers. p.61

Nazi schools All children went to school until they were 14. All schools had the same curriculum: PE took up a sixth of school time. Lessons taught Nazi views; for example, race studies taught Aryan superiority. Girls studied cooking and needlework. p.61

Nazi youth movements were also planned to make Germany strong. *Pimpfen* (Little Fellows, 6–14) and *Jungvolk* (Hitler Youth, 14–18) were for boys. They trained them for the army. The League of German Maidens was for girls. It taught motherhood. p.61

Edelweiss Pirates was an anti-Nazi youth group. It had 2,000 members by 1939. p.61

Nazi views about women Nazis thought women should focus on the traditional *kinder, küche, kirche* (children, kitchen, church). They frowned on women working, or wearing make-up or trousers. Some women felt devalued by Nazi policies. p.62

Women and work There were about 100,000 female teachers in Germany in 1933. The Nazis wanted women at home, and forced many women out of professions such as teaching and law. This created jobs for men and reduced unemployment. p.62

Women and marriage The Law for the Encouragement of Marriage (1933) lent couples who married 1000 marks (a month's wages) if the wife left work. For each child, they were let off a quarter of the loan. This boosted marriage, large families and women staying at home. p.63

Women as mothers The German Women's Enterprise supported the Nazi policy of large families. It gave classes and radio broadcasts on good motherhood. It gave the Mother's Cross to women with children: bronze for 4–5; silver for 6–7; gold for 8 or more. p.63

The *Lebensborn* programme aimed to produce 'racially pure' Germans. It found 'racially pure' women for SS men to get pregnant. In just one *Lebensborn* home, from 1938–41, 540 single women gave birth to babies fathered by SS men. p.63

Nazi economic policy made industry serve the needs of the state. For example, iron and steel production trebled 1933–39. This made Germany more self-sufficient. p.65

The Four Year Plan (1936) Hitler's plan to change the economy to make Germany ready for war in four years. As a result, arms spending went from 3.5 billion to 26 billion marks, and the army grew from 100,000 to 900,000 between 1933 and 1939. p.65

The German Labour Front (DAF) was the state-run Nazi replacement for trades unions. It set working hours and wages. Under the DAF, working hours went up by an average of 6 hours a week. p.64

Key Topic summary

From 1933 to 1939, the Nazi Party came to control all aspects of daily life in Germany. They tried to create a 'perfect' state where people willingly followed Nazi policies.

Propaganda and censorship were key tools in this. The Nazis took control of the education system. They set the curriculum, censored the textbooks and sacked teachers who protested. Boys were taught to become workers and soldiers, girls to become wives and mothers.

Women were discouraged from doing paid work and encouraged to be mothers at the heart of a traditional family. While the Nazis stressed the importance of the family, they set up so many state-run activities for children and adults that families actually spent little time together.

edexcel key terms

kinder, küche, kirche (children, kitchen, church) is the phrase that sums up Nazi policies towards women. They felt men and women should have different focuses in their work.

Aryan Hitler invented the Aryan race. 'Aryans', to the Nazis, were the 'original, pure' Germans – blonde, blue eyed and healthy. They aimed to make the new Germany an Aryan country.

ghettos were walled off areas in cities where Jewish people were forced to live as part of the Nazi policy of cutting Jewish people off from the rest of the community.

The Reich Labour Service (RAD) gave work to the unemployed. All young men had to do 6 months in the RAD from 1935. They did work vital to the state, like farm work and public buildings and, by 1939, had built 7,000 miles of autobahn. p.64

Unemployment caused hardship and discontent, so Hitler kept it down with schemes like the RDF and army spending. Taking jobs from women and Jews also increased employment for men. So unemployment fell from 6 million to 1 million 1933–38. p.65

Standard of living Wages rose 20% and sales of consumer goods by 45% from 1933–38. But food prices rose too, and people worked 6 hours more a week. Car ownership trebled in the 1930s; few Volkswagens were made: the factories soon moved to war production. p.66–67

The SdA (Beauty of Labour) aimed to please workers and keep their support. It controlled working conditions like meals and safety standards. p.66

The KdF (Strength through Joy) ran sports centres and social activities, such as theatre trips and holidays, for workers. As a result, KdF became the world's largest tour operator in the 1930s. p.66

Nazi views on race In *Mein Kampf* Hitler set out the Nazi hierarchy of race. 'Pure' Western Europeans were 'Aryans' (Hitler's invented race). Then came races such as eastern European Slavs. Next were 'sub-humans' (for example black people and the disabled). Gypsies and Jews were *Lebensunwertes* (unworthy of life). p.68

First racial policies The Nazis believed Jews weakened Germany. From 1933, they persecuted Jews. They organised boycotts of Jewish businesses. Then Jews could not work in government or the armed forces. They were banned from restaurants. p.68

The Nuremberg Laws (1935) said Jews were no longer German citizens, so could not vote or have passports. From 1938, Jews had to register their possessions and carry identity cards. Jewish professionals, like doctors, could not have Aryan clients. p.69

Kristallnacht (the Night of Broken Glass) Over the night of 9 November 1938 the Nazis took revenge for the shooting of a Nazi official in Paris by a young Jew. Nazi official figures say 814 shops, 171 homes and 191 synagogues were destroyed and about 100 Jews killed. p.69

Jews imprisoned After Kristallnacht, 20,000 Jews were sent to concentration camps. In 1939, all Jews had to move into ghettos: walled-off areas of cities that kept them apart from other people. Housing and food supplies to the ghettos were bad. p.70

Other targets Nazis wanted to purify Germany. So they also persecuted gypsies and homosexuals; they were sent to concentration camps. Disabled people were sent to state 'care' homes, where many died from deliberate neglect. p.71

ResultsPlus
Top tip

When choosing SuperFacts to support a statement, don't use all the SuperFacts you know on the topic. Choose the most relevant. So, in a question about economic problems in Germany 1919–22 only use SuperFacts that cover those dates. Do not discuss economic problems generally.

Need more help?
You can find a longer explanation of each SuperFact in your Edexcel textbook, *Germany 1918–39*. Look for this symbol, which will give you the page number.

Answering questions: Question 1 (a)

What you need to do

Question 1 (a) will always ask '**What can you learn from Source A about [something]**'. The best answers:

- not only extract **information** from the source
- but will also make **inferences** from the source *[see Top tip box]*
- and **support** those inferences with detail from the source.

Note: make sure you answer the question – after **about** comes the **subject**. You can't just make *any* inference from the source, it has to be about the *something* in the question.

Here is a possible **source**, **question** and **answer** for you to study.

> Hitler was filled with joy. He saw war as a way to unite all Germanic people. He joined the German Army and saw harsh times. Out of 3,600 men in his regiment, only 611 survived the first week. A corporal, he was awarded the Iron Cross for bravery. Wartime boosted his confidence. He called it 'the most memorable period of my life'.

Source A: From a GCSE textbook, *The Making of the Modern World, Germany 1918–39.*

Question: What does Source A tell us about Hitler's opinion of the First World War?

Inference	Supporting detail
Source A tells me that Hitler approved of the First World War.	I can infer this because it says that Hitler 'saw war as a way to unite all Germanic people', so he believed it would have benefits.

Now test yourself

(i) Write in the box below to show you can write **supporting detail** using this question:

What does Source A tell us about fighting in the First World War?

Source A tells me fighting was very fierce during the First World War.	**[Supporting detail]**

(ii) Write in the box below to show you can write **an inference** using this question:

What does Source A tell us about Hitler's experience of war?

[Inference]	I can infer this because Source A says that Hitler was awarded a medal, the war boosted his confidence and he called it the most memorable time of his life.

ResultsPlus
Top tip

An **inference** is a judgement that can be made by studying the source, but is not directly stated by it.

A **supported inference** is one that uses detail from the source to prove the inference.

Consider this example:

Source A: 'The furious head teacher told Jimmy that his behaviour was disgraceful, and that he had broken several school rules.'

Question: *What does Source A tell us about Jimmy?*

Information: Source A tells us that Jimmy had broken several school rules. [This is directly stated in the source, so it's not an inference.]

Inference: Source A tells me that Jimmy is in serious trouble and is likely to be punished. [The source does not directly tell us this, but we can infer that it is likely.]

A supported inference: Source A tells me that Jimmy is in serious trouble and is likely to be punished. I can infer this because Jimmy had broken several school rules and the head teacher was furious. [This is an inference, with details quoted from the source to support it.]

The answer

You can find suggested answers to the tasks numbered i), ii) etc. on page 74.

Answering questions: Question 1 (b)

What you need to do

Question 1(b) will always ask you to '**describe**' something. The best answers will:

- **state** not one, or two, but **three** features of the thing being described
- give extra factual detail or an explanation to **support** each feature.

How you do it

Take this question as an example:

Describe the punishments inflicted upon Germany in the Treaty of Versailles.

The SuperFacts will help us. Let's start with the SuperFact about **reparations**.

First we **state** the punishment.	One punishment inflicted on Germany was reparations.
Next we **support** the statement with extra detail or an explanation.	These were set at £6,600 million. This damaged German industry and government finances.

We've written this in **two sentences**, rather than one, to make it obvious to the examiner that we are **stating** a punishment and then **supporting** it with detail.

Now test yourself

(i) Write in the box below to show you can **provide supporting detail**.

Another punishment inflicted on Germany was military restrictions.	**[Supporting detail]**

(ii) In the box below, **state a punishment that fits the supporting detail**.

[Statement]	For example, about 13% of German land was given to its neighbours, including Alsace and Lorraine. It also lost 11 colonies in Africa.

These three examples, written in a paragraph, make a top answer to the exam question.

SuperFacts

German reparations were set at £6,600 million by the Treaty of Versailles. This damaged German industry and government finances.

The German armed forces, although not defeated in the war, were limited at Versailles to 100,000 soldiers (with no tanks or planes). The navy was limited to 6 battleships, 6 cruisers, 24 smaller ships and no submarines. This was very unpopular.

German land was taken by the Treaty of Versailles. Around 13% was given to its neighbours, including Alsace and Lorraine, Eupen and Malmedy, Danzig, West Prussia, and Posen. Germany also lost 50% of its iron and 15% of its coal reserves and 11 colonies in Africa. Accepting all this made the Weimar Republic unpopular.

The answer

You can find suggested answers to the tasks numbered i), ii) etc. on page 74.

Answering questions: Question 1 (c)

Question 1 (c) will always ask you to '**explain the effects**' of something.

What you need to do

The best answers will:

- state not one, but **two** effects
- **support** each effect with extra factual **detail** to write a developed statement
- use this detail to **explain how** each effect happened
- and show **links** or connections between the effects.

How you do it

Take this question as an example:

Explain the effects of the Treaty of Versailles on Germany 1918–23.

The SuperFacts on pages 56–57 will provide us with the information to answer this question. The titles of the relevant SuperFacts have been listed on this page to help you.

The SuperFacts suggest the following **effect** and **supporting detail**.

Effect	Supporting detail
One effect on Germany of the Treaty of Versailles was economic problems.	For example, reparations were set at £6,600 million. This damaged German industry and government finances.

Notice how we have made it very clear to the examiner how we are answering the question. We have:

- used **two** sentences, one for the **effect** and one for the **supporting detail**.
- started each sentence with 'signposts' to show what we are doing, by saying **'One effect was ...'** and **'For example ...'**

Use this approach when you write answers.

Now test yourself

The SuperFacts suggest another effect was **political problems**. Using this second effect, write in the boxes below to show that you can set out the **effect** and **supporting detail**. [You can check your answer in the top box on page 67.]

Effect	Supporting detail
(i)	(ii)

SuperFacts

The Treaty of Versailles The new Weimar government had to accept the Treaty. But this caused unrest. Germans called it a *diktat* because they were not part of the negotiations. They said that, by accepting it, the new government had given Germany a 'stab in the back' (*dolchstoss*) – and called them 'the November Criminals'.

Political problems The new Weimar government was blamed for Versailles and the economic problems. Many German workers supported left-wing parties, like the communists (KPD). Many ex-soldiers and landowners supported right-wing parties.

Political unrest over Versailles and the economic problems led to frequent strikes and protests. Between 1919 and 1922, there were 376 political murders.

The Spartacists, a communist group, led a huge uprising in Berlin in 1919. They thought the Weimar Republic was run by the middle-class. They wanted workers' councils to run the country. The government ended the revolt violently, using the *Freikorps* (anti-communist private armies formed after the war by ex-officers).

The Kapp Putsch (1920), led by Wolfgang Kapp, was a right-wing revolt to get the Kaiser back into power: 5,000 rebels took control of Berlin. The government promoted a general strike by workers. The city was paralysed and the revolt failed.

Making the answer better

But this is not enough. The best answers will **explain how** the effect happened.

Here is an example of how you can use supporting detail to explain how the effect happened. This time, we have used **political problems** as our example.

Effect and supporting detail	Explanation of how the effect happened
One effect on Germany of the Treaty of Versailles was political problems. The new Weimar government had to accept the Treaty. But this caused unrest.	People said the new government had given Germany a 'stab in the back'; they called them 'the November Criminals'. The Treaty caused political problems because it made many German workers support left-wing parties, like the KPD, while many soldiers and landowners supported right-wing parties. Some people felt so strongly that they supported uprisings like the Spartacist revolt in 1919 and the Kapp Putsch in 1920.

Now test yourself

(iii) Write in the box to show that you can explain how the effect happened.

Effect and supporting detail	Explanation of how the effect happened
One effect on Germany of the Treaty of Versailles was economic problems. For example, reparations were set at £6,600 million. This damaged German industry and government finances.	(iii)

[You can check your answer on page 74.]

The final touch

The very best answers show links between effects. So, now try this.

(iv) Write a paragraph to show:

- how the economic problems caused by the Treaty of Versailles made the political problems worse.

[If you find this hard, there is a **Hint for (iv)** on page 74. You can also check the answer there.]

(iv)

SuperFacts

German reparations were set at £6,600 million by the Treaty of Versailles. This damaged German industry and government finances.

German land was taken by the Treaty of Versailles. Around 13% of German land was given to its neighbours, including Alsace and Lorraine, Eupen and Malmedy, Danzig, West Prussia, and Posen. Germany also lost 50% of its iron and 15% of its coal reserves and 11 colonies in Africa. Accepting all this made the Weimar Republic unpopular.

Economic problems The Weimar government was bankrupt: Germany's gold reserves had been spent on the war. Its income was drained by reparation payments. It had also lost the land with its richest coal and iron reserves. Later it faced serious inflation.

The French occupied the Ruhr (1923) when Germany could not pay its reparations. They took raw materials, industrial machines and manufactured goods. The Ruhr contained many factories and around 80% of Germany's coal, iron and steel production, so Germany's economic problems were made worse.

Hyperinflation meant German money became almost worthless. A loaf of bread in 1919 cost 1 mark; in 1922, 200 marks; and in 1923, 100,000 million marks. By November 1923, it cost 200,000 million marks. In 1918, you could exchange 20 marks for £1. By 1923, you needed 20 billion marks for £1.

All Germans suffered as vital goods were hard to purchase. Many workers became unemployed. The pensions and savings of the middle-classes became worthless. This made the government even more unpopular.

ResultsPlus
Top tip

The best 1(d) answers will always:

- identify not one, but at least **two** causes
- give **details** to explain the causes
- **explain how** the causes made the outcome happen
- show how the causes are **linked**
- and /or explain which of the causes was **more important**.

SuperFacts

The Great Depression (began 1929) changed German politics. From 1929, the economy worsened, unemployment and unrest grew. Chancellor Brüning's government could not cope. He tried raising taxes and banning protests. Both failed. This boosted support for extreme parties: by September 1930, the Nazis had 107 Reichstag seats.

The Nazis gained support, more than other parties, because Hitler was an excellent speaker who impressed people at spectacular rallies; Nazi propaganda had simple messages like 'Work and Bread'; the SA made the Nazis seem strong and organised and broke up rival meetings. The NSDAP had 400,000 members by 1930.

The Nazis appealed to workers by promising work and bread; to the middle-class as a strong, moral, party; to farmers and businesses as protection against communism. Nazi propaganda targeted groups like women and young people.

Answering questions: Question 1 (d)

Question 1(d) will always ask you to '**Explain why**' something happened.

On this page, we are going to answer a question, step by step.

You can test yourself by doing the same, for a different question, on the opposite page.

Question: Explain why support for the Nazi Party grew 1929–33.

First, we need to identify **two causes**. We have chosen these.

One reason why Nazi support grew was the failure of Brüning's government.

Another reason why Nazi support grew was the popular appeal of the Nazi Party.

Next, we need to use **detailed information** to explain the causes.

[As above, then] For example, the Great Depression had caused unemployment and unrest in Germany. Chancellor Brüning's government could not cope with these.

[As above, then] For example, Hitler was an excellent speaker, there were spectacular rallies and the Nazi party seemed strong and organized.

Next, we need to explain **how** the causes made support for the Nazi Party grow.

[As above, then] Brüning's failure helped the Nazis grow because Germans turned to other parties. Brüning tried to raise taxes, to help the poor, and he tried to ban protests, to quiet unrest. Both failed. People needed an alternative. So support for the Nazis grew to 107 Reichstag seats.

[As above, then] All this increased Nazi support because Nazis appealed to all kinds of Germans: to workers by promising work and bread; to the middle-class as a strong, moral, party; to farmers and businesses as protection against communism. Nazi propaganda targeted groups like women and the young. As a result of this, the NSDAP had 400,000 members by 1930.

Finally, we need to show that these two causes are **linked** and/or **prioritise** them.

[As above, then] The appeal of the Nazis was the most important cause. It is true that the Nazis only came to power because Brüning failed. In this sense, the two causes are linked. But the appeal of the Nazis was the most important because, if they had no appeal, Germans would have turned to another party, like the Communist Party, instead.

Now test yourself

On the opposite page, we have answered an '**Explain why**' question, step by step. On this page, you can test yourself by doing the same for a different question.

Before you start, re-read our answers on the opposite page. Note that we have used carefully chosen words at the start of key sentences to make it clear to the examiner how we are answering questions. These words are called **signposts**. Try to use signpost words in your answer too.

Question: Explain why the Munich Putsch (1923) failed.

First, you need to identify **two causes**. We have done this to start you off.

One reason the Munich Putsch failed was because Hitler did not have the support of local leaders.

Another reason why the Munich Putsch failed was because the Nazis were too weak.

(i) and (ii) So use d**etailed information** to explain each of the two causes.

(i)

(ii)

(iii) and (iv) Next, you need to explain **how** the causes made the Munich Putsch fail.

(iii)

(iv)

(v) Finally, you need to show that your two causes are **linked** and/or **prioritise** them.

(v)

SuperFacts

Events of the Munich Putsch Hitler and 600 SA stormed a meeting of Bavarian state leaders and forced them to accept a Nazi takeover. Next day, the state leaders, no longer being physically threatened, called out the local police and army. The Nazis tried to take over the city; but state troops defeated them. Goering was wounded, 16 Nazis were killed, and Hitler was captured.

The Munich Putsch failed Firstly, this was because Hitler did not have the support of local Bavarian leaders. Secondly, the Nazis were too weak: they had only 2,000 rifles and they were outnumbered by Bavarian troops.

Need more help?

If you need more help with this type of question, then refer to the textbook on page 43.

Answering questions: Question 2(a) and 2(b)

What you need to do

In the examination, you have to answer **either** 2(a) or 2(b).

Both questions will ask you to '**Explain how…**' something happened. For example:

- ***Explain how the Nazi Party changed in the years 1920–28.***
  or
- ***Explain how Hitler dealt with the problem of unemployment 1933–39.***

How you do it

The technique for answering the question is always the same.

The best 2 (a) and (b) answers will always:

Describe a change or an action	and	give an explanation of why this answers the question.

So let's answer the following question together, using the SuperFacts on this page.

Explain how the Nazis increased the persecution of Jews.

An answer could start like this. Fill in the blanks at (i) and (ii) to show you understand.

One way the Nazis persecuted the Jews was by spreading Nazi views on race.	This increased the persecution of Jews because in *Mein Kampf*, Hitler portrayed the Jews as Lebensunwertes, unworthy of life. This encouraged the mistreatment of Jews and led to persecution.
Another way they persecuted Jews was the Nuremberg Laws.	This increased the persecution of Jews because… (i)
Another way they persecuted Jews was… (ii)	This increased persecution of Jews because by 1938 20,000 Jews had been placed in prisons. In 1939, all Jews had to move into ghettos, walled off areas of cities, where conditions were very bad.

Final step!

The best answers will show that all these ways of increasing persecution were **linked**.

For example, an answer to this question could finish like this…

These ways of increasing persecution were linked. For example, one way - spreading views that Jews were inferior - set the scene for all the other ways, like the Nuremberg Laws stopping Jews voting. Another way that they were linked was making Jews register their possessions prepared the way for confiscating all Jewish possessions when they were sent to concentration camps.

SuperFacts

Nazi views on race In *Mein Kampf* Hitler set out the Nazi hierarchy of race. 'Pure' Western Europeans were Aryans (Hitler's invented race). Then came races such as eastern European Slavs. Next were 'sub-humans' (for example black people and the disabled). Gypsies and Jews were *Lebensunwertes* (unworthy of life).

The Nuremberg Laws (1935) said Jews were no longer German citizens, so could not vote or have passports. From 1938, Jews had to register their possessions and carry identity cards. Jewish professionals, like doctors, could not have Aryan clients.

Jews imprisoned After Kristallnacht, 20,000 Jews were sent to concentration camps. In 1939, all Jews had to move into ghettos: walled-off areas of cities, that kept them apart from other people. Housing and food supplies to the ghettos were bad.

ResultsPlus

Top tip

Notice how, in our answers, we use **signposts** – phrases like *'one way'* or *'another way'* or even *'these ways ... are linked'*. This shows the examiner how you are answering the question, and makes your answer easier to understand.

Test yourself

Here is another '**Explain how…**' question:

Explain how the Nazis changed the position of women in society 1933–39.

Using the SuperFacts printed on this page, fill in the boxes below to create an answer.

One way the Nazis changed the position of women was spreading their views about women.	*This changed the position of women because …* (iii)
Another way the Nazis changed the position of women was by their policies about marriage and motherhood.	*This changed position of women by …* (iv)
Another way the Nazis changed women's position was by their policies about women and … (v)	*This changed the position of women by …* (vi)

These ways of changing the position of women were linked. For example, … (vii)

Another example of a link between the ways of changing the position of women was) (viii)

SuperFacts

Nazi views about women Nazis thought women should focus on the traditional *kinder, küche, kirche* (children, kitchen, church). They frowned on women working, or wearing make-up or trousers. Some women felt devalued by Nazi policies.

Women and work There were about 100,000 female teachers in Germany in 1933. The Nazis wanted women at home, and forced many women out of professions such as teaching and law. This created jobs for men and reduced unemployment.

Women and marriage The Law for the Encouragement of Marriage (1933) lent couples who married 1000 marks (a month's wages) if the wife left work. For each child, they were let off a quarter of the loan. This boosted marriage, large families and women staying at home.

Women as mothers The German Women's Enterprise supported the Nazi policy of large families. It gave classes and radio broadcasts on good motherhood. It gave the Mother's Cross to women with children: bronze for 4–5; silver for 6–7; gold for 8 or more.

The answer

You can find suggested answers to the tasks numbered i), ii) etc. on page 74.

Answering questions: Question 3(a) and 3(b)

Questions 3(a) and 3(b) follow the same format. You have to answer **either** 3(a) **or** 3(b).

Questions 3(a) and 3(b) will be about **causes** or **effects**.

They will ask you to make a judgement about causes or effects. So they could say:

- ***Was [something] the main cause of…?***
- ***Was [something] the worst effect of…?***
- ***etc.***

The questions may talk about **reasons** (meaning **causes**) and will always give you some '**information to help you with your answer**'. For example:

Was the Enabling Act the main reason Hitler was able to keep such strong control over Germany 1933–39?

> ***You may use the following information to help you with your answer.***
> - ***The Enabling Act***
> - ***The Gestapo***
> - ***Repression of churches***
> - ***Propaganda***

A good way to start is to show that you know **all** of the four factors in the box above are reasons why Hitler was able to control Germany. Make sure you signpost each of them for the examiner (see Top tip box for an example of signposting phrases). We have written a paragraph on the first factor. You write a similar paragraph on each of the others, marked (i), (ii) + (iii).

In the margin, you will see the titles of the SuperFacts that will help you.

The Enabling Act was one cause of Hitler's strong control of Germany. The Enabling Act was an act passed in March 1933 which said that Hitler could make laws without the consent of the Reichstag. The Enabling Act helped Hitler to keep strong control because the Reichstag could no longer stop him passing any laws he wanted.

The Gestapo was another cause of Hitler's strong control because…(i)

Propaganda was another… (ii)

Repressing the churches was also a cause … (iii)

SuperFacts

The SuperFacts you will need for this activity are on pages 60–61. The titles of the relevant SuperFacts are:

The Enabling Act
The Gestapo
The German Law Courts
Concentration camps
The Concordat failed
Some Protestants
Propaganda
Joseph Goebbels
Hitler banned trade unions

ResultsPlus Top tip

Notice some phrases in our paragraph on the Enabling Act are signpost phrases (The Enabling Act was one cause …). They are used to ensure the examiner knows exactly how you are answering the question. Use similar phrases in your paragraphs.

If you are having trouble with your paragraphs, look on page 74 for help.

If you don't feel you know enough about all of the bullet points to write about each of them, you could add any other cause which you think was important in helping Hitler control Germany.

Now the examiner knows that we realise a number of the factors that helped Hitler keep control.

Two steps to go!

Now we can make a **judgement** on the key part of this question.

Was the Enabling Act the main reason ...?

Here are two possible views. We have completed the first one. You complete the other.

The Enabling Act was the most important reason Hitler had such strong control of Germany because it meant he could pass any laws he wanted. So even if propaganda didn't persuade people about his policies, he could pass the laws anyway. It was also more important than controlling churches because they had no political power. It was more important than the police state because the only reason he could set up the Gestapo was the Enabling Act allowed him to do it.

The Gestapo was the most important reason in keeping control of the country because ... (v)

ResultsPlus
Top tip

1. Don't forget to base your answers on the SuperFacts.
2. Don't forget to **signpost** your answers.
3. You can **agree** or **disagree** with the question. In this case, you can say the Enabling Act **was** the most important reason. You can say it **wasn't**. The main thing is that you back up your opinion with an argument based on the facts.
4. If you are arguing that one cause is the most important **you must compare it to other causes, to show it was more important.**
5. If you need to check your answers as you go along, take a peek at page 74.

Final step!

The very best answers will see that, no matter how important **one** cause was, it was probably **not enough on its own**. One cause can be the most important, but most things in history depend on a combination of causes. We have written one final paragraph saying this. You complete the bottom box to write your own version.

The Gestapo was the most important reason why Hitler had such strong control over Germany, but it was not enough alone because if propaganda failed to work, everyone could have turned against him ... So the Gestapo was important, but it was not enough on its own.

But the Enabling Act was not enough on its own ... (vi)

ResultsPlus
Watch out!

Question 3 is one on which your skills of **written communication** will be judged.

To get to the top of each level of the mark scheme you have to:

- write effectively
- organise your thoughts coherently
- spell, punctuate and use grammar well.

Answers: Germany 1918–39

Question 1 (a)

i) *I can infer this because Source A says out of 3,600 men in his regiment, 611 survived the first week.*

ii) *Source A tells me that Hitler enjoyed the experience of war.*

Question 1 (b)

i) *For example, its army was cut to 100,000 men and it could not have submarines.*

ii) *A third punishment was that territory was taken from Germany.*

Question 1 (c)

iii) *Reparations caused even more economic problems when the government began to print more and more money to make the payments. This made prices go up fast. By 1923, even a loaf of bread cost 100,000 marks.*

[Hint] Look at the last SuperFact on page 67.

iv) *The economic problems caused by the Treaty of Versailles affected everyone. Essential goods were hard to find. Workers lost their jobs. Middle-class people had their savings made worthless by hyperinflation. All these economic problems are linked to the political problems because they made the government more unpopular, so it was harder to govern.*

Question 1 (d)

i) *On the previous night, Hitler and 600 SA had stormed a meeting of Bavarian leaders and told them to accept a Nazi takeover. They agreed under pressure. But the next day, they changed their minds.*

ii) *They had only 2,000 rifles and they were outnumbered by Bavarian troops.*

iii) *This was vital since, instead of the state helping them, the Nazis were opposed by state police and army. This was a key reason why it failed.*

iv) *This weakness was a direct reason why the Putsch failed. The Nazis tried to take over the city, but state troops defeated them. Goering was shot, 16 Nazis were killed and Hitler arrested.*

v) *The two causes were linked. The Nazis were weak without the support of the Bavarian leaders. If those leaders had supported the Putsch with the state police and the state army, then the Nazis would surely have succeeded. This suggests that the Bavarian leaders changing their minds was the most important reason for the failure of the Putsch.*

Question 2 (a) + (b)

i) *... it took away their passports and stopped them from voting.*

ii) *... by locking them up.*

iii) *... it affected the way women were regarded in society. The Nazis believed women should look after their families and not meddle in politics. Some women felt insulted by these policies.*

iv) *... giving them official recognition for getting married and having large families. For example, they gave a medal, the Mother's Cross, to women with four or more children.*

v) *... work.*

vi) *... forcing them out of professions such as teaching and law to create jobs for men and reduce employment.*

vii) *... spreading Nazi views about women focusing on children, kitchen and church paved the way for all their other reforms, like getting them out of jobs.*

viii) *... that any policy encouraging earlier marriage and more children, like loans for married couples, was bound to help the Nazi policy of keeping women in the home. So some policies reinforced other policies.*

Question 3 (a) + (b)

i) *... it spied on people and had wide powers to arrest people. By 1939, it had arrested 150,000 people for opposing the Nazis.*

ii) *... way Hitler kept control. This was a different kind of control. He and Goebbels used clever ways to persuade people that the Nazi way was right, like cheap radios, theatre, films and spectacular rallies.*

iii) *... because after the Concordat failed, Hitler made it impossible for Catholics to oppose him. He controlled Catholic schools and imprisoned priests.*

iv) *... by banning trade unions and strikes in 1933. This was because strikes could threaten his power. It removed a way of opposing him.*

v) *... it's one thing to pass a law with the Enabling Act, but people could ignore it. So in the end Hitler needed to rely on the Gestapo to force people to support him. It was more important than propaganda because persuasion doesn't always work; concentration camps were more persuasive!*

vi) *... even though Hitler could use it to pass new laws. But if, through propaganda, the Gestapo or friendly priests, he could get people to agree with his laws, they were more likely to work. The Enabling Act therefore relied on all the other causes too.*

Overview: Russia 1917–39

1917

Russia fighting the First World War

- shortages
- inflation
- transport problems
- discontent with the government.

December 1917: Treaty of Brest Litovsk with Germany. Bolsheviks take Russia out of the war.

Tsar rules

February 1917: February Revolution
Tsar abdicates

Provisional Government rules

October 1917: October Revolution
Provisional Government overthrown

Bolshevik Party rules

1918–28

Russia fighting a civil war 1918–22

Bolsheviks = Reds

Different opponents + foreign aid = Whites

- shortages
- inflation
- transport problems
- many skilled and professional workers emigrate
- discontent with the government.

1918: Bolshevik Party renamed the **Communist Party**; Russia renamed the Russian Republic.

1922: Russian Republic becomes the Soviet Union.

- War Communism controls supplies.
- The Cheka controls political opposition.

1924: Lenin dies.
1924–28: Stalin gets rid of opponents, e.g. Trotsky, and takes power.

1928–39

Stalin rules

introduces:

collectivisation

- large, state controlled farms
- mechanisation
- no *kulaks*
- opposition on a wide scale, crushed.

industrialisation

- state control of industry
- Gosplan
- Five-Year Plans
- production targets
- Stakhanov and Stakhanovites
- lack of quality control.

controls by:

terror

- secret police
- purges
- show trials
- labour camps.

censorship

propaganda

Key Topic summary

Russia in 1917 was a huge country, full of many different nationalities. Nicholas II, the Tsar, ruled without sharing power. He and a small group of rich nobles had all the land and power, and almost all the wealth.

The Tsar was unpopular and took Russia into a war that made life harder and the Tsar even more unpopular. In February 1917, there was a revolution. The Tsar abdicated. A temporary government, the Provisional Government, was set up to run Russia until a new government (the Constituent Assembly) was elected in November.

The Provisional Government, because it was only temporary, did not make enough changes. It did not even take Russia out of the war. It soon had many opponents.

edexcel key terms

conscription when a country's government makes a rule that people of a certain age have to join the army.

soviet an organisation of workers or soldiers. Soviets began as strike committees, and were usually radical, wanting change.

abdicate to give up your power over something, usually a country.

SuperFacts Key Topic 1
The collapse of the Tsarist regime 1917

SuperFacts are the key bits of information. Learn them and ask someone to test you.

Russia in 1917 covered a sixth of the world's land. Travel was hard: unpaved roads, and few railway lines. In the 1897 census, under half the 125.6 million people spoke Russian (the language of government). All this made the Tsar's government weak. p.7

Peasants made up 93.7 million of the 125.6 million population in 1897 census. They had hard lives in Tsarist Russia. Over a half had no land or homes of their own. Much of their land was poor quality and their farming methods were old-fashioned and inefficient. p.7

Industries grew, as did factory towns. About 50% of factory workers lived in Moscow, the biggest industrial city. Workers had bad housing (often 10 to a room). The work was hard, the hours were long, and the working conditions were often dangerous. p.8

Tsar Nicholas II ruled Russia in 1917. He was an indecisive man. He came from the Romanov family that had ruled Russia since 1613. He had a Council of Ministers from the noble families to advise him, but he made all the decisions and passed all the laws. p.8

The Duma was a parliament created by Nicholas II after the 1905 Revolution. It was supposed to meet regularly and advise the Tsar. The Duma failed because Nicholas II changed the voting regulations to make sure that the Duma was full of monarchists who supported him. He then stopped calling the Duma at all. p.9

Revolutionary opponents of the Tsar wanted him overthrown. The Social Democrats (the biggest group) thought the revolution would be led by workers in towns. In 1917, they split into Bolsheviks (led by Lenin) and Mensheviks (several leaders). p.9

The First World War broke out in 1914 and Russia sided with Britain and France against Germany. The war was popular at first; only 21 deputies in the Duma opposed it, and strikes almost stopped in the first year. p.10

An unpopular war Transport problems weakened the army. Soldiers were badly equipped – shortages of rifles meant they had to take from the dead. In 1915, 2 million soldiers were killed, wounded or captured; there were food shortages in the cities. p.10

The Tsar took command of the army in 1915, after criticism of the war. He failed to make things better. He left the government in the hands of his (German) wife who made bad decisions. All this made the Tsar increasingly unpopular. p.10

Effects of the war Military failure made the war unpopular. People hated conscription, and army demands on food and farm animals. Food production fell and shortages got worse. From 1914–16, people got 25% less food and infant mortality doubled. p.11

The February Revolution broke out in St Petersburg after a very cold winter. On February 21, some workers were locked out of the Putilov Works. Over the next 2 days strikes and demonstrations grew and protests broke at against the shortages, especially of bread. The police and troops could not stop them, so they continued to grow. p.12

The Tsar's reactions The Tsar did not come back from the front to take command. He sent a telegram ordering the general in charge of St Petersburg to stop the riots. p.12

Troops were told to fire on demonstrators on February 26. Some refused and changed sides. Others fired but did not return next day. Some troops changed sides (with their weapons) and organised the capture of weapons factories, boosting the revolution. p.13

On 27 February the Duma met to decide who to support: the Tsar or the revolution. The revolution needed leaders to succeed. The Petrograd Soviet and 12 Duma members set up the Provisional Government to run the country until elections could be held. p.14

The Tsar abdicated The Tsar tried to return to St Petersburg, but it was too late. Revolutionaries controlled the railway. He abdicated in favour of his brother, Prince Michael, who refused the crown and accepted the Provisional Government. p.14

The Provisional Government was weak because it saw itself as temporary, so did not want to make many laws; it only controlled a part of Russia; it was the army and the soviets, especially the St Petersburg Soviet, who were keeping it in power. p.14

The Provisional Government failed to take Russia out of the war, to fix the food and fuel shortages, to redistribute property more equally, and to improve the working conditions of factory workers. It merely set a date for elections to the new Constituent Assembly, for November 1917. p.16

Lenin and other revolutionaries returned to Russia because the Provisional Government made free speech and political organisations legal. Leaders like Lenin helped opposition parties to grow and speak against the government. p.17 & 18

Lenin's 'April Theses' of 1917 included not working with the Provisional Government and working towards control of industry and agriculture by the soviets. p.18

Lenin said the Provisional Government had to be overthrown and pushed the Bolsheviks to accept his policies when they might otherwise have co-operated. p.18

Bolshevik support grew as faith in the Provisional Government fell and the Petrograd Soviet lost support for working with it. Lenin made inspiring speeches with slogans like 'Peace, Land, Bread', stressing the failings of the Provisional Government. p.18 & 19

The Red Guard were Bolshevik-led private armies of workers: by July 1917 there were 10,000 Red Guards in Petrograd. 'The July Days' of 1917 were an unplanned rising in Petrograd, where the Provisional Government ordered troops to fire on demonstrators. They then arrested Bolshevik leaders and members of the Red Guard. p.17

Kornilov's Revolt (August 1917) was an attempt by General Kornilov to stop unrest in the countryside and pull back the growing power of the soviets. He wanted martial law, and thought that Kerensky, leader of the Provisional Government, agreed to this. He and his troops marched on Petrograd to take charge. p.20

The significance of Kornilov's revolt But Kerensky came down on the side of the soviets and armed the Bolshevik Red Guard to stop Kornilov and his army. Pro-soviet activists persuaded his troops not to attack. Kornilov and 7,000 others were arrested. The Red Guard did not give back their weapons once Kornilov was beaten. p.20

Top tip

When using SuperFacts to support a statement, make sure you do not just produce a list of facts. Always say **how** the detail supports the statement.

Need more help?
You can find a longer explanation of each SuperFact in your Edexcel textbook, *Russia 1917–39*. Look for this symbol, which will give you the page number.

SuperFacts Key Topic 2
Bolshevik takeover and consolidation 1917–24

Key Topic summary
The revolution of October 1917 brought the Bolsheviks to power. Unlike the Provisional Government, they acted quickly to take Russia out of the war and made reforms.

However, opponents of the Bolshevik revolution joined to fight them in civil war, aided by Russia's allies in the First World War who were angry because Russia had left the war and who disliked Bolshevik ideas.

The Bolsheviks won the civil war, but famine followed. This, and the measures they were forced to take to control the country and food supplies during the war, made the Bolsheviks (now re-named the Communist Party) a repressive government.

SuperFacts are the key bits of information. Learn them and ask someone to test you.

By October 1917, the Provisional Government seemed about to fall. Lenin, fearing the Petrograd Soviet would gain power in a second revolution, returned to Petrograd, to plan a Bolshevik revolution. Trotsky was leader of the Petrograd Soviet's Military Revolutionary Committee. He secretly persuaded army units to support him. p.25

The October Revolution began on the night of 24 October. The Provisional Government was arrested. The Council of People's Commissars was set up to rule, temporarily, by decree. Some Congress of Soviets members rejected the Bolsheviks and walked out. On 26 October, the rest announced a new, Bolshevik, government. p.25

The Bolsheviks succeeded because the Provisional Government did not act decisively (they did not disband the Red Guard); they had military strength (10,000 Red Guards and army support); they took over key parts of the city, such as the phone, telegraph and rail links, which stopped the Provisional Government getting help. p.26

The Bolsheviks' first decrees abolished capital punishment, began talks to leave the war, gave land to the peasants, and gave control of factories to the workers. In the November elections for the Constituent Assembly (the new government), the Bolsheviks won 175 seats, but the Socialist Revolutionary Party won 370 seats. p.28

The Treaty of Brest–Litovsk (March 1918) took Russia out of the war. Lenin needed to keep his promise of peace and had a civil war to fight. But Russia paid a high price, giving up large areas of agricultural and industrial land in Poland and the Ukraine: 80% of its coalmines, 50% of its industry, 26% of its railways, and 27% of its farmland. The treaty angered Russia's allies, who gave help to the Bolsheviks' opponents. p.29

Civil war broke out because many groups opposed the Bolsheviks. The war lasted from 1917 to 1921. The Bolsheviks (the Reds) held key central areas of Russia, including St Petersburg and Moscow. Their enemies (the Whites) could attack from all sides, but had to move troops and supplies long distances around the central area. p.30

The Whites came from many groups: Kornilov and Denikin led a Volunteer Army to bring back the Tsar; Kerensky led a Provisional Government army; the Czech Legion were Czech soldiers from the Tsar's army. The Whites had more troops and supplies (partly from Russia's old allies Britain, France, Japan and Italy). p.30

The Red Army was organised by Trotsky. He conscripted soldiers and used officers who had been in the Tsar's army to train them. Most units had a political commissar to educate the troops in Bolshevik ideas and report any disloyalty. No similar ideals united the Whites – they just wanted to get rid of the Bolsheviks. p.30

The Whites advanced all through 1918 and most of 1919, seeming sure to win. The most dangerous time for the Reds was on 14 October 1919: Denikin's army was just 300 km from Moscow and White troops were close to Petrograd. Only a fierce counter-attack, led by Trotsky, saved Petrograd. p.31

edexcel key terms

decree an order that has the force of law, from someone who is part of the government.

Cheka The Bolshevik secret police who could arrest political opponents and imprison them, or shoot them, without trial.

Central Executive Committee (CEC) The people chosen from the national Congress of Soviets to appoint the Council of People's Commissars and oversee their actions.

Council of People's Commissars (CPC) ran the 18 ministries that ran the country. They made the laws but the CEC and Congress of Soviets had to approve them.

The Reds recovered during late 1919 and 1920. Foreign aid stopped at the end of the First World War. The Whites were spread too thinly around Red territory. Their troops deserted to the Red Army. The Czech Legion went home (handing over some Whites they had captured to the Reds). p.31

The Cheka The Bolsheviks used the Cheka (secret police) to stop political opposition during the civil war. By 1919, the Cheka had arrested 87,000 people and shot 8,389 without trial in the 'Red Terror'. Civil rights suffered. p.32

War Communism organised farming and industry to serve the war. Peasants had crops and animals taken; industry was run by the state; strikes were banned; the state ran banks and fixed wages and prices. It helped the war effort. But peasants grew less food (37% of 1913 output). Food supplies fell; so prices rose and money lost its value. p.33.

The Bolsheviks won because the Cheka controlled opposition; War Communism controlled supplies; the Red Army, motivated by political commissars, had a shared political motivation (the Whites didn't); the Whites lost money and supplies when foreign aid stopped, and they lost men to the more motivated Red Army. p.32

Effects of the civil war Human suffering (casualties, food shortages); physical damage to road and rail links, farmland, factories; emigration of skilled workers; loss of support for Bolsheviks. p.33

Bolshevik political changes during the war In 1919, the Bolsheviks changed the name of the Party to the Communist Party. Russia became the Russian Socialist Federative Soviet Republic (Russian Republic) in 1918, and the Soviet Union in 1922. p.34

A new government The Constitution of 10 July 1918 set up a new government. Local soviets elected regional soviets, who elected a national Congress of Soviets. The Congress chose the Central Executive Committee (CEC), who chose the Council of People's Commissars (CPC), who made the laws. p.34

A new society The new constitution gave all land to the people. All businesses with more than 10 workers were run by the state, for the people. It promised free education and health care, free speech and a free press (suspended during the civil war). p.34

The crisis of 1921 The civil war was won but its effects were severe. Farm production in 1920 was 37% of its 1913 levels. There was such a severe famine that some people became cannibals; there were riots in the countryside and strikes in the cities. p.36

The Kronstadt Mutiny (1921) Sailors at the navy base of Kronstadt, who had supported all the Russian revolutions, mutinied. They demanded an end to the Red Terror, a new election, free speech and freedom for all political prisoners. This mutiny showed the Communists how unpopular they were and forced some changes. p.36

The New Economic Policy (NEP) War Communism caused hardship. This led to unrest. So the state let peasants keep some produce and sell the rest (paying a tax on profits). Factories with under 20 workers could be privately run for a profit. People (known as NEPmen) could open profit-making shops. p.36

Results of the NEP Factories came back into use. In 1921, 90% of cotton mills were not working; by 1922, 90% of them were working again. In 1922–23 production rose – grain by 6.3%, coal by 4.2%. Profits rose too, increasing confidence in the economy. p.37

Be careful not to confuse the Red Guard and the Red Army.

The **Red Guard** were workers' fighting units set up by the Bolsheviks. They shared ideals, but had no uniform, some weapons, and some training. They never had more than 10,000 members.

The **Red Army** was set up and run by Trotsky in January 1918 to fight for the Bolshevik government during the civil war. Many of the officers came from the Tsar's old army, as did many of its soldiers. Each army unit had a political commissar to explain Bolshevik ideas and watch for opposition.

Need more help?

You can find a longer explanation of each SuperFact in your Edexcel textbook, *Russia 1917–39*. Look for this symbol, which will give you the page number.

SuperFacts Key Topic 3
The nature of Stalin's dictatorship 1924–39

Key Topic summary
When Lenin died, in 1924, several members of the Politburo wanted to lead the Party. Many people thought Trotsky would become the leader, but it was Stalin. Stalin got rid of all his rivals, step by step, over several years. By 1928, he was clearly in charge.

Stalin's secret police arrested political opponents. These opponents were imprisoned, exiled or shot. They either had no trial or had public 'show trials' that always found defendants guilty.

Stalin used a combination of propaganda and censorship to control the information that people got and affect the way they thought.

SuperFacts are the key bits of information. Learn them and ask someone to test you.

Lenin did not name a successor Lenin did not think one person should dominate the Party. In theory, the Council of People's Commissars (CPC) ran the Soviet Union in the 1920s, not Lenin (although he always got his way).The leadership contestants were Stalin, Trotsky, Kamenev, Rykov, Zinoviev, Bukharin and Tomsky. p.41

Lenin's *Testament* was written during his last illness to be read to the Congress of Soviets after he died. He discussed the strengths and weaknesses of several Party members, including the two main leadership contenders, Trotsky and Stalin. p.41

Stalin's strengths Stalin was ambitious and could be charming. He was a good organiser and planner. He made friends in the Politburo and stayed close to Lenin in Moscow while Trotsky was away with the Red Army. As General Secretary, he appointed many officials and chose people who would support him. p.42

Trotsky was very able, but too self-confident and preoccupied with administration, according to Stalin. He did not cultivate allies on the Politburo as effectively as Stalin and was not as well known. He was very popular with the Red Army. p.42

Stalin eased Trotsky out He made the funeral speech for Lenin (Trotsky was told late and did not rush back to Moscow). Stalin plotted with Zinoviev, Kamenev and other Politburo members to: force Trotsky to resign as Minister for War (1925), expel him from the Politburo (1926), and the Communist Party (1927), and exile him (1929). p.43

Removing other rivals Stalin plotted with other Politburo members against Zinoviev and Kamenev once Trotsky was losing support. He pushed them into an alliance with Trotsky in1926, then had them expelled from the Communist Party as traitors. p.43

The Soviet Union was a police state before Stalin came to power. The Cheka became the 'reformed' GPU, then the OGPU. All did the same job – using terror to stop political opposition. They could arrest, torture, and imprison without trial. The OGPU could also send people into organisations and factories to look for 'sabotage'. p.44

Prison camps for political prisoners, usually in towns or cities, began under the Cheka. Under Stalin, the camps moved to isolated parts of the country and were much bigger. The Cheka had sent about 250,000 prisoners to camps by 1920. In 1938, there were about 7,000,000 people in camps, run by a department called the *Gulag*. p.44

Purges, the clearing out of political opponents from various groups, began in 1934. Failures anywhere, from factories to government offices, were often blamed on 'sabotage by enemies of the state', not incompetence – often the real cause. p.45

Groups purged by the OGPU included teachers, engineers, scientists, factory workers, the armed forces, the Politburo, and even the OGPU itself. So many were purged from 1936 to 1938 that this period was called the Great Terror. Those purged were usually executed, sent to labour camps, or sent into exile. p.45

Show trials started in 1936 when sixteen 'Old Bolsheviks' were tried for killing Kirov. The accused were always found guilty. At first, people did not realise the trials were unfair, because the accused often confessed. The trials helped Stalin – they made people feel the state was in danger and less likely to criticise him. p.46

edexcel key terms

the purges were hunting out supposed political opponents of the government ('enemies of the state') and shooting them, exiling them, or sending them to prison camps run by a secret police department called the *Gulag*.

show trials were trials for crimes such as treason where the judges always found the defendants guilty, and even defendants who were innocent sometimes pleaded guilty.

Bad effects The purges created an atmosphere of fear and suspicion; killed about 1 million people and imprisoned about 7 million; removed many skilled workers from factories; the state lost useful people (93 of the 139 members of the central Committee, 15 of the best generals of the Red Army). p.47

Good effects From the point of view of the state, the good effects were that people were mainly too frightened to oppose the state. The government was full of people who were completely loyal to Stalin. p.47

Millions were purged In 1939, about 3.5 million people were imprisoned. About 1.3 million of these were in labour camps. Historians disagree over the statistics that are available (estimates of numbers purged in the Red Army range from10%–50%). p.47

Stalin used propaganda for many purposes: to turn people against his enemies, to get people to accept plans such as collectivisation, to get people to work harder and put up with hardships, and to build a 'cult of Stalin'. p.48

Propaganda methods varied: posters, radio, plays, cinema, and banners with slogans. Officials travelled the country with propaganda films and posters, giving talks in towns and villages. Each new policy had its own propaganda campaign to persuade people to accept it. p.48

The 'cult of Stalin' showed Stalin as the father of his country, almost god-like. This increased his power, since many people believed it. Stalin said he was less important than the Soviet Union and its people, but encouraged the cult. Images of Stalin were everywhere. Newspaper reports praised him daily. p.50

The 1936 Constitution was described as 'democratic'; people could vote for members of the Supreme Soviet. It gave people rights such as free speech and free healthcare. It gave powers to Soviet republics, saying their local laws were to be respected. p.51

Effect of the 1936 Constitution It made little difference. The Supreme Soviet seldom met, the Politburo ruled. People had to vote for a member of the Communist Party – it was the only one. Civil rights were ignored 'in the interest of national security'. p.51

The state censored everything It controlled the media (newspapers and radio broadcasts were told what to report). It changed the past (photos were censored to remove Stalin's enemies such as Trotsky). It had a huge official department that changed official records to show what it wanted people to believe. p.52

Censorship produced an official culture Stalin controlled the culture so it could be understood by everyone. His censors banned 'high' (hard to understand) music, plays or films; they made sure that only approved 'low' culture was made public. p.52

Education was free; at first it stressed basic literacy and numeracy. But Stalin made schools spread propaganda; teachers were purged unless they taught Stalinist views. Schools also censored the past; textbooks were changed to suit the official view. p.48

When choosing SuperFacts to support a statement, read the question carefully and consider the limits it puts on the information you use. If you are asked for **one** cause, action, or decision, give just one, explained. Do not give more than one: you will get no more marks.

Need more help?
You can find a longer explanation of each SuperFact in your Edexcel textbook, *Russia 1917–39*. Look for this symbol, which will give you the page number.

Key Topic summary

Stalin saw the West as the enemy of the USSR. He thought the USSR could only survive by becoming strong and self-sufficient. He wanted the USSR to industrialise fast.

Stalin needed to feed the workers in the rapidly growing industrial towns. Soviet agriculture was not efficient, and had been disrupted by the problems of war and civil war. Stalin wanted to move to collectives – large, mechanised, state-controlled farms. There was considerable resistance to collectivisation from the peasant farmers.

The state controlled all aspects of life in the USSR. The communist ideal was an equal society. But in the USSR, how good a life you had depended on how willing you were to co-operate with the state.

SuperFacts Key Topic 4
Economic and social changes 1928–39

SuperFacts are the key bits of information. Learn them and ask someone to test you.

Stalin wanted industrialisation and collectivisation to make the Soviet Union safe from Western aggression. He wanted higher industrial output and enough grain to feed town workers. He also wanted surplus grain to earn money from grain exports. p.57

Collectivisation was joining small farms and villages together into big farms called *kolkhozy*, run by peasant committees. Stalin wanted, eventually, to make all these farms *sovkozy* (huge collective farms run by a state manager). p.57 & 58

Collectives The average collective had about 80 hectares of land worked by 'brigades' of about 15 families. The state set working hours and work, usually 140 days a year, farming and repairing roads. It also provided homes and equipment. p.58

Mechanisation, using tractors and, from 1931, combine harvesters was possible on collectives. By 1935, the Soviet Union was exporting grain. p.57 & 62

Objections to collectivisation Peasants did not like losing independence; or having a committee telling them when to work and what to do (and fining them if they disobeyed). They did not like losing their land; handing over their farms, animals and equipment. *Kulaks* objected the most – they had the most to lose. p.60

Many peasants refused to collectivise So, from 1928, the state enforced it. Peasants responded by killing their animals and hiding crops, seed and equipment. 50% of the pigs and 25% of the cows in the Soviet Union were killed during 1929–33. p.61

Stalin's reaction He sent officials into the countryside to find hidden crops and meat from the animals. If the peasants resisted, he sent in the army. p.61

Kulaks were richer peasants, created by the NEP. They used profit from selling surplus crops to get more land and hire workers. Stalin wanted to get rid of the *kulaks*: under communism all peasants should be equal. Collectivisation would do this. p.58

Dekulakisation The army arrested *kulaks* and sent them to labour camps; 600,000 farms were *dekulakised* in 1930–31. Anyone who objected was called a *kulak* (no matter how poor they were). After 1932, any peasant who would not join a collective was treated as a *kulak*. This was how Stalin removed opposition to collectives. p.61

Failures of collectivisation The worst failure was the famine of 1932–33, when about 3 million people starved to death. Discontented peasants on collectives did not always work hard, or use machinery properly. In 1935 Stalin finally offered a compromise: he allowed peasants an acre of land apiece to farm for themselves. p.62

Successes of collectivisation By 1935, over 90% of Soviet farmland was collectivised and the steep fall in crop and animal production was reversed. In 1928, 63 million tons of grain was produced; 56 million tons in 1932, and 75 million tons in 1935. In the same years, the number of pigs went from 22 million to 10.9 million to 17 million. p.62

Gosplan was set up in 1921; it was the State Planning Committee. It had the job of making industrialisation work. From 1928, it set Five-Year Plans for industrial growth. There were national targets; but every factory had a production target too. p.64

edexcel key terms

Gosplan was the State Planning Committee. It was set up in 1921 to make industrialisation work. It developed a huge bureaucracy to deal with this. The amount of administration needed to get parts for a factory or get permission to change the way things worked slowed industry down.

kulaks were richer peasants, created by the NEP, which allowed peasants to sell surplus crops. They used the profit from selling surplus crops to get more land. Some of them even hired workers.

The First Five-Year Plan (1928–32) focused on heavy industry: iron, coal, steel and electricity. It was said to have reached its targets in four years – but these were reduced targets. The original target was missed; it was not reached until the late 1940s. p.64

The Second Five-Year Plan (1933–37) focused on heavy industry and set targets for tractor and combine harvester production. It started a year early (before the First Five-Year Plan finished) and was more realistic, and so it met its targets. p.64

The Third Five-Year Plan (1938–41) was the first to have 'luxury' items such as bikes and radios. But from 1939 production was geared towards preparing for war. p.64

Alexei Stakhanov was a miner said to have dug 102 tons of coal in a 6-hour shift (the target was 7 tons). Gosplan arranged this (it was prepared in advance, other miners took the coal away) as propaganda to encourage other workers to imitate him. p.65

The Stakhanovite Movement encouraged workers to compete to produce more (like Stakhanov). They were sent into factories to show ordinary workers more efficient, higher, production. From 1934 workers were paid by piecework, not set wages. The state rewarded high production with better housing and rations. p.65

Increased productivity We only have state statistics, often exaggerated. However, industrial production certainly rose. The statistics say from 1928 to 1936 iron production went from 3.3 to 6.2 million tons. Coal went from 35.4 to 64.3 million tons. p.66

Industrial quality suffered at first – due to the drive for high productivity. Workers were often badly trained; factories were inefficient and had few safety features. p.66

Quality improved e.g. the Stalingrad Tractor Factory, built June 1930. Target: 500 tractors a month. Made by end of September: 43. Average life of a tractor: 70 hours. BUT by 1939 it worked better and produced over half the tractors in the USSR. p.66 & 67.

Social inequality existed, despite the emphasis communism placed on equality. State officials got a better standard of living. In 1939, state officials were allowed 6.7 square metres of housing space per person. The average was 4.3 square metres. Those not in favour with the state had to wait longer for nursery places, operations etc. p.68

Ethnic minorities At first, the state welcomed local languages and diversity. But from 1932, they were seen as 'counter-revolutionary', mainly because the republics were most resistant to collectivisation. The state imposed a universal Russian culture ('Russification'), and Russian became compulsory in schools from 1938. p.68

Religion was officially allowed Actually, religion was frowned on and atheism was the norm. People were sent to labour camps for religious beliefs; priests were purged. In 1915 Russia had 54,000 churches. By 1940 all but 400 had been destroyed. p.69

Women were seen as equal citizens They had equal voting rights to men. They were equal at work and had equal pay for equal work, as well as equal opportunities to work. In 1928, there were 3 million working women. In 1940 there were over 13 million. p.70

ResultsPlus
Top tip

When choosing SuperFacts to support a statement, read the question carefully and consider the limits it puts on the information you use. Question 1a) asks, 'What can you learn from the source about...?' This is the one question where you should not use SuperFacts at all. It is asking what you can learn from the source, not what you know.

Need more help?

You can find a longer explanation of each SuperFact in your Edexcel textbook, *Germany 1918–39*. Look for this symbol, which will give you the page number.

Answering questions: Question 1 (a)

What you need to do

Question 1 (a) will always ask '**What can you learn from Source A about [something]**'. The best answers:

- not only extract **information** from the source
- but will also make **inferences** from the source *[see Top tip box]*
- and **support** those inferences with detail from the source.

Note: make sure you answer the question – after **about** comes the **subject**. You can't just make *any* inference from the source, it has to be about the *something* in the question.

Here is a possible **source**, **question** and **answer** for you to study.

Source A: From a GCSE textbook, *The Making of the Modern World, Russia 1917–39.*

> The Russian Empire in 1917 was huge…it covered a sixth of all the land in the world. Roads were unpaved and thick with mud for much of the year. Railways connected a fraction of the country. Russia had 125 million people. Of these only 55 million spoke Russian. There were hundreds of different nationalities living in very different ways.

What does Source A tell us about the government of Russia in 1917?

Inference	Supporting detail
Source A tells me that governing Russia was difficult.	I can infer this because it says it covered a sixth of the land in the world and there were many nationalities living in very different ways.

Now test yourself

i) Write in the box below to show you can write **supporting detail** using this question.

What does Source A tell us about transport in Russia in 1917?

Source A tells me that transport was slow in Russia in 1917.	[Supporting detail]

ii) Write in the box below to show you can write a**n inference** using this question:

What does Source A tell us about communicating information in Russia in 1917?

[Inference]	I can infer this because Source A says that Russia was very big, there were lots of different nationalities and less than half the population even spoke Russian.

ResultsPlus

Top tip

An **inference** is a judgement that can be made by studying the source, but is not directly stated by it.

A **supported inference** is one that uses detail from the source to prove the inference.

Consider this example:

Source A: 'The furious head teacher told Jimmy that his behaviour was disgraceful, and that he had broken several school rules.'

Question: *What does Source A tell us about Jimmy?*

Information: Source A tells us that Jimmy had broken several school rules. [This is directly stated in the source, so it's not an inference.]

Inference: Source A tells me that Jimmy is in serious trouble and is likely to be punished. [The source does not directly tell us this, but we can infer that it is likely.]

A supported inference: Source A tells me that Jimmy is in serious trouble and is likely to be punished. I can infer this because Jimmy had broken several school rules and the head teacher was furious. [This is an inference, with details quoted from the source to support it.]

The answer

You can find suggested answers to the tasks numbered i), ii) etc. on page 94.

Answering questions: Question 1 (b)

What you need to do

Question 1(b) will always ask you to '**describe**' something. The best answers will:

- **state** not one, or two, but **three** features of the thing being described
- give extra factual detail or an explanation to **support** each feature.

How you do it

Take this question as an example:

Describe the ways the Bolsheviks fought the civil war of 1917–21.

The SuperFacts will help us. Let's start with the SuperFact about the **Red Army**.

First we **state** one way the war was fought.	One way they fought the war was with the Red Army.
Next we **support** the statement with extra detail or an explanation.	This was run by Trotsky. He conscripted soldiers and trained them with officers from the Tsar's army.

We've written this in **two sentences**, rather than one, to make it obvious to the examiner that we are **stating** a way the war was fought and then **supporting** it with detail.

Now test yourself

(i) Write in the box below to show you can **provide supporting detail**.

Another way they fought the war was by using the Cheka.	**[Supporting detail]**

(ii) In the box below, **state a way they fought the war that fits the supporting detail**.

[Statement]	This helped the Bolshevik war effort because it took crops and animals from peasants and banned strikes.

These three examples, written in a paragraph, make a top answer to the exam question.

SuperFacts

The Red Army was organised by Trotsky. He conscripted soldiers and used officers who had been in the Tsar's army to train them. Most units had a political commissar to educate the troops in Bolshevik ideas and report any disloyalty. No similar ideals united the Whites – they just wanted to get rid of the Bolsheviks.

The Cheka The Bolsheviks used the Cheka (secret police) to stop political opposition. By June 1919, the Cheka had arrested 87,000 people and shot 8,389 without trial in the 'Red Terror'. Civil rights suffered.

War Communism organised farming and industry to serve the war. Peasants had crops and animals taken; industry was run by the state; strikes were banned; the state ran banks and fixed wages and prices. This helped the war effort. But peasants grew less food (37% of 1913 output). Food supplies fell; so prices rose and money lost its value.

The answer

You can find suggested answers to the tasks numbered i), ii) etc. on page 74.

SuperFacts

The Bolsheviks' first decrees abolished capital punishment, began talks to leave the war, gave land to the peasants, and gave control of factories to workers. In the November elections for the Constituent Assembly (the new government), the Bolsheviks won 175 seats, but the Socialist Revolutionary Party won 370 seats.

The Treaty of Brest–Litovsk (March 1918) took Russia out of the war. Lenin needed to keep his promise of peace and had a civil war to fight. But Russia paid a high price, giving up large areas of agricultural and industrial land in Poland and the Ukraine: 80% of its coalmines, 50% of its industry, 26% of its railways, and 27% of its farmland. The treaty angered Russia's allies, who gave help to the Bolsheviks' opponents.

A new government The Constitution of 10 July 1918 set up a new government. Local soviets elected regional soviets, who elected a national Congress of Soviets. The Congress chose the Central Executive Committee (CEC), who chose the Council of People's Commissars (CPC), who made the laws.

A new society The new constitution gave all land to the people. All businesses with more than 10 workers were run by the state, for the people. It promised free education and health care, free speech and a free press (suspended during the civil war).

Answering questions: Question 1 (c)

Question 1 (c) will always ask you to '**explain the effects**' of something.

What you need to do

The best answers will:

- state not one, but **two** effects
- **support** each effect with extra factual **detail** to write a developed statement
- use this detail to **explain how** each effect happened
- and show **links** or connections between the effects.

How you do it

Take this question as an example:

Explain the effects on Russia 1917–21 of the Bolsheviks coming to power.

The SuperFacts on the left will provide us with the information to answer this question.

The SuperFacts suggest the following **effect** and **supporting detail**.

Effect	Supporting detail
One effect on Russia of the Bolsheviks coming to power was a series of political changes.	Russian citizens were given new rights and freedoms, and the ownership of land and factories changed.

Notice how we have made it very clear to the examiner how we are answering the question. We have:

- used **two** sentences, one for the **effect** and one for the **supporting detail**.
- started each sentence with 'signposts' to show what we are doing, by saying 'One effect was ...' and 'For example ...'

Use this approach when you write answers.

Now test yourself

The SuperFacts suggest another effect was **a long, hard civil war**. Using this effect, write in boxes (i) and (ii) below to show that you can set out the **effect** and **supporting detail**. [You can check your answer in the first box on page 87.]

Effect	Supporting detail
(i)	(ii)

Making the answer better

But this is not enough. The best answers will **explain how** the effect happened.

Here is an example of how you can use supporting detail to explain how the effect happened. This time, we have used **change during the civil war** as our example.

Effect and supporting detail	Explanation of how the effect happened
One effect on Russia of the Bolsheviks coming to power was a long, hard civil war. It lasted until 1921. Russians suffered food shortages and lost political freedoms.	The civil war happened because many groups in Russia were opposed to the Bolsheviks. The civil war had many casualties: it caused damage to property; it also brought food shortages. This is how the civil war happened, bringing hardship.

Now test yourself

(iii) Write in the box to show that you can explain how the effect happened.

Effect and supporting detail	Explanation of how the effect happened
One effect on Russia of the Bolsheviks coming to power was a series of political changes. Russian citizens were given new rights and freedoms and the ownership of land and factories changed.	(iii)

[You can check your answer on page 94.]

The final touch

The very best answers show links between effects. So, now try this.

(iv) Write a paragraph to show how the two effects of the Bolsheviks coming to power – the civil war and political changes – were linked.

[If you find this hard, there is a [**Hint for (iv)**] on page 94. You can also check the answer there.]

SuperFacts

Civil war broke out because many groups opposed the Bolsheviks. The war lasted from 1917 to 1921. The Bolsheviks (Reds) held key central areas of Russia, including St Petersburg and Moscow. Their enemies (the Whites) could attack from all sides, but had to move troops and supplies long distances around the central area.

The Red Army was organised by Trotsky. He conscripted soldiers and used officers who had been in the Tsar's army to train them. Most units had a political commissar to educate the troops in Bolshevik ideas and report any disloyalty. No similar ideals united the Whites - they just wanted to get rid of the Bolsheviks.

The Cheka The Bolsheviks used the Cheka (secret police) to stop political opposition during the civil war. By 1919, the Cheka had arrested 87,000 people and shot 8,389 without trial in the 'Red Terror'. Civil rights suffered.

War Communism organised farming and industry to serve the war. Peasants had crops and animals taken; industry was run by the state; strikes were banned; the state ran banks and fixed wages and prices. This helped the war effort. But peasants grew less food (37% of 1913 output). Food supplies fell; so prices rose and money lost its value.

Effects of the civil war Human suffering (casualties, food shortages); physical damage to road and rail links, farmland, factories; emigration of skilled workers; political damage (loss of support for Bolsheviks).

The answer

You can find suggested answers to the tasks numbered i), ii) etc. on page 74.

Answering questions: Question 1 (d)

ResultsPlus

Top tip

The best 1(d) answers will always:

- identify not one, but at least **two** causes
- give **details** to explain the causes
- **explain how** the causes made the outcome happen
- show how the causes are **linked**
- and /or explain which of the causes was **more important**.

Question 1(d) will always ask you to '**Explain why**' something happened.

On this page, we are going to answer a question, step by step.

You can test yourself by doing the same, for a different question, on the opposite page.

Explain why Stalin won the struggle for power after Lenin died in 1924.

First, we need to identify **two causes**. We have chosen these.

One reason why Stalin won the struggle for power was his strengths.

Another reason why Stalin won the struggle for power was Trotsky's weaknesses.

Next, we need to use **detailed information** to explain the causes.

[As above, then] For example, Stalin was ambitious and could be charming; he was a good organiser and planner.

[As above, then] For example, Trotsky was too self-confident (according to Stalin).

Next, we need to explain **how** the causes helped Stalin to win the struggle for power.

[As above, then] Stalin's strengths meant he made friends in the Politburo. As General Secretary, he appointed many officials and chose people who would support him. This gave him many supporters in the struggle for power when Lenin died.

[As above, then] Trotsky's self-confidence meant that, when he did not rush back to Moscow for Lenin's funeral, people thought it was arrogance. He was preoccupied with administration so he did not cultivate allies on the Politburo as well as Stalin. All this reduced his support in the struggle for power.

Finally, we need to show that these two causes are **linked** and/or **prioritise** them.

[As above, then] The two causes are linked because Stalin's ambition meant he exploited Trotsky's weaknesses. For example Stalin cultivated the support of Zinoviev and Kamenev; they supported Stalin because Trotsky had not cultivated them. The main cause was probably Stalin's ambition because, without him taking the initiative, Zinoviev and Kamenev may have decided to support Trotsky despite his weaknesses.

SuperFacts

Stalin's strengths Stalin was ambitious and could be charming. He was a good organiser and planner. He made friends in the Politburo and stayed close to Lenin in Moscow while Trotsky was away with the Red Army. As General Secretary, he appointed many officials and chose people who would support him.

Trotsky was very able, but too self-confident and preoccupied with administration, according to Stalin. He did not cultivate allies on the Politburo as effectively as Stalin and was not as well known. He was very popular with the Red Army.

Stalin eased Trotsky out He made the funeral speech for Lenin (Trotsky was told late and did not rush back to Moscow). Stalin plotted with Zinoviev, Kamenev and other Politburo members to: force Trotsky to resign as Minister for War (1925), expel him from the Politburo (1926) and the Communist Party (1927) and exile him (1929).

Now test yourself

On the opposite page, we have answered an '**Explain why**' question, step by step. On this page, you can test yourself by doing the same for a different question.

Before you start, re-read our answers on the opposite page. Note that we have used carefully chosen words at the start of key sentences to make it clear to the examiner how we are answering questions. These words are called **signposts**. Try to use signpost words in your answer too.

Explain why Stalin was able to become a dictator in the Soviet Union by 1939.

First, you need to identify **two causes**. We have done this to start you off.

One reason why Stalin was able to become a dictator was his suppression of opposition.
Another reason why Stalin was able to become a dictator was the use of propaganda.

(i) and (ii) So use **detailed information** to explain each of the two causes.

(i)

(ii)

(iii) and (iv) Next, you need to explain **how** the causes helped Stalin to become a dictator.

(iii)

(iv)

(v) Finally, you need to show that your two causes are **linked** and/or **prioritise** them.

(v)

SuperFacts

Groups purged by the OGPU included teachers, engineers, scientists, factory workers, the armed forces, the Politburo, and even the OGPU itself. So many were purged from 1936 to 1938 that this period was called the Great Terror. Those purged were usually executed, sent to labour camps, or sent into exile.

Show trials started in 1936 when sixteen 'Old Bolsheviks' were tried for killing Kirov. The accused were always found guilty. At first, people did not realise the trials were unfair, because the accused often confessed. The trials helped Stalin – they made people feel the state was in danger and be less likely to criticise him.

Millions were purged In 1939, about 3.5 million people were imprisoned. About 1.3 million of these were in labour camps. Historians disagree over the statistics that are available (estimates and numbers purged in the Red Army range from 10% – 50%).

Stalin used propaganda for many purposes: to turn people against his enemies, to get people to accept plans such as collectivisation, to get people to work harder and put up with hardships, and to build a 'cult of Stalin'.

Propaganda methods varied: posters, radio, plays, cinema, and banners with slogans. Officials travelled the country with propaganda films and posters, giving talks in towns and villages. Each new policy had its own propaganda campaign to persuade people to accept it.

SuperFacts

Collectives The average collective had about 80 hectares of land worked by 'brigades' of about 15 families. The state set working hours and work, usually 140 days a year, farming and repairing roads. It also provided homes and equipment.

Mechanisation using tractors and, from 1931, combine harvesters, was possible on collective farms. By 1935 the Soviet Union was exporting grain.

Objections to collectivisation Peasants did not like losing independence; or having a committee telling them when to work and what to do (and fining them if they disobeyed). They did not like losing their land; handing over their farms, animals and equipment. *Kulaks* objected the most – they had the most to lose.

The Stakhanovite Movement encouraged workers to compete to produce more (like Stakhanov). They were sent into factories to show ordinary workers more efficient, higher, production. From 1934 workers were paid by piecework, not set wages. The state rewarded high production with better housing and rations.

Women were seen as equal citizens They had equal voting rights to men. They were equal at work and had equal pay for equal work, as well as equal opportunities to work. In 1928, there were 3 million working women. In 1940 there were over 13 million.

ResultsPlus
Top tip

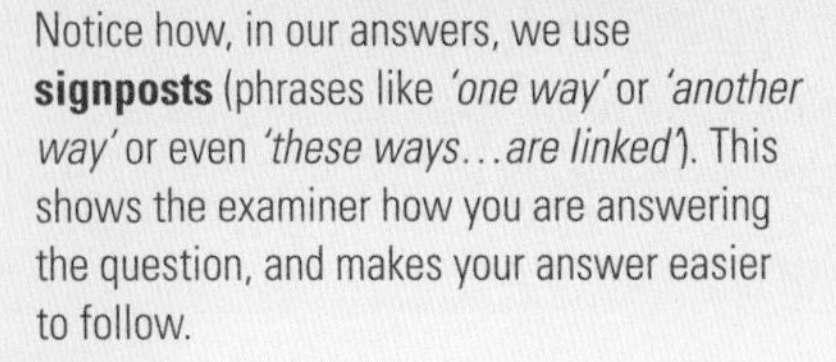

Notice how, in our answers, we use **signposts** (phrases like *'one way'* or *'another way'* or even *'these ways…are linked'*). This shows the examiner how you are answering the question, and makes your answer easier to follow.

Answering questions: Question 2(a) and 2(b)

What you need to do

In the examination, you have to answer **either** 2(a) or 2(b).

Both questions will ask you to '**Explain how…**' something happened. For example

- ***Explain how agriculture changed in the Soviet Union 1924–39.***

  or
- ***Explain how the Five-Year Plans changed the Soviet Union 1928–39.***

How you do it

The technique for answering the question is always the same.

The best answers will:

Describe a change or an action	and	give an explanation of why this answers the question.

So let's answer the following question together, using the SuperFacts on this page.

Explain how working conditions in the Soviet Union changed under Stalin.

An answer could start like this. Fill in the blanks at (i) + (ii) to show you understand.

One way working conditions changed was that peasants' farms were collectivised.	This changed their working conditions because the state now set their working hours and work - many peasants did not like this. Their work also became more mechanised.
Another way working conditions changed was the new production targets.	These changed working conditions because … (i)
Another way working conditions changed was … (ii)	This change was that they now got equal pay for equal work and they had more chances to work. 13 million of them were in work by 1939.

Final step!

The best answers will show that all these ways of increasing persecution were **linked**.

For example, an answer to this question could finish like this…

These changes in working conditions were linked. They all show ways that, under Stalin, the state controlled working conditions more and more – setting wages for peasants and factory workers, production methods, targets and job opportunities.

Test yourself

Here is another '**Explain how...**' question.

Explain how daily life changed in Stalin's Soviet Union before 1939.

Using the SuperFacts printed on this page, fill in the boxes below to create an answer.

One way daily life changed was that social inequality grew.	This changed daily life because .... (iii)
Another change to daily life was that religion was discouraged.	This changed daily life because ... (iv)
Another way daily life changed was ...(v)	This changed daily life because ... (vi)

These changes in daily life were linked.
For example,... (vii)

SuperFacts

Social inequality existed, despite the emphasis communism placed on equality. State officials got a better standard of living. In 1939, state officials were allowed 6.7 square metres of housing space a person. The average was 4.3 square metres. Those not in favour with the state had to wait longer for nursery places, operations, etc.

Religion was officially allowed Actually, religion was frowned on and atheism was the norm. People were sent to labour camps for religious beliefs; priests were purged. In 1915 Russia had 54,000 churches. By 1940 all but 400 had been destroyed.

Ethnic minorities At first, the state welcomed local languages and diversity. But from 1932, they were seen as 'counter-revolutionary', mainly because the republics were most resistant to collectivisation. The state imposed a universal Russian culture ('Russification'), and Russian was compulsory in schools from 1938.

The answer

You can find suggested answers to the tasks numbered (i), (ii) etc. on page 94.

SuperFacts

The SuperFacts you will need for this activity are on pages 82–83. The titles of the relevant SuperFacts are:

Stalin wanted collectivisation and industrialisation

Collectivisation
Collectives

Failures of collectivisation
Successes of collectivisation

Mechanisation

Gosplan
The First Five-Year Plan 1928–32
The Second Five-Year Plan 1933–37
The Third Five-Year Plan 1938–41

Alexei Stakhanov
The Stakhanovite Movement

Increased productivity
Industrial quality suffered at first

Quality improved

Answering questions: Question 3(a) and 3(b)

Questions 3(a) and 3(b) follow the same format. You have to answer **either** 3(a) **or** 3(b).

Questions 3(a) and 3(b) will be about **causes** or **effects**.

They will ask you to make a judgement about causes or effects. So they could say:

- ***Was [something] the main cause of ...?***
- ***Was [something] the worst effect of ...?***

The questions may talk about **reasons** (meaning **causes**) and will always give you some '**information to help you with your answer**'. For example:

Were Stalin's 5-Year Plans the main reason for the improvement in the economy of the Soviet Union 1924–39?

You may use the following information to help you with your answer.

- ***Collectivisation of agriculture***
- ***Mechanisation of agriculture***
- ***The Five-Year Plans***
- ***The Stakhanovite Movement***

A good way to start is to show that you know **all** the four factors in the box above are reasons why the Soviet economy improved. Make sure you signpost each of them for the examiner (see Top tip box for an example of signposting phrases). We have written a paragraph on the first factor. You write a similar paragraph on each of the others, marked (i), (ii) + (iii).

On the left, you will see the titles of the SuperFacts which will help you.

Collectivisation was one cause of improvement in the Soviet economy. Collectivisation was the process of joining small farms together into bigger units, averaging 80 hectares. By 1935, over 90% of Soviet farmland was collectivised. Grain production rose from 63 to 75 million tons 1928-35. This improved the economy because there was enough grain to feed town workers and earn money from grain exports.

Mechanisation of agriculture was another cause of improvement in the Soviet economy. Mechanisation... (i)

The Five-Year Plans were another cause ... (ii)

The Stakhanovite Movement was another... (iii)

ResultsPlus
Top tip

Notice some phrases in our paragraph on Collectivisation are signpost phrases (Collectivisation was one cause ...). They are used to ensure the examiner knows exactly how you are answering the question. Use similar phrases in your paragraphs.

If you are having trouble with your paragraphs, look on page 94 for help.

Need more help?

If you are having trouble with your paragraphs, look on page 94 for help.

Now the examiner knows that we realise **all** the factors helped the Soviet economy.

If you know any **other** causes which helped the economy to improve, you can include these too. Study the relevant SuperFacts and explain one **extra** cause below.

Another cause for improvement in the Soviet economy by 1939 was... (iv)

Two steps to go!

Now we can make a judgement on the key part of this question:

Were the 5-Year Plans the main reason ...?

Here are two possible views. We have completed the first one. You complete the other.

Collectivisation was the main reason for (or cause of) improvement in the Soviet economy because it enabled the Soviet Union to produce more food. First of all, this helped exports: they were exporting grain by 1935. But it also meant that there was plenty of food to feed the workers in the towns. If the famine of 1932 had continued, the factory workers would have starved. Or they would have had to import food. Either way, the economy depended on better food supplies.

The Five-Year Plans were the most important cause of improvement in the Soviet economy because... (v)

Final step!

The very best answers will see that, no matter how important **one** cause was, it was probably **not enough on its own**. One cause can be the most important, but most things in history depend on a combination of causes. We have written one final paragraph saying this. You complete the bottom box to write your own version.

But the Stakhanovite Movement was not enough on its own. True, it did help boost production. But encouraging workers to produce more and paying them piecework rates meant they didn't care about the quality of what they made. Tractors from the Stalingrad Tractor Factory only lasted an average of 70 hours at first. To help the economy they had to improve quantity AND quality. So the Stakhanovite Movement was not enough on its own.

But the Five-Year plans were not enough on their own because... (vi)

ResultsPlus
Top tip

You can **agree** or **disagree** with the question. In this case, you can say the 5-Year Plans **were** the most important reason. You can say they **weren't**. The main thing is that you back up your opinion with an argument based on the facts.

If you are arguing that one cause is the most important **you must compare it to other causes, to show it was more important.**

Don't forget to **signpost** your answers.

ResultsPlus
Watch out!

Question 3 is one on which your skills of **written communication** will be judged.

To get to the top of each level of the mark scheme you have to:

- write effectively
- organise your thoughts coherently
- spell, punctuate and use grammar well.

The answer

You can find suggested answers to the tasks numbered (i), (ii) etc. on page 94.

Answers: Russia 1917–39

Question 1 (a)

i) *I can infer this because Source A says mud covered roads for much of the year and there were few railways.*

ii) *Source A tells me that communicating information in Russia was very difficult.*

Question 1 (b)

i) *For example the Cheka stopped all political opposition. By June 1919 they had arrested 87,000 people.*

ii) *A third way the Bolsheviks fought the war was by using War Communism.*

Question 1 (c)

iii) *One set of political changes came about through the first Bolshevik decrees. One of these, for example, abolished capital punishment. Other political changes came about through the Constitution of July 1918. This gave all land to the people and required all businesses with 10 or more workers to be run by the state.*

[Hint] *Look at the SuperFact about the Cheka.*

iv) *One effect of the Bolsheviks coming to power – the civil war – worsened the other effect – political change. This was because, fighting a civil war, the Bolsheviks had to stop opposition. So they used the Cheka to arrest and kill political rivals. Civil rights therefore suffered.*

Question 1 (d)

i) *For example, OGPU arrested political opponents in purges and convicted them in show trials.*

ii) *For example, he used posters, radio, plays, cinema and banners with slogans.*

iii) *The show trials helped Stalin – they made people feel the state was in danger and less likely to criticise him.*

iv) *This helped Stalin become a dictator because each new policy had its own propaganda campaign to persuade people to accept it.*

v) *The two causes were linked. This is because the show trials were a form of propaganda: they convinced people the country was under threat from Stalin's enemies and he was right to suppress them. Suppressing the opposition was the main reason Stalin could be a dictator. His propaganda was only believed because there was no opposition to argue against it.*

Question 2 (a) + (b)

i) *workers were now paid by piecework, not by set wages. They could also get rewards like better housing and rations for higher production.*

ii) *equal working conditions for women.*

iii) *only people like state officials got benefits. They got 6.7 square metres of living space when the average was only 4.3 sqm. Those not in favour with the state had to wait longer for nursery places, operations, etc.*

iv) *people could not openly be religious. Although religion was officially allowed, actually it was not. Some people were sent to labour camps for their religious beliefs. There were only 400 churches left by 1940.*

v) *ethnic minorities were mistreated.*

vi) *Russian culture was imposed on people. For example, Russian became compulsory in all the schools of the Soviet Union from 1938.*

vii) *... all the changes are the result of the state controlling the daily lives of people. In the Soviet Union under Stalin, the state decided what your culture should be, what religious beliefs you should have and how you were housed. So all the changes are linked; they have a common root.*

Question 3 (a) + (b)

i) *... involved the use of tractors and, from 1931, combine harvesters, on the larger farms. This helped the Soviet economy because, by 1935, they were exporting grain.*

ii) *... of improvement in the Soviet economy. A government agency called Gosplan set targets for raising industrial output. There were three 5-Year Plans. The third was disrupted by war. But the first two met their targets, so this improved the Soviet economy.*

iii) *... cause of improvement in the Soviet economy. This was when industrial workers tried to copy Alexei Stakhanov and raise their production. By 1934, teams of Stakhanovites were sent to spread more efficient ways of working and workers were paid by piecework. This was good for the Soviet economy because production went up, e.g. from 3.3 to 6.2 million tons in iron.*

iv) *... that the quality of factory production improved. The Stalingrad Tractor factory, for example, was supposed to produce 500 tractors per month at first, but it managed only 43 in three months. But by 1939 it was producing half the tractors in the country.*

v) *... Gosplan set national targets and gave each factory a production target too. The First and Second plans focused on heavy industry; the Third plan included 'luxury' items. So the 5-Year Plans were vital. They set the pace of change and boosted key industries.*

vi) *... the economy needed improvements in industry AND agriculture to be healthy. Without collectivisation to make farming more efficient, the factory workers would have starved. Or they would have needed to import food. Either way, 5-Year Plans to increase industrial output depended on a healthy food supply from farming – so they may have been the most important reason, but they*

2C Overview: The USA 1919–41

1919–29

At the end of the First World War

There was an economic boom that affected:

- new industries making consumer products (such as radios and cars)
- leisure industries (such as the movies)
- the stock market and share trading.

Boosted by

- hire purchase schemes
- bank loans and mortgages
- mass production methods.

No boom benefits for:

- farmers (overproducing after the war, prices dropping)
- old industries (e.g. coal lost customers to electricity)
- black people and others in worst-paid jobs.

Became powerful in parts of the USA in the 1920s

- gangsters (who exploited Prohibition)
- the Ku Klux Klan and other racist groups in the South.

1929–33

The Depression

had several underlying causes:

- overproduction by businesses and farmers
- too much buying on credit
- rising unemployment
- falling farm prices.

President Hoover's government

- believed in *laissez faire* for too long
- gave too little help too late
- became very unpopular.

worsened by the Wall Street Crash, which led to:

- industries going bankrupt
- banks going bankrupt
- people losing their savings
- people losing homes and goods when can't pay loans.

1933–41

President Roosevelt's New Deal

introduces measures aimed at:

1932–35: recovery

- all banks closed, inspected and the financially sound ones re-opened
- temporary government agencies (Alphabet Agencies) to fund state projects.

1935-41: reform (Second New Deal)

- temporary agencies replaced with permanent ones
- federal social security scheme set up for unemployed
- federal funding of low-cost housing.

opposition from:

- Republicans
- business that objected to NRA regulation
- people, such as Huey Long, who wanted more reform.

SuperFacts Key Topic 1
The US economy 1919–41

SuperFacts are the key bits of information. Learn them and ask someone to test you.

World War I helped the US economy During and after the war, the USA earned income from lending money to Europe; British borrowing had risen to $4,277 million. The USA had not suffered war damage; its factories had been expanded for war production. It had also taken over some of Europe's trade markets, such as supplying cotton to Japan. p.8

Rising farm prices A bushel of wheat cost $0.9 in 1915 and $2.16 in 1919, because the war disrupted production in Europe. US farmers were encouraged to raise production to supply Europe. Some even borrowed money to mechanise production. p.8 & 9

Trade dominance In the early 1920s, the USA produced 70% of the world's petrol, 55% of its cotton and 30% of its wheat. It also saw itself as the world's banker. p.9

Isolationism After the war, the USA did not want to get caught up in world politics again. It refused to join the League of Nations, despite the fact that it was the US president, Woodrow Wilson, who had pushed for the League. p.10

The Emergency Tariff Act (May 1921) put taxes on some foreign goods imported into the USA (such as wheat and sugar) to encourage Americans to buy US goods. Some other countries then put tariffs on US goods, making them more expensive. Sales of goods, such as wheat, to Europe fell. This hit US farmers. p.10

Rising number of immigrants From 1900–20, 12.5 million Europeans emigrated to the USA, as did 1.5 million people from Canada, Asia and Mexico. Prejudice against immigrant communities in the USA was rising. Isolationism and prejudice caused the government to submit to pressure to restrict immigration. p.11

The Emergency Quota Act (1921) restricted immigration from any country to 3% of the number of immigrants from that country already living in the USA according to the census of 1910. This made the biggest cut in immigrants from Eastern Europe and Italy, the groups there was most prejudice against. p.11

The Immigration Act (1924) set a limit on immigration. It was 150,000 a year. p.11

Mass production In 1924, Henry Ford's moving assembly line system cut the time it took to produce a car from 12 hours to 1 hour 33 minutes. The price of a Ford car dropped from around $850 in 1908 to around $300 (for an improved car) in 1926. p.12

Car production In 1915, there were 1 million cars in the USA. In 1939, there were 28 million. About 400,000 km of road was built in the USA in the 1920s. This affected how much people travelled for work, shopping and holidays. p.13

The importance of the car industry By 1929, over 4 million workers depended on the car industry (from garage workers to those in industries providing raw materials). By 1929, 75% of all new leather, glass and rubber in the USA went into making cars. p.13

Key Topic summary

There was an economic boom in the USA during the First World War, as the USA supplied food and war goods to its allies in Europe. It also lent these allies money. After the war, the USA continued to lend money and send supplies to a war-devastated Europe.

After the war, there was a boom in new consumer goods, such as radios and cars, thanks to mass production methods and hire-purchase schemes (that allowed people to spread the cost of goods over months or years). Successful companies made such high profits that many ordinary people began to buy shares in them.

Some people did not share the boom. Farmers, now over-producing (as European agriculture recovered and there was less demand for food), suffered as prices fell. Older industries, such as the coal industry, lost out to new industries such as electricity.

edexcel key terms

shares People can buy shares in a company for a price that changes over time. The more shares they have, they more they have to pay. If the company makes a profit, the people who bought the shares (shareholders) get a share of the profit based on the number of shares they have.

stock market A place where shares are bought and sold – the biggest stock market in the USA was in New York, on Wall Street.

laissez faire is the idea that the government should not interfere in the way that people run their businesses and their lives. A *laissez faire* policy will not try to control business, but neither will it help the poor or people with other social problems.

The hire-purchase system allowed people to buy more consumer goods than they had money for, by paying in instalments over a set period of time. However, they did have to keep up their regular payments. p.14

Consumer goods In 1921, there were 5,000 fridges made in the USA. In 1929, there were 890,000. In 1923, there were 190,000 radios made in the USA. In 1929, there were 4,980,000. With mass production, prices of these goods fell. Now more people could afford them, so demand rose. p.14

Wage rises The average wage rose by 8% in the 1920s. Some wages dropped – so others must have risen by more than 8%. For example, the average teacher's wage nearly doubled between 1919 and 1930. It rose from $15.5 to $29.9 a week. p.10 &19

Buying shares In 1926, about $450 million was spent on share trading in the USA. By mid-1929, this had risen to $1,125 million. p.10

Making a profit from shares As share prices rose, even ordinary people began to buy shares to make a profit. The price of a share in a radio company rose from $0.94 on 3 March 1928 to $5.05 on 3 September 1929. Share prices rose because profits, especially for producers of consumer goods (such as radios) were rising rapidly. p.16

'Buying on the margin' is buying shares with borrowed money, hoping to make a profit by selling them quickly at a higher price. This was risky, even when people did it with their own money. But during the boom, banks started to do it with their investors' money, too. Even bankers thought share prices would just keep on going up. p.17

Falling farm prices In 1919, a bushel of wheat cost $2.16. In 1929, it cost $1.04. Demand fell because Europe was growing its own crops again and tariffs made US wheat more expensive. But farmers went on producing at wartime levels, instead of cutting output as demand fell. p.18

Older industries did not share the boom of the 1920s. For example, coal mining declined as people turned to electricity for power, light and heat. Railways also suffered as road transport grew in popularity. p.18

Farm workers About 40% of US workers in the 1920s were farmers or farm workers. The average wage for a farm worker fell from $13.5 a week in 1919 to $7.5 in 1930. Many farm workers lost their jobs as farmers brought in bigger machines. p.18

Black workers did not share the boom of the 1920s. Many worked in farming, which was not a boom industry, or in poorly paid industrial jobs. They were discriminated against in most places and often 'last hired, first fired'. p.19

ResultsPlus
Top tip

When using SuperFacts to support a statement, make sure you do not just produce a list of facts. Always say **how** the detail supports the statement.

Need more help?
You can find a longer explanation of each SuperFact in your Edexcel textbook, *The USA 1919–41*. Look for this symbol, which will give you the page number .

SuperFacts Key Topic 2
US society 1919–29

SuperFacts are the key bits of information. Learn them and ask someone to test you.

Consumerism As wages grew, people had more time and money to spend on goods and leisure. Industry made new goods to buy, such as radios, fridges and cars, and advertising made these seem desirable. By 1925, 2,700,000 families had a radio. p.23

Advertising boosted the sales of consumer goods. Adverts were everywhere, e.g. in newspapers, on billboards and, from 1922, on the radio. People responded by spending money, borrowing if necessary, to keep up with what other people had. p.23

Jazz music was part of the leisure boom. It swept from the South to the North during the 1920s, as black people moved to cities like New York and Chicago. Jazz, and new dances, like the Charleston, seemed to represent the new, freer, era. p.24

Sport became a leisure industry, especially for the wealthy middle class, with radio broadcasts of boxing and baseball and newly built golf courses and tennis courts. p.24

The movies The cinema was the fastest-growing leisure industry, even more so when 'talkies' started in 1927. By 1922, movies were making $4 million a week in ticket sales. p.24

Movie stars earned huge amounts of money. In 1916, Mary Pickford (the highest-earning movie star) was paid $10,000 a week. The average wage was $13 a week. p.24

The Hays Code (1930) responded to the criticism that the movies caused immorality. Its rules aimed to stop the movies 'lowering the moral standards' of moviegoers. p.25

Prohibition was made law by the 18th Amendment to the Constitution. It came into effect in 1920. It prohibited the making, transport and sale of alcohol in all US states. p.26

Illegal drinking became common Millions of people still wanted to drink. It soon became clear that people would break Prohibition if they could. Illegal 'speakeasies' sprang up. Better speakeasies served 'bootleg' alcohol, smuggled in from Mexico. Bad ones served home-brewed 'moonshine' that could be dangerous to drink. p.26

Organised crime had been in the USA for a long time, but was boosted by Prohibition. Gangsters took over the sale of alcohol. The gangster Al Capone made $105 million profit from crime in 1927 – $60 million of that was from speakeasies. Gangs were wealthy and powerful; they used the profits of crime to bribe police, judges and local officials. p.26

Reasons for the growth of organised crime Prohibition (which increased profit), the war (trained people to kill), cheaper cars (quick getaways), its profitability (could afford bribes), the ruthlessness of the gangsters (intimidated people). p.27

Gang wars sprang up as powerful rival gangs fought each other to control cities such as Chicago (e.g. the St Valentine's Day Massacre of 7 Moran gang members by Capone's Gang in 1929). There were about 400 gang-related killings in Chicago in 1929. p.27

Key Topic summary

In the boom years of the 1920s, there was a huge rise in consumerism, encouraged by the growth of advertising. More and more people wanted consumer goods such as radios, washing machines, and cars. They also wanted to spend money in their leisure time, going to sports events or the movies.

Women got the vote in 1920. Many had more independence after the war. Young working women, nicknamed 'flappers', dressed more daringly and did things only men had done in the past, like drinking and smoking.

The 1920s saw a growth in organised crime, encouraged by Prohibition – the government ban on alcohol. There was also a great deal of prejudice against immigrants, black people, and those who challenged the status quo.

edexcel key terms

consumerism is the desire to buy more things, usually inessential goods (such as radios and cars), rather than essential goods (such as basic food).

Prohibition is the name given to the period in the USA (1920–32) when it was illegal to make, sell or transport alcohol in the USA.

Jim Crow Laws were laws passed by some Southern states to enforce segregation between black and white people.

Effects of the war on women The fact that women worked so successfully during the war led to their getting the vote in 1920 (19th Amendment). They were paid less and some lost jobs to returning men after 1918, but many stayed on. This started a trend. For example, women white-collar workers rose from 1.9 million in 1910, to 3.3 million in 1920 and 4.7 million in 1930. p.28

'Flappers' was the name given to some young, independent women in the 1920s. They earned their own money, and behaved with a freedom formerly reserved for men. They drove cars, drank in speakeasies, cut their hair in a short 'bob', and wore shorter, less restricting (so more revealing) clothes. p.29

Women consumers took advantage of the new, labour-saving appliances in the 1920s (like washing machines and fridges) to make their lives easier. Some married women even continued to go out to work, though this was disapproved of. p.29

Racism was part of everyday life. All over the USA, black people did the poorest paid jobs and were 'last hired, first fired'. Racism existed in the North, but was more severe, violent and legally enforced in the South. p.30

Jim Crow laws enforced segregation – making black people use separate transport, cafés, toilets, drinking fountains, etc. Black schools, situated in the poorer parts of town, got less state money than white ones. p.30

Black people had the right to vote but were often prevented from voting in the South by tricks or threats. p.30

Many black people moved north as a result of Southern racism, to cities like New York (black population in Harlem in 1920, 33%; in 1930 70%). p.30

Racist violence also happened across the USA but more often in the South. Black people were beaten up, their homes burned and they were murdered or lynched (killed by a mob for a supposed crime). p.32

The Ku Klux Klan was a racist organisation It wanted America to be a WASP (white, Anglo-Saxon, Protestant) nation. It mainly targeted black people, although it also persecuted Jews, immigrants, and Catholics. In some Southern states the police, the law courts and local government were full of Klan members. p.33

The Sacco and Vanzetti case was an example of prejudice against immigrants. The two immigrants were executed despite unclear evidence. It showed legal prejudice; the judge wanted a guilty verdict. The public debate showed wider prejudice; e.g. thinking of all immigrants as poor, lacking in skills, involved with crime or communist. p.34

The 'Monkey Trial' (1925) showed how people's religious convictions caused intolerance. John Scopes, a teacher in Dayton, Tennessee, was put on trial for introducing the evolutionary ideas of Charles Darwin. Teaching anything contrary to the Creation story in the Bible was banned in Tennessee. He was found guilty. The law was not repealed until 1967. p.35

Be careful when you write about the **Ku** Klux Klan. It is **not** the **Klu** Klux Klan, although many people, even some textbook authors, make the mistake of putting an 'l' in the first word because there is an 'l' after the 'K' in the next two words!

Need more help?
You can find a longer explanation of each SuperFact in your Edexcel textbook, *The USA 1919–41*. Look for this symbol, which will give you the page number.

Key Topic summary

The 1920s boom had several weaknesses. It relied heavily on the production of consumer goods, and on loans. The stock market boom relied on stock prices continuing to rise and, again, many investors depended on loans.

In 1929, the price of shares fell rapidly, in what became known as the Wall Street Crash. The economic effects of this crash were felt world-wide, but most heavily in the USA. Banks had been investing peoples' savings in shares, and with the fall of share prices, ran out of money. They began calling in loans, which many people could not repay, because they had lost their jobs as businesses failed,

Soon many Americans were living in desperate poverty and growing increasingly angry, and the government did little or nothing to help them or end the crisis.

SuperFacts Key Topic 3
The USA in Depression 1929–33

SuperFacts are the key bits of information. Learn them and ask someone to test you.

Unemployment problems Unemployment rose (from 0.8 million in 1926 to 2 million in 1928), partly because mass production needed fewer workers. Rising unemployment meant more people chasing fewer jobs, so bosses cut wages. Unemployment and falling wages meant people had less money to spend so demand for goods fell. p.39–41

Trade problems Trade tariffs cut world trade, causing a drop in profits from exports. Farmers, desperate to make money, overproduced, driving prices down more (wheat $1.4 to $1 a bushel 1925–28). No government control of credit (hire purchase or bank loans); too much borrowing and too many shares bought on credit. p.39–41

Herbert Hoover became president in 1929 He was a Republican who believed in *laissez faire* (the government not interfering in business or social issues). p.40

Causes of the Wall Street Crash (October 1929) In September 1929, doubts about the economy meant share sales rose, so share prices fell. As more people sold, prices fell more. On 24 October, panic set in. 13 million shares were sold. Prices kept falling. Some bankers bought $250 million worth of shares, hoping to stop the drop. They failed. p.42

Share prices hit bottom in November 1929 Radio company shares worth $0.94 a share in March 1928 were worth $5.05 in September 1928, but $0.28 in November. p.42

Effects of the Wall Street Crash People, businesses and banks lost huge sums (much of it borrowed). Things worsened when banks could not get loans repaid. By 1933, 5,000 banks closed; one, the Bank of New York, lost the savings of 400,000 people. p.43

More effects Many people could not pay hire purchase or bank loans; they had to give the bank their homes and became homeless. Companies went bankrupt. Sales of goods fell, unemployment rose from 3% in 1929 to 15% in 1931. p.44

The Depression spreads worldwide The US had to lend less and called for loans to be repaid. This caused a worldwide depression and cut demand for US exports. p.44

Hoover and the Depression Hoover believed in *laissez faire*, so his government did little. When it did act, it only gave a limited amount of money or help, soon used up. Shanty towns of temporary homes for the unemployed appeared in cities and were nicknamed 'Hoovervilles' to underline Hoover's inaction. p.46 & 48

Federal Farm Board (July 1929, before the Crash): set up with $500 million to help farmers by buying surplus crops. At first, the crops were destroyed rather than used to feed the unemployed. The money ran out in 1932 and the Board shut. p.47

Smoot-Hawley tariff (1930) increased tariffs on imports to make people buy US goods to create jobs. But imports **and** exports fell, harming trade and employment. In 1929, US exports were worth $2,341 million dollars. In 1932, this had fallen to $784 million. p.47 & 52

National Credit Corporation The NCC was set up in 1931 by banks and businesses to lend money to restore confidence. It did not want to take risks. It only lent $10 million of its $500 million fund, so the government made it disband. p.47

edexcel key terms

slump A slump is when the economy has a drop in activity. Unemployment rises, wages fall and prices fall. There is less buying and selling, so businesses do badly.

depression A depression is when an economy does not get out of a slump. Unemployment rises rapidly, wages fall and many businesses collapse. 'The Depression' refers to the world-wide depression of the late 1920s and the 1930s.

hobo A hobo is a homeless person who is constantly on the move, looking for work, but not finding it.

Reconstruction Finance Corporation (RFC) was set up in 1932 to replace the NCC. It was government funded and run. In July 1932, it was given an extra $300 million under the Emergency Relief and Construction Act, for farm projects and public works. p.47

Federal Home Loan Bank Act (1932) was passed to lend money to people in trouble with loans on their homes. Of 41,000 applications, only three were accepted. p.47

The Dust Bowl During WWI, the Great Plains were ploughed up for arable crops. Farmers grew wheat year after year, impoverishing the soil. In the 1920s over-farming made things worse. New farm machinery dug deep into the soil. The 1931 drought was the last straw. Winds blew away all the fertile top-soil causing a dust bowl. p.50

Impact of the Dust Bowl Farmers could not grow crops or raise animals on the dusty soil. Farms went bankrupt and laid off workers. Men and boys became migrants looking for work; there were 1–2 million hobos at this time. p.50

Migrant workers (people who travel from place to place looking for work) became more common as people became more desperate for work. In towns, they lived in 'flophouses' (slum housing where many workers shared a room) and ate at soup kitchens. Migrant farm workers lived in tents or in their cars. p.50

Help for the unemployed before 1932 came only from charities and 'relief agencies'. These gave small amounts to those who passed poverty tests (which included investigating homes and sometimes even weighing children). Other charities set up 'soup kitchens' to provide a hot meal. Al Capone, the gangster, ran one in Chicago. p.48

Government unpopularity By 1932 (a presidential election year) the government and President Hoover were very unpopular. The government finally passed some laws to help solve the crisis. Some said this was because of the election, others that the government saw *lassez faire* wasn't working. But it was too little, too late. p.52

Who resented the government? The unemployed and the poor, for the lack of help (by the time the federal work projects were set up unemployment had reached over 12 million). The relief agencies because they were losing the battle which the government claimed to be winning. Businesses because the extra trade tariffs made trade fall. p.52

The Bonus Army were people who were owed bonus money from the First World War. It was due to be paid in 1945. Many were unemployed and living in Hoovervilles. In May 1932, about 15,000 of them (some with their families) marched to Washington to ask for the bonus money to be paid early. p.53

Debating what to do Congress was split. The House of Representatives voted to pay the bonuses early. But the Senate voted against, 62 votes to 18. So Hoover told the Bonus Army to go home and offered them loans to get there. Some went, but about 10,000 stayed and continued to march and demonstrate. p.53

The use of force In July, police were told to drive the Bonus Army out of Washington. They refused. Hoover sent in the army. There was fighting in which four of the marchers were killed and hundreds injured. Hoover became even more unpopular. p.53

ResultsPlus
Top tip

When choosing SuperFacts to support a statement, read the question carefully and consider the limits it puts on the information you use. Question 1a) asks, 'What can you learn from the source about...?' This is the one question where you should not use SuperFacts at all. It is asking what you can learn from the source, not what you know.

Need more help?

You can find a longer explanation of each SuperFact in your Edexcel textbook, *The USA 1919–41*. Look for this symbol, which will give you the page number.

SuperFacts Key Topic 4
FDR and the New Deal 1933–41

Key Topic summary
Roosevelt replaced Hoover as president in 1933 and set to work with Congress to produce laws to aid recovery from the Depression – the New Deal. Various agencies were set up with billions of federal dollars to fund state projects to provide work for the unemployed, relief for the poor and homeless, stability for banks, and help for farmers.

The New Deal had achieved a lot by 1935, but it faced criticism from some businessmen, politicians, ordinary people, and even the Supreme Court. Most opponents worried about the growth of federal control, but others felt the reforms had not gone far enough.

In 1935, the New Deal moved into its second phase, from temporary solutions to aid recovery to more permanent systems (such as unemployment benefit) to set up long-term reform.

SuperFacts are the key bits of information. Learn them and ask someone to test you.

Franklin D Roosevelt became president in 1933 His aims were: to get people back to work, to build confidence in banks, and to provide help for those in need. He explained his policies in a series of radio broadcasts ('fireside chats'). In his first 100 days in government, Roosevelt and Congress passed laws focused on these aims. p.57 & 58

Emergency Banking Act (March 1933) closed all banks for government inspection. Only financially sound banks reopened (5,000 after 3 days, more later). Confidence was restored – there was no rush for money. Banks agreed not to call in loans so fast. p.59

Reforestation Relief Act (March 1933) set up the Civilian Conservation Corps (CCC). It held work camps for male volunteers aged 17–23, fed them and gave them wages of $30 a month. In return they dug ditches and reservoirs and replanted forests. p.59

Agricultural Adjustment Act (May 1933) set up the Agricultural Adjustment Administration (AAA). It began by buying up surplus crops and animals; this raised prices and farm incomes. Then it tackled over-production by giving subsidies to farmers to grow less. It regulated the output of all major crops: corn, wheat, cotton, tobacco and milk. p.59

Federal Emergency Relief Administration (FERA) began in May 1933 to provide relief work with a budget of $3 billion. It set up the Civil Works Administration (CWA); which organised useful public building projects all over the USA. It cut unemployment. By January 1934, about 4 million people were working on CWA projects. p.59 & 60

Tennessee Valley Authority (TVA) was set up in May 1933 to run land development in the Tennessee Valley (104,000 square km over seven states). It gave the unemployed work building dams to stop flooding **and** created a water reserve **and** generated electricity for rural areas. CCC projects in the area stopped soil erosion, and taught better farming practices. p.59 & 60

Home Owners' Refinancing Act (June 1933) extended the time limit on home loans, reducing monthly payments for those struggling to pay mortgages. p.59

The National Recovery Administration (NRA) (set up by the 1933 National Industrial Recovery Act) helped working conditions. Employers linked to the NRA agreed to protect conditions for workers (minimum wage, 8-hour day, no child labour). Joining was voluntary, but businesses with the NRA blue eagle symbol were popular. p.59

The Public Works Administration (PWA), set up by the 1933 National Industrial Relief Act, ran large building projects. It had a budget of $3.3 billion for public works; most was for large building projects. It was temporary; the PWA closed when the money was spent. p.59

The Alphabet Agencies had huge federal budgets; some taxpayers resented this. The agencies gave money to the state governments, as grants; this reduced the resentment. But the agencies controlled what the money was spent on; the states suggested the relief projects, the agencies decided which projects to support. p.60

edexcel key terms

The Hundred Days is the phrase used to refer to the first 100 days of Roosevelt's time as president. During this time he and Congress worked together to pass a huge amount of legislation.

Alphabet Agencies The many agencies set up under the New Deal and the Second New Deal that aimed to solve the social and economic problems of the 1930s. They are called the Alphabet Agencies because they were usually referred to by an acronym (the initial letter short form) of the agency name (e.g. CCC for Civilian Conservation Corps).

General opposition to the New Deal Some people opposed the cost (federal spending went from $4.7 billion in 1931 to $6.7 billion). Some businesses resented NRA rules: they wanted to run their companies without interference. Some worried about federal power: they said the federal government was taking power from the states, and this was against the Constitution. p.62 & 64

Republican opposition Some Republicans wanted *laissez faire* policies: they didn't think it was the government's job to run the economy. Some opposed government interference in people's lives: they preferred to be left to cope. Some opposed the growth of state power: they feared that this was a step on the road to communism. p.62

Some opponents felt reforms did not go far enough They wanted radical policies, such as nationalising the banks, and bringing in pensions and unemployment benefit. One of these was Huey Long, Governor and Senator for Louisiana. His support had helped Roosevelt win the 1932 election; his criticism was therefore very damaging. p.62

Opposition from the Supreme Court The Alphabet Agencies were taken to court for being unconstitutional by not keeping the separation of powers. In 1934, in the 'sick chicken case' the Supreme Court ruled the NRA unconstitutional. Other rulings against the New Deal followed, including one against the AAA. p.63

Recovery by 1935 The banking system was now stable. Tax income was rising ($1.9 billion 1933, $2.9 billion 1934). Unemployment was falling (12.8 million 1933, 10.6 million 1935). p.64

The Second New Deal and unemployment The Second New Deal began in 1935; this focused on long-term reforms. So the WPA (Works Progress Administration) replaced the PWA, giving training, not just unskilled work. Roosevelt also proposed a social-security system that would pay benefits to the unemployed from 1937. p.66

The Second New Deal and homelessness The Resettlement Administration (RA) built new communities for the homeless in towns and in the countryside. The Federal Housing Administration (FHA) cleared slums and provided affordable housing. p.66 & 67

Taking on the Supreme Court Roosevelt challenged the Supreme Court, suggesting adding new judges. There was little support for the plan, but as existing judges died off, Roosevelt supporters were elected who backed New Deal agencies like the WPA. p.66

Dust Bowl conditions worsened 1935–36 In 1936, the FSA (Farm Security Administration) set up camps with food for those affected. Its Soil Conservation Service worked to fertilise the land and stop the Dust Bowl growing. p.67

The Second World War began in September 1939. The USA did not join the war at once, but supplied the Allies with weapons, ammunition and food. This boosted production. Roosevelt decided to re-arm the USA, which boosted industry and employment. The war helped the USA recover from the Depression. p.67

Recovery by 1941 Unemployment was down (10.6 million 1935, 5.6 million 1941). There was more training as well as jobs. The WPA spent $8.5 billion from 1935–41 and the CCC spent $1.2 billion in rural areas. Homelessness was down: the FHA built 120,000 homes for families on low income. Welfare improved: the FSA spent $128 million on relief 1935–41. p.68

Lack of recovery? Critics said: the WPA favoured some areas of the USA; recovery was slow (no social security payments until 1937); 1938 was a bad year (unemployment rose to 10 million) and the Second World War ensured recovery, not the New Deal. p.68

The Alphabet Agencies can be confusing and can seem a huge amount to learn. Lean the acronym (initial letter short form) of the agency name (e.g. AAA not Agricultural Adjustment Agency). It will be quicker to write in the exam. Make sure you also learn a key word to link to the acronym so that you remember what it did (agriculture).

To distinguish between the PWA (came first, a temporary organisation) and the WPA (came later, permanent), remember that 'P' comes before 'W' in the alphabet, and the agency beginning with P comes first.

Need more help?

You can find a longer explanation of each SuperFact in your Edexcel textbook, *The USA 1919–41*. Look for this symbol, which will give you the page number.

Answering questions: Question 1 (a)

What you need to do

Question 1 (a) will always ask '**What can you learn from Source A about [something]**'. The best answers:

- not only extract **information** from the source
- but will also make **inferences** from the source *[see Top tip box]*
- and **support** those inferences with detail from the source.

Note: make sure you answer the question – after **about** comes the **subject**. You can't just make *any* inference from the source, it has to be about the *something* in the question.

Here is a possible **source**, **question** and **answer** for you to study.

Source A: From a GCSE textbook, *The Making of the Modern World, The USA 1919–41*.

> [During the First World War] … they expanded their farms, often taking out loans to buy new land and machinery. They also ploughed up land previously used for grazing cattle and sheep and grew wheat instead. By the early 1920s the USA was producing 30% of the world's wheat, 75% of its corn and 55% of its cotton.

What does Source A tell us about US farm profits in the First World War?

Inference	Supporting detail
Source A tells me that farm profits went up.	I can infer this because it says that farmers took out loans to buy new land and machinery. Profits must have been high for the farmers to make money and pay back the loans.

Now test yourself

(i) Write in the box below to show you can write **supporting detail** using this question.

What does Source A tell us about US farming after the First World War?

Source A tells me that US farming exports were booming after the war.	**[Supporting detail]**

(ii) Write in the box below to show you can write an inference using this question.

What does Source A tell us about US wheat production in the First World War?

[Inference]	I can infer this because Source A says that US farmers ploughed up land which they previously used for grazing cattle and sheep and used it for wheat instead.

An **inference** is a judgement that can be made by studying the source, but is not directly stated by it.

A **supported inference** is one that uses detail from the source to prove the inference.

Consider this example:

Source A: 'The furious head teacher told Jimmy that his behaviour was disgraceful, and that he had broken several school rules.'

Question: *What does Source A tell us about Jimmy?*

Information: Source A tells us that Jimmy had broken several school rules. [This is directly stated in the source, so it's not an inference.]

Inference: Source A tells me that Jimmy is in serious trouble and is likely to be punished. [The source does not directly tell us this, but we can infer that it is likely.]

A supported inference: Source A tells me that Jimmy is in serious trouble and is likely to be punished. I can infer this because Jimmy had broken several school rules and the head teacher was furious. [This is an inference, with details quoted from the source to support it.]

The answer

You can find suggested answers to the tasks numbered (i), (ii) etc. on page 114.

Answering questions: Question 1 (b)

What you need to do

Question 1(b) will always ask you to '**describe**' something. The best answers will:

- **state** not one, or two, but **three** features of the thing being described
- give extra factual detail or an explanation to **support** each feature.

How you do it

Take this question as an example:

Describe the key features of the 1920s consumer boom in the USA.

The SuperFacts will help us. Let's start with the SuperFact about **Wage rises**.

First we **state** the consumer boom.	One feature of the consumer boom was people having extra wages to spend on consumer goods.
Next we **support** the statement with extra detail or an explanation.	Average wages in the US rose by 8% in the 1920s. Some rose even more. The average weekly wage of a teacher rose from $15 to $30 dollars 1919–30.

We've written this in **two sentences**, rather than one, to make it obvious to the examiner that we are **stating** a feature of the boom and then **supporting** it with detail.

Now test yourself

(i) Write in the box below to show you can **provide supporting detail**.

Another feature of the consumer boom in the USA was rising sales of consumer goods for the home.	**[Supporting detail]**

(ii) In the box below, **state a feature of the boom which fits the supporting detail**.

[Statement]	This system allowed people to buy more consumer goods than they had money for by paying in instalments over a set period of time.

SuperFacts

The hire-purchase system allowed people to buy more consumer goods than they had money for by paying in instalments over a set period of time. However, they did have to keep up their regular payments.

Consumer goods In 1921, there were 5,000 fridges made in the USA. In 1929, there were 890,000. In 1923, there were 190,000 radios made in the USA. In 1929, there were 4,980,000. With mass production, prices of these goods fell. Now more people could afford them so demand rose.

Wage rises The average wage rose by 8% in the 1920s. Some wages dropped – so others must have risen by more than 8%. For example, the average teacher's wage nearly doubled between 1919 and 1930. It rose from $15.5 to $29.9 a week.

The answer

You can find suggested answers to the tasks numbered (i), (ii) etc. on page 114.

Answering questions: Question 1 (c)

Question 1 (c) will always ask you to '**explain the effects**' of something.

What you need to do

The best answers will:

- state not one, but **two** effects
- **support** each effect with extra factual **detail** to write a developed statement
- use this detail to **explain how** each effect happened
- and show **links** or connections between the effects.

How you do it

Take this question as an example:

Explain the effects of Prohibition in the USA.

The SuperFacts on the left will provide us with the information to answer this question.

The SuperFacts suggest the following **effect** and **supporting detail**.

Effect	Supporting detail
One effect of Prohibition was that illegal drinking became common.	*Millions of people still wanted to drink. It soon became clear that people would break Prohibition if they could.*

Notice how we have made it very clear to the examiner how we are answering the question. We have:

- used **two** sentences, one for the **effect** and one for the **supporting detail**.
- started each sentence with 'signposts' to show what we are doing, by saying 'One effect was ...' and 'For example ...'

Use this approach when you write answers.

Now test yourself

The SuperFacts suggest another effect was **powerful, organised crime**. Using this second effect, write in the boxes below to show that you can set out the **effect** and **supporting detail**. [You can check your answer in the top box on page 107.]

Effect	Supporting detail
(i)	(ii)

SuperFacts

Prohibition was made law by the 18th Amendment to the Constitution. It came into effect in 1920. It made illegal the making, transport and sale of alcohol in all US states.

Illegal drinking became common Millions of people still wanted to drink. It soon became clear that people would break Prohibition if they could. Illegal 'speakeasies' sprang up. Better speakeasies served 'bootleg' alcohol, smuggled in from Mexico. Bad ones served home brewed 'moonshine' that could be dangerous to drink.

Organised crime had been in the USA for a long time, but was boosted by Prohibition. Gangsters took over the sale of alcohol. The gangster Al Capone made $105 million profit from crime in 1927 – $60 million of that was from speakeasies. Gangs were wealthy and powerful; they used the profits of crime to bribe police, judges and local officials.

Reasons for the growth of organised crime Prohibition (which increased profit), the war (trained people to kill), cheaper cars (quick getaways), its profitability (could afford bribes), the ruthlessness of the gangsters (intimidated people).

Making the answer better

But this is not enough. The best answers will **explain how** the effect happened.

Here is an example of how you can use supporting detail to explain how the effect happened. This time, we have used **organised crime** as our example.

Effect and supporting detail	Explanation of how the effect happened
One effect of Prohibition in the USA was the growth of powerful, organised crime. Organised crime had existed in the USA for a long time, but it was boosted by Prohibition.	Organised crime was boosted because gangsters took over the sale of alcohol. Gangs became wealthy. They also became powerful, because they used their profits to bribe police, judges and local officials.

Now test yourself

(iii) Write in the box to show that you can explain how the effect happened.

Effect and supporting detail	Explanation of how the effect happened
One effect of Prohibition was that illegal drinking became common. Millions of people still wanted to drink. It soon became clear that people would break Prohibition if they could.	(iii)

[You can check your answer on page 114.]

The final touch

TThe very best answers show **links** between effects. So, now try this.

(iv) Write a paragraph to show how the two effects of Prohibition – the **illegal drinking** and o**rganised crime** – were linked.

[To help you, there is a [**Hint for (iv)**] on page 114. You can also check the answer there.]

ResultsPlus
Top tip

So, in summary, a good answer to Q1(c) would always look like this.

Question
1(c) What were the effects of [something]?

Answer
One effect of [something] was…
+
More information on this effect
+
Explanation of **how** [something] caused this effect.
Another effect of [something] was…
+
More information on this effect.
+
Explanation of **how** [something] caused this effect.
These two effects were linked because…

ResultsPlus
Top tip

The best 1(d) answers will always:

- identify not one, but at least **two** causes
- give **details** to explain the causes
- **explain how** the causes made the outcome happen
- show how the causes are **linked**
- and /or explain which of the causes was **more important**.

SuperFacts

Effects of the war on women The fact that women worked so successfully during the war led to their getting the vote in 1920 (19th Amendment). They were paid less and some lost jobs to returning men in 1918, but many stayed on. This started a trend. For example, women white-collar workers rose from 1.9 million in 1910, to 3.3 million in 1920 and 4.7 million in 1930.

'Flappers' was the name given to some young, independent women in the 1920s. They earned their own money, and behaved with a freedom formerly reserved for men. They drove cars, drank in speakeasies, cut their hair in a short 'bob', and wore shorter, less restricting (so more revealing) clothes.

Women consumers took advantage of the new, labour-saving appliances in the 1920s (like washing machines and fridges) to make their lives easier. Some married women even continued to go out to work, though this was disapproved of.

Answering questions: Question 1 (d)

Question 1(d) will always ask you to '**Explain why**' something happened.

On this page, we are going to answer a question, step by step.

You can test yourself by doing the same, for a different question, on the opposite page.

Question: Explain why the lives of women changed during the 1920s.

First, we need to identify **two causes**. We have chosen these.

> One reason why women's lives changed was the effects of the First World War.
>
> Another reason why women's lives changed was new lifestyles in leisure and home-life.

Next, we need to use **detailed information** to explain the causes.

> **[As above, then]** For example, many women worked during the war.
>
> **[As above, then]** For example, some young women became 'flappers' and many women took advantage of new, labour-saving consumer goods.

Next, we need to explain **how** the causes made women's lives change.

> **[As above, then]** This changed women's lives because it set a trend. The number of women in work continued to increase. For example, numbers of female white-collar workers rose from 3.3 million in 1920 to 4.7 million in 1930. It also led the government to give women the vote in 1920.
>
> **[As above, then]** Flappers changed women's lifestyles. They drove cars, drank in speakeasies, cut their hair short and wore revealing clothes. Labour-saving machines in the home also changed women's lives. They encouraged some married women to stay in employment.

Finally, we need to show that these two causes are **linked** and/or **prioritise** them.

> **[As above, then]** The two causes are linked because women who worked were more independent. They didn't rely on men for their money, so they could break the normal rules for women's lives and live differently, like flappers. In addition, jobs for women and new labour-saving machines in the home combined to make it possible for married women to work. The jobs gave them the opportunity to work, the machines gave them the time. So the causes are linked, but women going to work seems to be the most important cause, since all the other changes flowed from this.

Now test yourself

On the opposite page, we have answered an '**Explain why**' question, step by step. On this page, you can test yourself by doing the same for a different question.

Before you start, re-read our answers on the opposite page. Note that we have used carefully chosen words at the start of key sentences to make it clear to the examiner how we are answering questions. These words are called **signposts**. Try to use signpost words in your answer too.

Explain why life was so difficult for black people in the USA in the 1920s.

First, you need to identify **two causes**. We have done this to start you off.

One reason why life was so difficult for black people was the Jim Crow laws.

Another reason why life was difficult for black people was the racist violence in the USA.

(i) and (ii) So use **detailed information** to explain each of the two causes.

(i)

(ii)

(iii) and (iv) Next, you need to explain **how** the causes made life difficult for black people.

(iii)

(iv)

(v) Finally, you need to show that your two causes are **linked** and/or **prioritise** them.

(v)

SuperFacts

Racism was part of everyday life. All over the USA, black people did the poorest paid jobs and were 'last hired, first fired'. Racism existed in the North, but was more severe, violent and legally enforced in the South.

Jim Crow laws enforced segregation – making black people use separate transport, cafés, toilets, drinking fountains, etc. Black schools, situated in the poorer parts of town, got less state money than white ones.

Black people had the right to vote but were often prevented from voting in the South by tricks or threats.

Many black people moved north as a result of Southern racism, to cities like New York (black population in Harlem in 1920, 33%; in 1930 70%).

Racist violence also happened across the USA but more often in the South. Black people were beaten up, their homes burned and they were murdered or lynched (killed by a mob for a supposed crime).

The Ku Klux Klan was a racist organisation. It wanted America to be a WASP (white, Anglo-Saxon, Protestant) nation. It mainly targeted black people, although it also persecuted Jews, immigrants, and Catholics. In some Southern states the police, the law courts and local government were full of Klan members.

The answer

You can find suggested answers to the tasks numbered (i), (ii) etc. on page 114.

SuperFacts

Causes of the Wall Street Crash (October 1929) In September 1929, doubts about the economy meant share sales rose, so share prices fell. As more people sold, prices fell more. On 24 October, panic set in. 13 million shares were sold. Prices kept falling. Some bankers bought $250 million worth of shares, hoping to stop the drop. They failed.

Share prices hit bottom in November 1929 Radio company shares worth $0.94 a share in March 1928 were worth $5.05 in September 1928, but $0.28 in November.

Effects of the Wall Street Crash People, businesses and banks lost huge sums (much of it borrowed). Things worsened when banks wanted loans repaid. By 1933, 5,000 banks closed; one, the Bank of New York, lost the savings of 400,000 people.

More effects Many people could not pay hire purchase or bank loans; they had to give the bank their homes and became homeless. Companies went bankrupt. Sales of goods fell, unemployment rose from 3% in 1929 to 15% in 1931.

Answering questions: Question 2(a) and 2(b)

What you need to do

In the examination, you have to answer **either** 2(a) or 2(b).

Both questions will ask you to '**Explain how...**' something happened. For example:

- ***Explain how people reacted to President Hoover's handling of the Wall Street Crash.***

  or
- ***Explain how underlying problems weakened the US economy by 1928.***

How you do it

The technique for answering the question is always the same.

The best 2 (a) and (b) answers will always:

Describe a change or an action	and	give an explanation of why this answers the question.

So let's answer the following question together, using the SuperFacts on this page.

Explain how the Wall Street crash affected ordinary people in the USA.

An answer could start like this. Fill in the blanks at (i) and (ii) to show you understand.

One way the Wall Street Crash affected ordinary people was that share prices fell.	This affected ordinary people because many people lost huge sums of money – much of it borrowed.
Another way the Wall Street Crash affected ordinary people was that banks, short of money, called in loans.	This affected people because ... (i)
Another way the Crash affected ordinary people was ... (ii)	This affected ordinary people because they lost their jobs. Unemployment rose from 3% in 1929 to 15% in 1931.

Final step!

The best answers will show that all these affects of the crash were **linked**.

For example, an answer to this question could finish like this...

The ways people were affected by the Crash were linked. They seem to follow on from each other. First falling share prices meant people and banks lost money. Then this meant the banks asked for loans to be repaid and this made people and companies bankrupt. Then this meant they had to sell their homes or sack their workers. It was all linked, like a row of dominoes falling over.

ResultsPlus
Top tip

Notice how, in our answers, we use **signposts** – phrases like *'one way'* or *'another way'* or even *'these ways ... are linked'*. This shows the examiner how you are answering the question, and makes your answer easier to understand.

Test yourself

Here is another '**Explain how…**' question:

Explain how ineffective Hoover's response was to the effects of the Wall Street Crash.

Using the SuperFacts printed on this page, fill in the boxes below to create an answer.

One response of Hoover to the effects of the Wall Street Crash was to give out money or help to those in need.	This was an ineffective response because …. (iii)
Another response of Hoover to the effects of the Wall Street Crash was the Smoot-Hawley tariff.	This was an ineffective response because … (iv)
Another of Hoover's responses was … (v)	This was ineffective because … (vi)

These ineffective responses were linked because… (vii)

SuperFacts

Hoover and the Depression Hoover believed in *laissez faire*, so his government did little. When it did act, it only gave a limited amount of money or help, which was soon used up. Shanty towns of temporary homes for the unemployed appeared in cities and were nicknamed 'Hoovervilles' to underline Hoover's inaction.

Federal Farm Board (July 1929, before the Crash) set up with $500 million to buy surplus crops. At first, the crops were destroyed rather than used to feed the unemployed. The money ran out in 1932, and the Board shut.

Smoot-Hawley tariff (1930) increased tariffs on imports to make people buy US goods to create jobs. But imports **and** exports fell, harming trade and employment. In 1929, US exports were worth $2,341 million dollars. In 1932, this had fallen to $784 million.

The answer

You can find suggested answers to the tasks numbered (i), (ii) etc. on page 114.

SuperFacts

The SuperFacts you will need for this activity are on pages 102–103. The titles of the relevant SuperFacts are:

Emergency Banking Act (March 1933)

Agricultural Adjustment Act (May 1933)

Tennessee Valley Authority (TVA)

Recovery by 1935

The Second New Deal and unemployment

The Second World War

Recovery by 1941

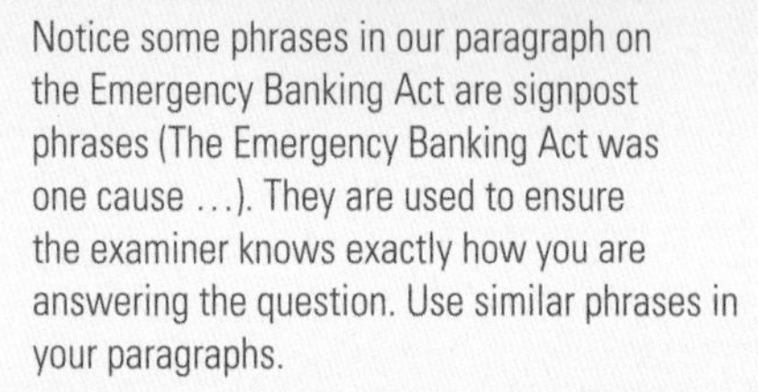

Notice some phrases in our paragraph on the Emergency Banking Act are signpost phrases (The Emergency Banking Act was one cause ...). They are used to ensure the examiner knows exactly how you are answering the question. Use similar phrases in your paragraphs.

If you are having trouble with your paragraphs, look on page 114 for help.

Need more help?

If you are having trouble with your paragraphs, look on page 114 for help.

Answering questions: Question 3(a) and 3(b)

Questions 3(a) and 3(b) follow the same format. You have to answer **either** 3(a) **or** 3(b).

Questions 3(a) and 3(b) will be about **causes** or **effects**.

They will ask you to make a judgement about causes or effects. So they could say:

- ***Was [something] the main cause of ...?***
- ***Was [something] the worst effect of ...?***

The questions may talk about **reasons** (meaning **causes**) and will always give you some '**information to help you with your answer**'. For example:

Was the Emergency Banking Act the main reason for the improvement in the US economy by 1941?

> ***You may use the following information to help you with your answer.***
> - ***The Emergency Banking Act***
> - ***The Agricultural Adjustment Act***
> - ***The Works Progress Administration (WPA)***
> - ***The outbreak of the Second World War***

A good way to start is to show that you know **all** of the four factors in the box above are reasons why the US economy improved. Make sure you signpost each of them for the examiner (see Top tip box for an example of signposting phrases). We have written a paragraph on the first factor. You write a similar paragraph on each of the others, marked (i), (ii) + (iii).

On the left, you will see the titles of the SuperFacts that will help you.

The Emergency Banking Act was one reason for improvement in the US economy. This Act was passed in March 1933 and closed all the banks. Government inspectors only re-opened them if they were financially sound. 5,000 banks were re-opened first; more were re-opened later. This restored confidence in the banks. There was no rush to take money out. The banks agreed not to call in loans so quickly. All this stabilised the banking system and this improved the economy.

The Agricultural Adjustment Act was another reason for improvement in the US economy. This ... (i)

The Works Progress Administration (PWA) was ... (ii)

The outbreak of the Second World War was another... (iii)

Now the examiner knows that we realise **all** the factors helped the US economy.

If you know any **other** causes which helped the economy to improve, you can include these too. Study the relevant SuperFacts and explain one **extra** cause below.

Another reason that the US economy improved in the 1930s was ... (iv)

ResultsPlus
Top tip

You can **agree** or **disagree** with the question. In this case, you can say the Emergency Banking Act **was** the most important reason. You can say it **wasn't**. The main thing is that you back up your opinion with an argument based on the facts.

If you are arguing that one cause is the most important **you must compare it to other causes, to show it was more important.**

Don't forget to **signpost** your answers.

Two steps to go!

Now we can make a judgement on the key part of this question:

Was the Emergency Banking Act the main reason?'

Here are two possible views. We have completed the first one. You complete the other.

The outbreak of the Second World War was the main reason for US economic recovery because the other reasons depended on government handouts. The AAA and the WPA only helped the economy because the government gave money for special projects. But that wasn't a real improvement if the jobs were not permanent. Real improvement in the economy didn't come until after 1939 when the US began making and selling arms and food for Europe. This makes the war the main reason for improvement.

The Emergency Banking Act (1933) was the main reason for US economic recovery because ... (v)

Final step!

The very best answers will see that, no matter how important **one** cause was, it was probably **not enough on its own**. One cause can be the most important, but most things in history depend on a combination of causes. We have written one final paragraph saying this. You complete the bottom box to write your own version.

But the Emergency Banking Act was not enough on its own because it only provided the foundation for recovery. It was just a starting point. Proper recovery needed more jobs, more production, more sales and more profits. These things only came with AAA and WPA projects and with production of wartime goods. The EBA was a start. But it was not enough alone.

But the outbreak of the Second World War would never have brought recovery from the 1930s depression on its own ... (vi)

ResultsPlus
Watch out!

Question 3 is one on which your skills of **written communication** will be judged.

To get to the top of each level of the mark scheme you have to:

- write effectively
- organise your thoughts coherently
- spell, punctuate and use grammar well.

The answer

You can find suggested answers to the tasks numbered (i), (ii) etc. on page 114.

Answers: USA 1919–41

Question 1 (a)

i) *I can infer this because Source A says that by the early 1920s the USA was producing 30% of the world's wheat, 75% of its corn and 55% of its cotton.*

ii) *Source A tells me that US wheat production in the First World War was going up.*

Question 1 (b)

i) *For example, in 1921, there were 5,000 fridges made in the USA. In 1929, there were 890,000.*

ii) *A third feature of the US consumer boom was the hire-purchase system.*

Question 1 (c)

iii) *Illegal drinking became possible as speakeasies sprang up. Better speakeasies served bootleg alcohol, smuggled in from Mexico. Bad ones served illegally brewed, home-made, 'moonshine'.*

[**Hint**] Use the information about Al Capone in the SuperFact on **Organised crime**

iv) *These two effects are linked. The illegal drinking produced the money for criminals to create powerful, organised gangs. For example, the gangster Al Capone made $60 million dollars from speakeasies in 1927. It was this kind of money from illegal drinking that funded organised crime.*

Question 1 (d)

i) *These laws enforced segregation.*

ii) *For example, there was an organisation called the Ku Klux Klan which wanted America to be a WASP nation (white, Anglo-Saxon, Protestant). They targeted blacks.*

iii) *Segregation meant that blacks had to use separate, usually worse facilities (transport, cafes, toilets, etc). Black schools, in poorer parts of town, got less state money.*

iv) *This made the lives of black people worse because their houses could be burned or they could be beaten up, murdered or lynched. This happened all over the US but was worse in the South.*

v) *The two causes were linked. If the Jim Crow laws treated blacks as different and gave them worse facilities, this gave out the message that the government thought blacks were inferior. This was bound to make some white people treat them badly. So the two causes were linked. But the Jim Crow laws were more important, because they affected everyone's attitude to blacks.*

Question 2 (a) + (b)

i) *... they had to sell their homes to pay off their debts. They became homeless.*

ii) *... some companies could not repay their bank loans and they became bankrupt.*

iii) *Hoover believed in* laissez-faire*, so his government did very little. Even when it did give money or help, it gave a limited amount which was soon used up.*

iv) *The increased tariffs were supposed to make imports dearer and make people buy US goods instead. This was meant to help unemployment. But exports fell too, so this actually made trade and employment worse.*

v) *... the Federal Farm Board.*

vi) *... although the Board bought up surplus crops from farmers, at first these were destroyed rather than used to feed the unemployed. Then, the money ran out in 1932 and the Board was shut.*

vii) *...* laissez faire *was the common factor. This meant that Hoover didn't really think it was the government's job to interfere and control the economy. He thought it would right itself. So* laissez faire *made all his responses – aid, tariffs and buying up crops – half-hearted.* Laissez faire *linked them all.*

Question 3 (a) + (b)

i) *... set up the AAA, which bought up surplus crops; this raised prices and farm incomes. It also reduced over-production by giving subsidies to farmers to grow less. It also regulated output of major crops: corn, wheat, cotton etc. This helped the economy by stabilising farming.*

ii) *... another reason the US economy improved in the 1930s. It was part of the New Deal, starting in 1935, which focused on long term reforms. The WPA replaced the PWA, giving training as well as work to the unemployed.*

iii) *... reason why the US economy improved in the 1930s. The war started in 1939. Even though the US did not join the war at once, it did supply the Allies with weapons, ammunition and food. This boosted US factory and farm production and helped employment.*

iv) *... the Tennessee Valley Authority. This started in May 1933; it ran projects to improve land in the Tennessee Valley covering 104,000 sq km in seven states. CCC workers stopped soil erosion. The unemployed built dams to stop flooding and create a water reserve. The dams also made electricity for rural areas. It was a boost to farms and jobs, so it helped improve the US economy.*

v) *... it restored confidence in the banks. All the other reasons for improvement would have failed without this. It kept people's savings safe and meant that industry and farming could borrow loans to expand. It provided the sound financial basis which was essential for recovery.*

vi) *... For one thing, it didn't come until 1939, too late to solve a problem that started in 1929 and was at its worst in 1933. For another thing, all those farms and factories supplying food and war goods depended on banks for loans. So the Second World War was a big boost to recovery, but it was not enough on its own.*

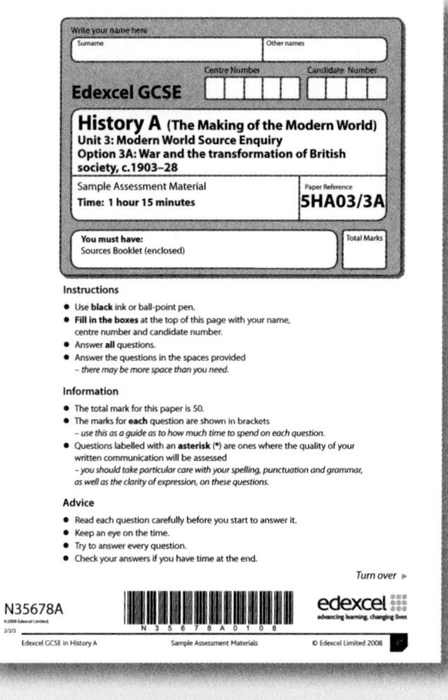

Write your name here

Surname | Other names

Centre Number | Candidate Number

Edexcel GCSE

History A (The Making of the Modern World)
Unit 3: Modern World Source Enquiry
Option 3A: War and the transformation of British society, c.1903–28

Sample Assessment Material
Time: 1 hour 15 minutes

Paper Reference
5HA03/3A

You must have:
Sources Booklet (enclosed)

Total Marks

Instructions
- Use **black** ink or ball-point pen.
- **Fill in the boxes** at the top of this page with your name, centre number and candidate number.
- Answer **all** questions.
- Answer the questions in the spaces provided – *there may be more space than you need.*

Information
- The total mark for this paper is 50.
- The marks for **each** question are shown in brackets – *use this as a guide as to how much time to spend on each question.*
- Questions labelled with an **asterisk** (*) are ones where the quality of your written communication will be assessed – *you should take particular care with your spelling, punctuation and grammar, as well as the clarity of expression, on these questions.*

Advice
- Read each question carefully before you start to answer it.
- Keep an eye on the time.
- Try to answer every question.
- Check your answers if you have time at the end.

Turn over ▸

N35678A

edexcel advancing learning, changing lives

Edexcel GCSE in History A | Sample Assessment Materials | © Edexcel Limited 2008

Edexcel GCSE

History A (The Making of the Modern World)
Unit 3: Modern World Source Enquiry
Option 3A: War and the transformation of British society, c.1903–28

Sample Assessment Material
Sources Booklet

Paper Reference
5HA03/3A

Do not return this Sources Booklet with the question paper.

Turn over ▸

N35678A

edexcel advancing learning, changing lives

Edexcel GCSE in History A | Sample Assessment Materials | © Edexcel Limited 2008

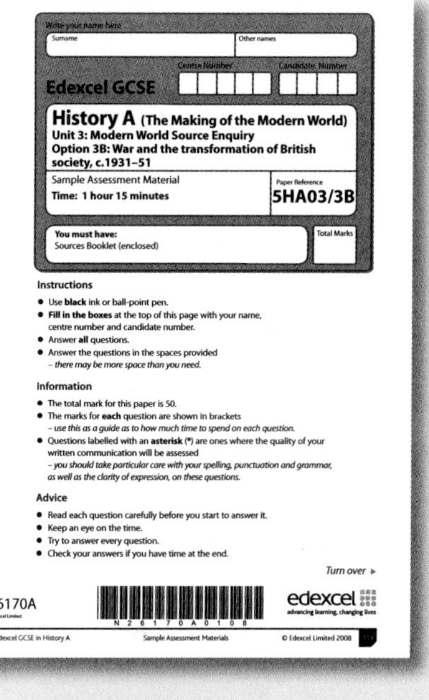

Write your name here

Surname | Other names

Centre Number | Candidate Number

Edexcel GCSE

History A (The Making of the Modern World)
Unit 3: Modern World Source Enquiry
Option 3B: War and the transformation of British society, c.1931–51

Sample Assessment Material
Time: 1 hour 15 minutes

Paper Reference
5HA03/3B

You must have:
Sources Booklet (enclosed)

Total Marks

Instructions
- Use **black** ink or ball-point pen.
- **Fill in the boxes** at the top of this page with your name, centre number and candidate number.
- Answer **all** questions.
- Answer the questions in the spaces provided – *there may be more space than you need.*

Information
- The total mark for this paper is 50.
- The marks for **each** question are shown in brackets – *use this as a guide as to how much time to spend on each question.*
- Questions labelled with an **asterisk** (*) are ones where the quality of your written communication will be assessed – *you should take particular care with your spelling, punctuation and grammar, as well as the clarity of expression, on these questions.*

Advice
- Read each question carefully before you start to answer it.
- Keep an eye on the time.
- Try to answer every question.
- Check your answers if you have time at the end.

Turn over ▸

N26170A

edexcel advancing learning, changing lives

Edexcel GCSE in History A | Sample Assessment Materials | © Edexcel Limited 2008

Edexcel GCSE

History A (The Making of the Modern World)
Unit 3: Modern World Source Enquiry
Option 3B: War and the transformation of British society, c.1931–51

Sample Assessment Material
Sources Booklet

Paper Reference
5HA03/3B

Do not return this Sources Booklet with the question paper.

Turn over ▸

N26170A

edexcel advancing learning, changing lives

Edexcel GCSE in History A | Sample Assessment Materials | © Edexcel Limited 2008

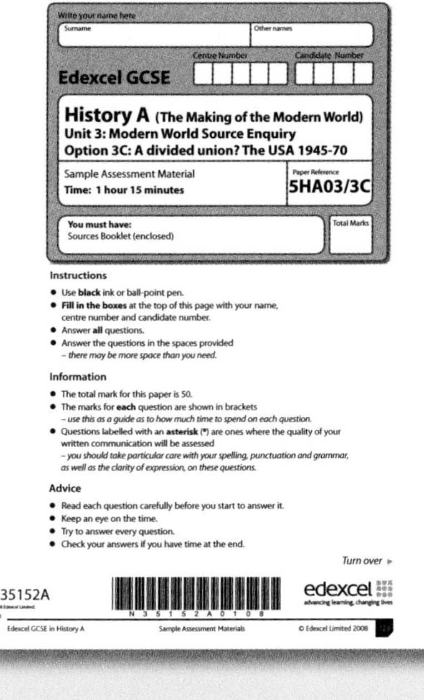

Write your name here

Surname | Other names

Centre Number | Candidate Number

Edexcel GCSE

History A (The Making of the Modern World)
Unit 3: Modern World Source Enquiry
Option 3C: A divided union? The USA 1945-70

Sample Assessment Material
Time: 1 hour 15 minutes

Paper Reference
5HA03/3C

You must have:
Sources Booklet (enclosed)

Total Marks

Instructions
- Use **black** ink or ball-point pen.
- **Fill in the boxes** at the top of this page with your name, centre number and candidate number.
- Answer **all** questions.
- Answer the questions in the spaces provided – *there may be more space than you need.*

Information
- The total mark for this paper is 50.
- The marks for **each** question are shown in brackets – *use this as a guide as to how much time to spend on each question.*
- Questions labelled with an **asterisk** (*) are ones where the quality of your written communication will be assessed – *you should take particular care with your spelling, punctuation and grammar, as well as the clarity of expression, on these questions.*

Advice
- Read each question carefully before you start to answer it.
- Keep an eye on the time.
- Try to answer every question.
- Check your answers if you have time at the end.

Turn over ▸

N35152A

edexcel advancing learning, changing lives

Edexcel GCSE in History A | Sample Assessment Materials | © Edexcel Limited 2008

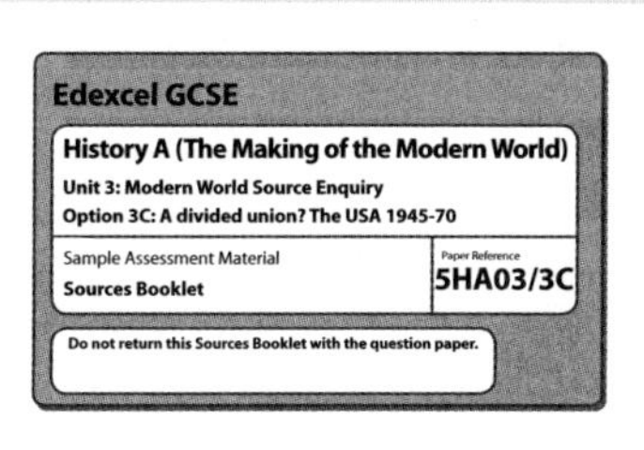

Edexcel GCSE

History A (The Making of the Modern World)
Unit 3: Modern World Source Enquiry
Option 3C: A divided union? The USA 1945-70

Sample Assessment Material
Sources Booklet

Paper Reference
5HA03/3C

Do not return this Sources Booklet with the question paper.

Turn over ▸

N35152A

edexcel advancing learning, changing lives

Edexcel GCSE in History A | Sample Assessment Materials | © Edexcel Limited 2008

Unit 3 Exam War and the transformation of British Society c.1903–28

The exam for Unit 3 is quite different from the other exam papers in Modern World History. This is because this paper tests your understanding of how historians use sources. There is less information for you to learn before you go into the exam. Instead you have to use the sources you are given in the exam to answer the questions. So, in Unit 3, it is not so much *how much you know, as what you know how to do*.

Sources are the raw material of history. Historians use them to work out what happened and why. But it isn't as simple as that. Historians need a range of skills to puzzle out the answers from lots of different sources, which may contradict one another, and even deliberately mislead. The exam tests that you have some of these skills.

There are five questions in the exam, and the good news is they will always test the same skills in the same order.

- **Question 1** tests your ability to understand a source and to make an **inference** from it.
- **Question 2** sees if you can understand the **purpose** of a source – why it was created or used.
- **Question 3** asks you to **cross-refer** between three sources.
- **Question 4** asks you to judge the **utility** or **reliability** of sources.
- **Question 5** gives you a hypothesis about what happened, and asks you to judge **how far the sources support or prove it**.

Because the exam is different, this section of the revision book is different too. There are no SuperFacts. Instead, the next three pages remind you of the general shape of the course you have studied. When you are given sources in the exam, it helps to be able to put them in context, and these three pages are designed to help you get the general overview you need.

Next, you have four pages to help you remember how to use sources. Finally, you practise answering questions.

Context

To understand the context of a source is to see how it fits into the background of things that were happening when it was created.

For example, Source B on page 170 shows a young mother voting in 1918. Someone who was shown the photograph and did not understand the context would be puzzled by it. Why is it important to show this person voting? Because she is pretty? Because she is teaching the children to vote?

Using the caption and the context provided by your revision, you will know that the 1918 election in Britain was the first one in which women over 30 could vote. That is how we know she is over 30 and why her voting had such significance.

Overview: War and the transformation of British society c.1903–28

In 1905, a new Liberal government came to power. It passed laws to provide support for the old, the unemployed and the sick. It provided children with school meals and medical services. It did not, however, give in to the pressure of women's groups (most famously the suffragettes) to give women the vote.

The First World War began in August 1914 and dragged on into 1918. It caused horrific loss of life often for very little gain (especially in the trenches of the Western Front in France). New weapons, such as tanks and gas, were used on both sides. The government used the 1914 Defence of the Realm Act (DORA) to control the news, industrial production, and food supplies (through rationing). It introduced conscription (forcing men to join the armed services) and punished those who would not join (conscientious objectors) severely.

During the war, millions of women took over the jobs men left to go to war. They helped the war and found a new independence, but after the war the government, unions and many ordinary people wanted women to resume the role of wives and mothers (they did get the vote). The government failed in their promise to build 'a land fit for heroes' after the war: unemployment rose and discontent and strikes followed.

key words

suffragettes were women who campaigned for the right of women to vote.

force-feeding was feeding hunger strikers by pushing a feeding tube down their throats into their stomach and pouring liquid food down it.

creeping barrage was attacking by firing artillery shells closer and closer to the enemy in stages. The infantry follow on behind the barrage, taking over the shelled area.

gas (in the context of this book) was various kinds of gas used against the enemy. Chlorine and phosgene gas caused suffocation; mustard gas ate away the lungs.

attrition (in the context of this book) is wearing the enemy down by constant attacks, hoping they will give up before you do.

censorship (in the context of this book) is stopping the publication of certain kinds of information.

propaganda is giving people information (which may or may not be true) to make them believe what you want them to believe.

munitions are weapons of war (the word is usually used to refer to ammunition).

Need more help?

You can find more about each key term, key word and key person in your Edexcel textbook, *War and the transformation of British society c.1903–28*. Look for this symbol, which will give you the page number.

key terms

Cat and Mouse Act p.15
Labour Exchange p.23

Schlieffen Plan p.28
Trench warfare p.30–31
the Western Front p.29

Defence of the Realm Act (DORA) p.45
conscription p.49
Pals battalions p.48
conscientious objectors p.50–51
rationing p.52–3
the 'Right to Serve' p.54
free speech p.45

merchant shipping p.52

key people and organisations

NUWSS (National Union of Women's Suffrage Societies) p.10
WSPU (Women's Social and Political Union) p.11
Emmeline Pankhurst p.11
Sylvia Pankhurst p.11
Christabel Pankhurst p.11
Emily Davison p.13
Lloyd George p.22

BEF (British Expeditionary Force) p.26
General Haig p.36
General Alfred von Schlieffen p.28
Lord Kitchener p.30

British Neutrality League p.50
WAAC (Women's Army Auxiliary Corps) p.56
WRAF (Women's Royal Air Force) p.56
WRNS (Women's Royal Naval Service) p.56

Viscountess Astor p.62

Colour coding

The information boxes on pages 117–19 use the same colour used to distinguish the Key Topics in your student textbook, so you know which key topic they come from.

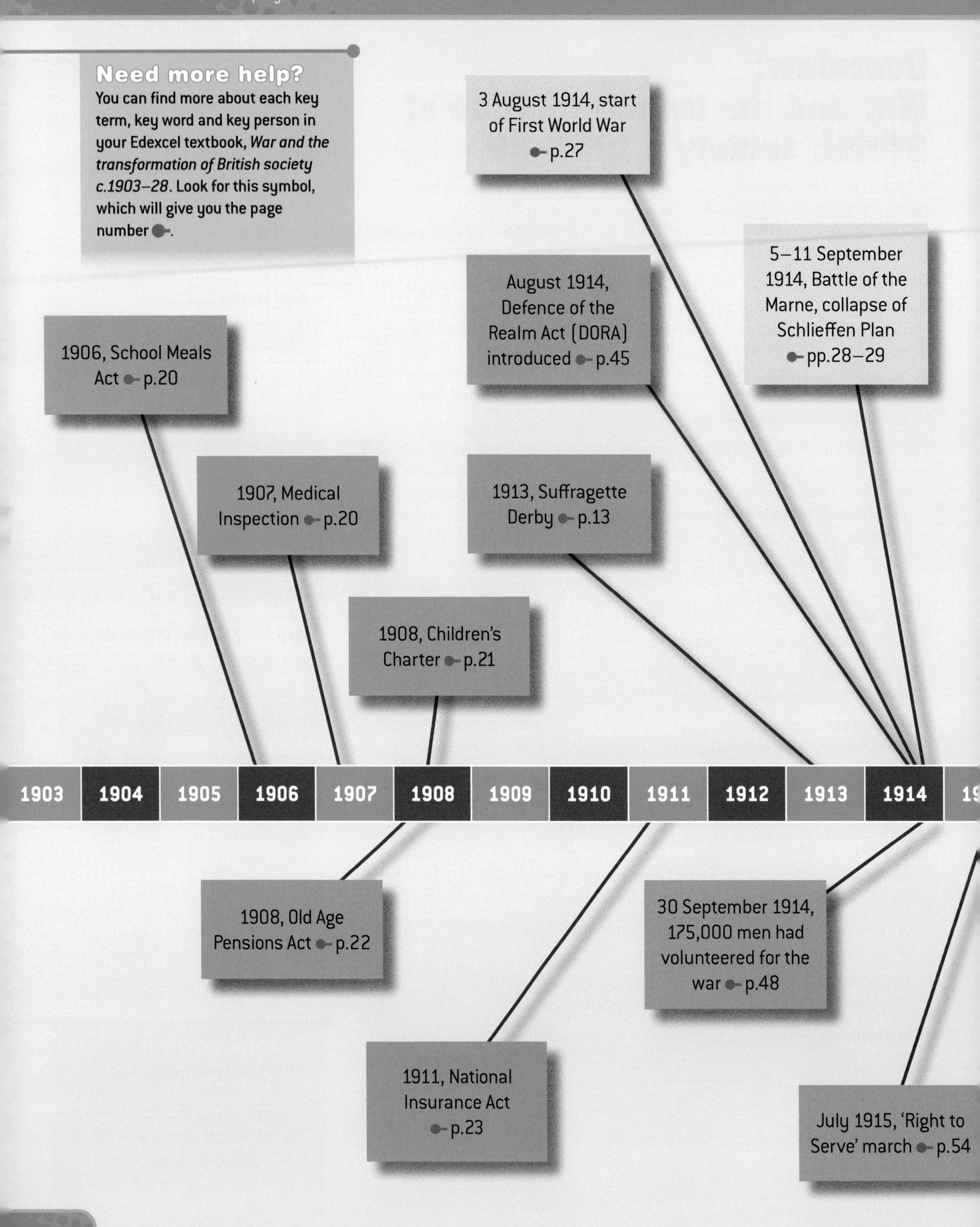
Need more help?
You can find more about each key term, key word and key person in your Edexcel textbook, *War and the transformation of British society c.1903–28*. Look for this symbol, which will give you the page number.
3 August 1914, start of First World War p.27
August 1914, Defence of the Realm Act (DORA) introduced p.45
5–11 September 1914, Battle of the Marne, collapse of Schlieffen Plan pp.28–29
1906, School Meals Act p.20
1907, Medical Inspection p.20
1913, Suffragette Derby p.13
1908, Children's Charter p.21
1903
1904
1905
1906
1907
1908
1909
1910
1911
1912
1913
1914
1908, Old Age Pensions Act p.22
30 September 1914, 175,000 men had volunteered for the war p.48
1911, National Insurance Act p.23
July 1915, 'Right to Serve' march p.54

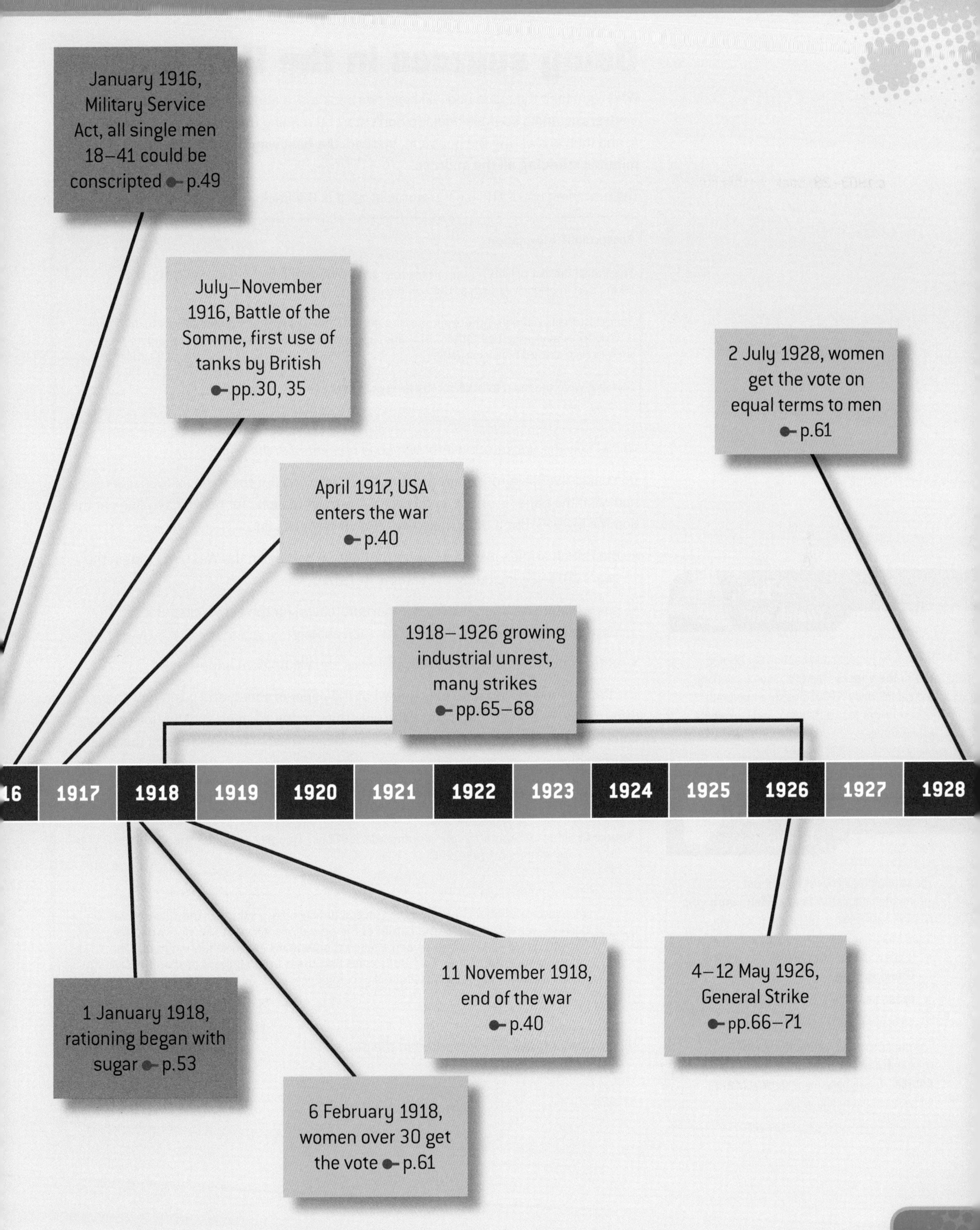
January 1916, Military Service Act, all single men 18–41 could be conscripted p.49
July–November 1916, Battle of the Somme, first use of tanks by British pp.30, 35
April 1917, USA enters the war p.40
1918–1926 growing industrial unrest, many strikes pp.65–68
2 July 1928, women get the vote on equal terms to men p.61
16
1917
1918
1919
1920
1921
1922
1923
1924
1925
1926
1927
1928
1 January 1918, rationing began with sugar p.53
6 February 1918, women over 30 get the vote p.61
11 November 1918, end of the war p.40
4–12 May 1926, General Strike pp.66–71

Using sources in the Unit 3 exam

When you take the exam you will have two booklets, a question booklet you write your answers in, and a sources booklet. Don't start by reading Question 1, looking at Source A, and then answering the question. **Instead, the best way to start is to spend a few minutes studying all the sources.**

The first thing you'll find isn't a source at all, it is the Background information.

> **Background information**
>
> The British armies played an important role on the Western Front in the years 1915-17, taking part in offensives such as the Somme in 1916.
>
> Some historians claim that the Somme was a disaster and have blamed commanders such as Haig for heavy casualties. Other historians suggest that factors other than commanders such as Haig caused heavy casualties.
>
> So, what were the main reasons for the heavy casualties?

This is how the Background information is presented in the paper.

Don't skip the Background information. It is there for a purpose. The examiner is telling you what the paper is about. In this case, the main reasons for heavy casualties at the Somme in 1916. But it does more than that. It also tells you:

- the British armies played an important part in battles on the Western Front in the years 1915–17, including the Somme in 1916
- some historians think the most important reason for the heavy casualties at the Somme was the role of commanders such as Haig
- other historians argue other reasons were equally or more important.

The Background information tells you what the paper is about, and gives you some information. It is also, importantly, the only thing in the sources booklet you can trust completely. You need to be prepared to consider how accurate a picture all the other sources give.

This brings us to the most important part of the paper – the sources.

> **Source C:** From a report by the Commander-in-Chief, Douglas Haig, to the British Government, 1 July 1916.
>
> Very successful attack this morning. Several (officers) have said that they have never been so well instructed of the nature of the operations. All went like clockwork. The battle is going very well for us and already the Germans are surrendering freely. The enemy is so short of men that he is collecting them from all parts of the line. Our troops are in wonderful spirits and full of confidence.

This is how sources are presented in the paper.

The source heading and caption are printed **above the source**. The next source heading and caption may follow directly underneath. Be careful not to mix them up, and look at the wrong source.

The caption tells you very important information about the source. **Make sure you read it carefully**. In this case, it tells you three important things:

- it is a report by the Commander-in-Chief, **Douglas Haig**
- **when** he made it – 1 July 1916
- he made it **for** the British government.

The caption comes before the source for a reason. **Read the caption first, then the source**. It will make more sense when you know who said it, and when.

Key skills for using sources

Inference

To make an inference is to work something out from a source that the source doesn't actually tell you or show you.

For example, look at Source B on page 170:

Source B **shows** you a young mother voting. The caption tells you she was voting in 1918 and the photo was used in news reports on women voting for the first time.

You can **infer** from Source B that women voting for the first time was an important, newsworthy, issue. The photo was used 'widely', that suggests a lot of news reports.

Now you try with Source E on page 171.

(i) Give an example of something Source E shows you.

(ii) Give an example of something you can infer from Source E.

Message and Purpose

Working out the message of a source is working out what the source shows you or tells you. Working out the purpose is going one step further. **Why** has the source shown or told you those things? What effect was the source intended to have?

For example:
The **message** of Source B is that women can now vote and the woman they have chosen is a respectable-looking young mother with her children, not a poor scruffy woman or even a very posh one.

The **purpose** of Source B could be to persuade women to vote. She's a nice, respectable 'ordinary' woman with nice kids. So it could be saying 'women like you should vote, not just suffragettes who campaigned for it'.

Now you try with Source F on page 171.

(iii) What is the message of Source F?

(iv) What is the purpose of Source F?

The sources

From now on, you will be using the sources for Britain 1903–28 on pages 170–71 of this book. Cut them out so you can have the pages in front of you while you work on the sources, without having to keep turning back and forth in the book. Be careful though – don't lose the pages, because you will need them for all the work on Unit 3.

Watch out!

Using the sources in the paper
Questions 1 to 4 all use specific sources. Question 5 asks you to use 'all the sources'. Be careful to use the sources referred to in the question. You won't get any credit for writing about Source E in a question that asks you about Sources A, B and C.

When you refer to a source, make it clear which one you mean.
Say, 'in Source A…' or 'Source D says…' If you want to quote from a source, to prove your point, put the bit of the source you are quoting in quotation marks.

So don't write:
Some people felt that married women shouldn't work after the war. They felt single women and widows should be given the work.

But do write:
Some people felt that married women shouldn't work after the war. So Mrs Pazzey (a married woman) actually wrote to the Daily Herald newspaper in October 1919, saying, "single women and widows should be given the work" (Source C).

Cross-referencing

Cross-referencing is when you compare two or more sources. One question in the exam (Question 3) will ask you to use (or cross-refer between) three sources in the question. In Question 5, you won't be able to get a good mark without cross-referencing.

When you cross-refer you need to look for things that agree, or things that don't agree, between the sources.

For example: Do Sources C, D and E support the view that women stopped working after the war to give the jobs to men?

They **do agree**

- because Source D shows that the employment rates for women were pretty much the same in 1911 and 1921. Yet we know that lots more women were working during the war. So they must have given up their jobs by 1921.
- because Source E shows a workshop after the war and all the workers that you can see in it are men.

But they **don't agree** as well

- because Source C is only saying that that is what should happen. It is a letter showing a person's opinion. It doesn't give any evidence to support the statement that that is what happened.

Now you try, with a different question and different sources. ***Do Sources A, C and F support the view that people wanted women to continue working after the war?***

(v) Ways they do support this view:

(vi) Ways they do not:

The answer

You can find suggested answers to the tasks numbered (i), (ii) etc. on page 164.

Cross-referencing won't give you the full answer to the question. It gives you the material to support your answer.

Utility (usefulness)

This is quite straightforward. The only thing to remember is, it depends on the question. So, starting with the question you want to answer, you just need to decide whether the source tells you anything useful or not.

For example:

How did the position of women change after the war?

Source A – useful

Source B – useful

Source C – not useful

Source D – useful

Source E – useful if you count their absence from the picture

Source F – useful.

Now you try, in the boxes on the right.

Reliability

Testing a source for reliability is about thinking whether you can believe it or not. What are the clues to look for?

- **Provenance** – who created the source and why?
- **Language** is a useful clue – often a biased source shows up in its choice of language.
- **Selection** is a very powerful clue – sources don't tell us everything, and the person who created the source probably chose what to include and what to leave out. This can be just as true of a photograph as of a written source. A photographer decides which bit of what is happening to photograph, and a newspaper editor decides which photograph to use. For example, in a demonstration they could choose to show thousands of people protesting peacefully, or a few people starting a fight with the police. The two photographs would give very different impressions of what happened.

Reliability affects what a source is useful for. An unreliable source might not be useful for facts – but it tells you useful things about the opinions of the person who created it.

Repeat the exercise you did for utility, this time for reliability.

(vii) Did women want changes after the war? Are the sources useful?

(viii) Did women go back to the way their lives were before the war once the war was over? Are the sources useful?

(ix) Did women want changes after the war? Are the sources reliable? Give reasons for your answers.

(x) Did women go back to the way their lives were before the war once the war was over? Are the sources reliable? Give reasons for your answers.

Answering questions: Question 1

What you need to do

Question 1 will always ask '***What does Source A tell us about* [something]**'.
The best answers:

- not only extract **information** from the source
- but will also make **inferences** from the source *[see Top tip box]*
- and **support** those inferences with detail from the source.

Note: make sure you answer the question – after **about** comes the **subject**. You can't just make *any* inference from the source, it has to be about the *something* in the question.

Let's practise. Study Source A (cut out from page 170).

What can you learn from Source A about the position of women after the war?

Inference	Supporting detail
I can learn from Source A that women must have been given the right to become MPs at some time before 1919.	I can infer this because Source A says 'In 1919, the first woman took her seat in the House of Commons.' The source doesn't say when women were given the right to be MPs but it must have been some time before 1919.

Now test yourself

(i) Here's another inference. You try writing the **supporting detail**.

I can learn from Source A that, at some stage before 1921, women must have been given the right to work in the lower levels of the civil service.	**[Supporting detail]**

(ii) Can you write out the **inference** that matches this supporting detail?

[Inference]	I can infer this because Source A says that in the early 1920s women had a 'string of successes'. Source A doesn't tell us what they were, but the examples of changes which it gives us couldn't really be called 'a string of successes' so there must have been others.

In the exam, one inference with support scores well. If you have time, find two or three.

ResultsPlus
Top tip

An **inference** is a judgement that can be made by studying the source, but is not directly stated by it.

A **supported inference** is one that uses detail from the source to prove the inference.

Consider this example:

Source A: 'The furious neighbour told Anna that her tennis ball had broken his window and he would tell her parents about her carelessness.'

Question: ***What can you learn from Source A about Anna?***

Information: Source A tells us that Anna broke a neighbour's window. [This is directly stated in the source, so it's not an inference.]

Inference: Source A tells me that Anna is likely to be in trouble with her parents. [The source does not directly tell us this, but we can infer that it is likely.]

A supported inference: Source A tells me that Anna is likely to be in trouble with her parents. She broke the neighbour's window and he was going to tell her parents. [This is an inference, with details quoted from the source to support it.]

The answer

You can find suggested answers to the tasks numbered (i), (ii), etc. on pages 164–65.

Answering questions: Question 2

What you need to do

Question 2 will always ask you to explain the **purpose** of a source.

How you do it

The best way to approach these questions is a two-step approach.

- First, use details in the source to explain what **message** it is giving out.
- Second, say **why** the author or photographer is putting out this message. The reason why they are doing it is their **purpose**.

Let's practice. Use Source B (cut out from page 170).

Why do you think this photograph was used in many news reports on women voting for the first time? Use detail from the source and your own knowledge to explain your answer.

Step 1 is to ask yourself what is the **message** in the photograph. For example:

- What impression does it give of the woman voting – and how does it do this?
- What impression of the woman's family does it give – and how does it do this?
- What impression of the people behind the ballot box does it give – and how does it do this?

(i) Now write a couple of sentences saying what message the photograph gives. Use details in the source to support your answer.

(i) The photo was probably used a lot because it gives a clear message. The message is ...

Step 2 is to ask yourself why people may have wanted to spread this message. For example, could the message in the photo...

- change views on who should vote?
- affect views about women?
- affect views on what role women should play in society?

(ii) Now explain why you think people published this photo widely. Use details from the source to support your answer.

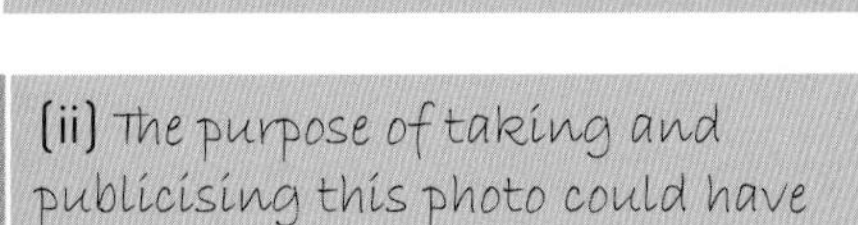
(ii) The purpose of taking and publicising this photo could have been to...

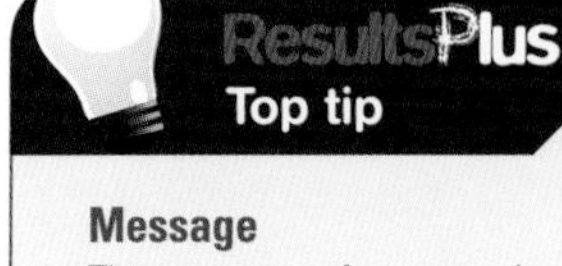

Message
The message of a source is:

- the impression it gives
- what it is trying to say.

For example, does Source B give the impression of:

- a trustworthy woman or a foolish one?
- a successful mother or a bad one?
- helpful or unhelpful voting officials?

Purpose
The purpose of a source is what the author/photographer, etc., was trying to achieve.

For Source B, for example, the people who took the photo or publicised it could have been trying to:

- change people's views about voting
- change people's views about women's rights
- change limits on which jobs women could have.

If you understand the **message** of a source, this gives you a clue to what its **purpose** may have been.

ResultsPlus Top tip

Note that we have used the key words *message* and *purpose* as signposts for the examiner at the start of the answers to steps (i) and (ii).

The answer

Model answers to these questions are given on page 164.

Answering questions: Question 3

Question 3 will ask you to study three sources and then ask if they support a view **or** agree about [something].

What you need to do

There are two stages to answering these questions. The best answers will:

- firstly, **cross-refer** what the sources say – i.e. compare what they say, to find ways in which they **do** and **do not** support the view stated
- secondly, consider **how convincingly** the sources support the view stated.

Test yourself

Let's practice. Use Sources A, B and C (cut out from page 170) to answer this question.

Do these sources support the view that people saw the role of women differently after the war? Explain your answer, using the sources and your own knowledge.

Firstly, let's practise **cross-referencing** between the sources.

We have done this below, showing ways in which the sources do support the view that people saw the role of women differently after the war.

There are some parts of Sources A, B and C which do support the view that people saw the role of women differently after the war. For example, Source A tells us that women were given the vote in 1918 and Source B supports this by showing a woman voting. Source A also supports the view that people saw the role of women differently by saying that the first woman MP was elected in 1919 and that women were allowed to work in the upper levels of the civil service after 1921. There is nothing in Source C which directly supports this view – though it shows there must have been some women who saw their role differently and decided to keep their jobs. If nobody thought that way and kept working, there would be no problem for this letter to protest about.

Now, you try. Write a paragraph saying how the sources **do not** support the view that people saw the role of women differently after the war.

(i) There are some parts of Sources A, B and C which do not support the view that people saw the role of women differently after the war. For example...

An answer like those we've produced so far, which cross-references information in different sources

- to show parts of the sources which **do support** the view
- **AND** show parts of the sources which **do not support** the view

would get a good mark in the exam. However, the best answers go one step further.

ResultsPlus

Top tip

Cross-referencing

Cross-referencing between two or more sources means checking what different sources say about the same thing.

So, if one source says that views about the role of women changed, then we can cross-reference this in the other sources. This means we can look to see if they say the same thing – or something different.

Cross-referencing helps you to make judgements.

- If you cross-reference between lots of sources and they all agree about something, this encourages you to believe it.
- If you cross-reference between lots of sources and they disagree, then you may have to be more careful about the judgement you make.

The final step

So far, our answer says **how much** support the sources give.
But sources can only really support the view in question if they are reliable.

Read about **reliability** in the Top tip box on this page.

Now consider the **provenance** and **content** of Sources A, B and C.

We've written our conclusions about the reliability of **Source C** for this question.

Source C is a letter written by someone who thinks women should go back to their old roles. This does not support the view that people saw the roles of women differently after the war. I trust this source to be telling me the truth about Isobel Pazzey's views. It is from a newspaper; they are unlikely to have made up the letter – especially since it names the writer. But we don't know if the view in this letter is typical of others at the time. The caption says there was a series of letters, but we don't know how many people agreed with this view. So it is strong evidence that SOME people hadn't changed their views on the role of women but not strong evidence about how many thought like this.

Now you write your conclusions about the reliability of **Source B** for this question.

(ii) *Source B is a photo of a woman voting.*

Now write your conclusions about the reliability of **Source A** for this question.

(iii) *Source A is a published book.*

The best candidates will round off this part of their answer with a **conclusion**.

This should be a very short summary of the answer's main points. It could look like this.

In conclusion, I think Source A is a reliable balanced source and I believe what it tells me. Sources B and C are not necessarily typical; they are giving true pictures of one side of what happened. Taken together, they give me a lot of reliable information about people's views on the role of women after the war.

ResultsPlus
Top tip

Reliability
The reliability of a source is how far you can trust what it says about the thing you are studying.
You can test the reliability of a source by looking at its **provenance** and **content**.

Provenance means:
- who wrote or produced it
- where and when
- what kind of source it is
- why it was produced (its *purpose*).

Content includes:
- the language it uses
- signs of exaggeration
- things it includes or leaves out
- how *typical* it is.

Asking these questions about a source will give you ideas about how reliable it is.

Typicality
Typicality is one aspect of the content of a source that affects how much you trust it.
- If information in a source is much the same as the information in other similar sources, then your source is typical. This would encourage you to trust it.
- If information in a source is very different from information in other similar sources then your source is not typical. This might lead you not to trust it.

ResultsPlus
Top tip

Note that we have used key words and phrases such as *'I trust this source to show me'*, *'it is evidence of'*, *'it doesn't tell me'*, and *'in conclusion'* as signposts for the examiner at the start of the answers to steps (i) and (ii).

The answer
Model answers to these questions are given on page 165.

Answering questions: Question 4

What you need to do

Question 4 will always ask you how **useful** sources are as evidence of... [a specified thing] or how **reliable** sources are as evidence of... [a specified thing].

How you do it

The technique for answering this type of question is always the same.

There are two issues to consider.

- Firstly, how much **useful** information do these sources contain?
- Secondly, how **reliable** is that information; how much do you trust it?

Now test yourself

Let's practice. Use Sources D and E (cut out from page 171) to answer this question.

How useful are Sources D and E as evidence of working opportunities for women after the war? Explain your answer.

Read the Top tip box about **utility** on this page.

Now write a paragraph to say how much useful and relevant information there is in Sources D and E.

(i) Sources D and E are useful, because they have relevant information about working opportunities for women after the war. For example...

However, there is a limit to how useful Sources D and E are. For example, they are not able to tell us...

Check your answer against the model answer on page 165 before you continue.

Utility

When you are asked about the utility of a source in the examination, you are always asked how useful two sources are as evidence of a particular thing. Always consider the usefulness of the sources in providing evidence of that particular thing.

Be careful to point out the evidence that the source provides **and** the things it doesn't tell us about that particular enquiry.

Notice how, in our answers, we use key phrases such as *'is useful because'*, *'we should be able to trust it because'*, or *'it is of limited use because'* as **signposts** for the examiner.

So far, our answer says **how much** useful information Sources D and E **do** and **don't** give. But this information is only useful if we can **trust** it.

So Step 2 of our answer involves saying whether the useful information is **reliable**.

Assessing their **provenance** and **content** will help you decide how much to trust them.

So, think about the **provenance** of Sources D and E. Write a paragraph saying if this makes you trust the information in these sources about women's work opportunities.

Remember, when we ask if the **provenance** of a source affects how much we *trust* it, we think about: • who wrote/produced it • where and when • what kind of source is it • why was it produced (its *purpose*).	(ii) The information in Sources D and E is only useful if we can trust it. In this case...

Now look at the **content** of sources D and E. Write a paragraph saying whether it makes you trust the information in the sources about women's work opportunities.

Remember, when we ask if the **content** of a source affects how much we can *trust* it, we look at: • the language it uses • signs of exaggeration • things it chooses to include and leave out • how *typical* is its content compared to other similar sources.	(iii) The information in Sources D and E is only useful if we can trust it. In this case...

Answers that assess how useful the sources are by setting out:

- how much **useful** and r**elevant information** they have
- and how **reliable** this information is

should be rewarded with marks in the top level.

Sometimes Question 4 will ask you only about **reliability**. For example, the question in this spread could have been: ***How reliable are Sources D and E as evidence of working opportunities for women? Explain your answer.***

In this case, to answer the question you would only need to include those parts of your answer to the question on this page – i.e. parts (ii) and (iii).

The answer

Model answers to the questions on these pages can be found on page 165.

Answering questions: Question 5

Question 5 will always:

- give you a **statement**
- then ask you ***'How far do the sources support this statement?'***

What you need to do

You should try to use **all the sources** in your answer.

The best answers to these kinds of questions will always look like this.

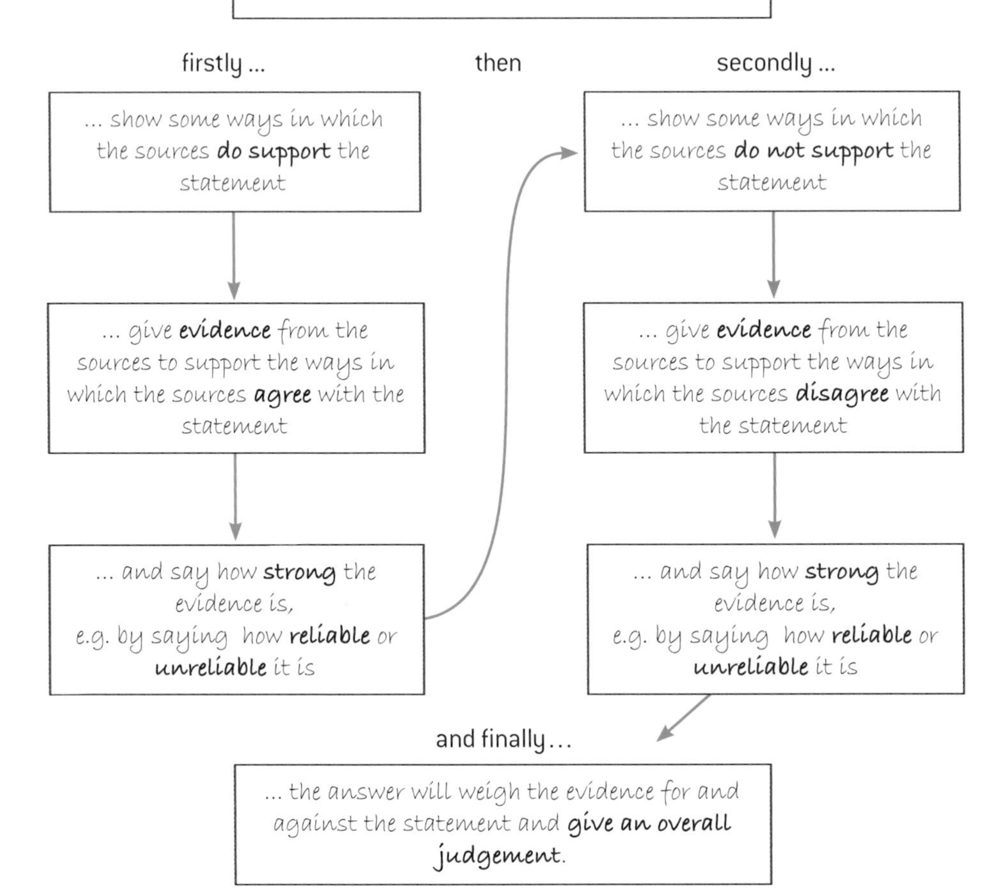

ResultsPlus
Watch out!

Quality of Written Communication

When your answer to Question 5 is marked, the quality of your written communication will always affect your mark.

To get to the top of each level of the mark scheme you have to:

- write effectively
- organise your thoughts coherently
- spell, punctuate and use grammar well.

Test yourself

Use all the sources (cut out from pages 170–71). Consider the following question:

The position of women was unchanged after the war.'

How far do the sources in this paper support this statement?

Use details from the sources and your own knowledge to explain your answer.

On the following page, we have provided an answer to this question. Your task is:

a) to cut out the paragraphs provided and sort them into the correct order
b) to fill in the missing parts of the paragraphs, to show that you understand how each kind of paragraph should be constructed.

Paragraph 1

For example, (i) ______________________ says that the popular view of women was still "as a mother and a wife. Source C supports this view. For example, it says (ii) ______________________

____

____

______________________.

Paragraph 2

The sources show that, in some ways, the position of women was unchanged.

Paragraph 3

However, there is also evidence in the sources that shows the position of women did change a little.

Paragraph 4

So, looking at all the sources, they provide strong evidence that in some ways the position of women was unchanged after the war, but that in other ways it did change. They show change and lack of change.

Paragraph 5

I think I can trust Sources A and C when they show the political position of women was changing, for the reasons I have already explained.

Paragraph 6

For example, Source A shows that the political position of women changed after the war. It tells us that (iii) ______________________

____

____

______________________.

Source C also tells us that some women – even married women – were staying on in their old jobs. We can tell this because (iv) ______________________

____

____

______________________.

Paragraph 7

These two sources appear to be more reliable evidence because they are very different kinds of sources, but they still support each other. Source A comes from a published book, which should be researched carefully; Source C is the view of a woman who put her name to her letter. So I think I can trust all of these to be true. Source E confirms them too, by showing (v) ______________________

____

______________________.

ResultsPlus
Top tip

Remember, when the question says:

'How far do the sources support this statement?'

Your answer looks like this:

Say that in some ways the sources **do support** the statement.

Give the **evidence** using as many sources as you can.

Assess **how strong** that evidence is.

Say that in some ways the sources **do not support** the statement.

Give the **evidence** using as many sources as you can.

Assess **how strong** that evidence is.

Give your **overall** judgement.

The answer

You can find suggested answers to the tasks numbered (i), (ii), etc. on page 165.

Unit 3 Exam War and the transformation of British society c.1931–51

The exam for Unit 3 is quite different from the other exam papers in Modern World History. This is because this paper tests your understanding of how historians use sources. There is less information for you to learn before you go into the exam. Instead you have to use the sources you are given in the exam to answer the questions. So, in Unit 3, it is not so much *how much you know, as what you know how to do*.

Sources are the raw material of history. Historians use them to work out what happened and why. But it isn't as simple as that. Historians need a range of skills to puzzle out the answers from lots of different sources, which may contradict one another, and even deliberately mislead. The exam tests that you have some of these skills.

There are five questions in the exam, and the good news is they will always test the same skills in the same order.

- **Question 1** tests your ability to understand a source and to make an **inference** from it.
- **Question 2** sees if you can understand the **purpose** of a source – why it was created or used.
- **Question 3** asks you to **cross-refer** between three sources.
- **Question 4** asks you to judge the utility or reliability of sources.
- **Question 5** gives you a hypothesis about what happened, and asks you to judge **how far the sources support or prove it**.

Because the exam is different, this section of the revision book is different too. There are no SuperFacts. Instead, the next three pages remind you of the general shape of the course you have studied. When you are given sources in the exam, it helps to be able to put them in context, and these three pages are designed to help you get the general overview you need.

Next, you have four pages to help you remember how to use sources. Finally, you practise answering questions.

Context

To understand the context of a source is to see how it fits into the background of things that were happening when it was created.

For example, Source B on page 172 is an extract from a book by the writer George Orwell. Someone with no context for the extract will be confused. What is the Means Test? Why are people 'reporting' their neighbours, and who to? Why does whoever is running the Means Test want to break up families?

Using the caption, background information, and the context provided by your revision, you will know that the Means Test was an investigation into the incomes of everyone in the household to make sure that they were 'in need' to get benefit payments from the government.

Overview:
War and the transformation of British society c.1931–51

In 1929, the US stock market collapsed, sending the already worsening US economy into a depression. The USA was important to world trade, and was lending many countries huge amounts of money. This meant the Depression rapidly spread worldwide. Britain was one of the countries affected. Trade dropped, industries suffered, and unemployment rose (from 1.5 million in 1929 to 3.3 million in 1931).

Britain and France went to war with Germany on 3 September 1939. The Second World War was fought on many fronts. It affected Britain not only in the loss of life of those fighting. Britain had to fight on the Home Front too – fighting shortages, the possibility of invasion and the bombing of British cities by German planes. Once the war ended, the government had to work to repair the damage and rebuild society, including making social reforms to help the poor and setting up a National Health Service to care for the sick.

Need more help?

You can find more about each key term, key word and key person in your Edexcel textbook, *War and the transformation of British society c.1931–51*. Look for this symbol, which will give you the page number.

key terms

National Insurance Benefit p.9
Hunger march p.9
The Means Test p.12
Special Areas p.12, 16

'Dunkirk spirit' p.28

Rationing pp.48–49

'Five Giants' pp.66–67
National Health Service p.70

key words

depression (in the context of this book) A period of long-term economic crisis, with high unemployment and falling wages and prices.

the dole Government benefit payments made to the unemployed who were not covered by the National Insurance Scheme or who had been unemployed for more than 15 weeks.

Blitzkrieg 'Lightning war' – the name given by the Germans to their rapid invasion tactics.

blackout (in the context of this book) Not showing any lights at all at night: from buildings, car lights or even lit cigarettes.

evacuee (in the context of this book) A child, elderly person or pregnant woman sent away from cities at risk from bombing to safer places in the countryside.

censorship (in the context of this book) Stopping the publication of certain kinds of information.

propaganda Giving people information (which may or may not be true) to make them believe what you want them to believe.

key people and organisations

NUWM (National Unemployed Workers' Movement) p.9 & 16
Stanley Baldwin p.9 & 20
The National Government p.12
NSS (National Shipbuilders' Security Ltd) p.16

Winston Churchill p.25
BEF (British Expeditionary Force) p. 25
LDF (Local Defence Force: later 'Home Guard') p.32
RAF (Royal Air Force) p.30
Luftwaffe (German air force) p.30
ARP (Air Raid Protection service) p.32

Ministry of Information p.46–7
Ministry of Food p.48–9
ATS, WAAF & Wrens p.50

William Beveridge p.66
BMA p.70

Colour coding

The information boxes on pages 133–35 use the same colour used to distinguish the Key Topics in your student textbook, so you know which key topic they come from.

Need more help?

You can find more about each key term, key word and key person in your Edexcel textbook, *War and the transformation of British society c.1931–51*. Look for this symbol, which will give you the page number.

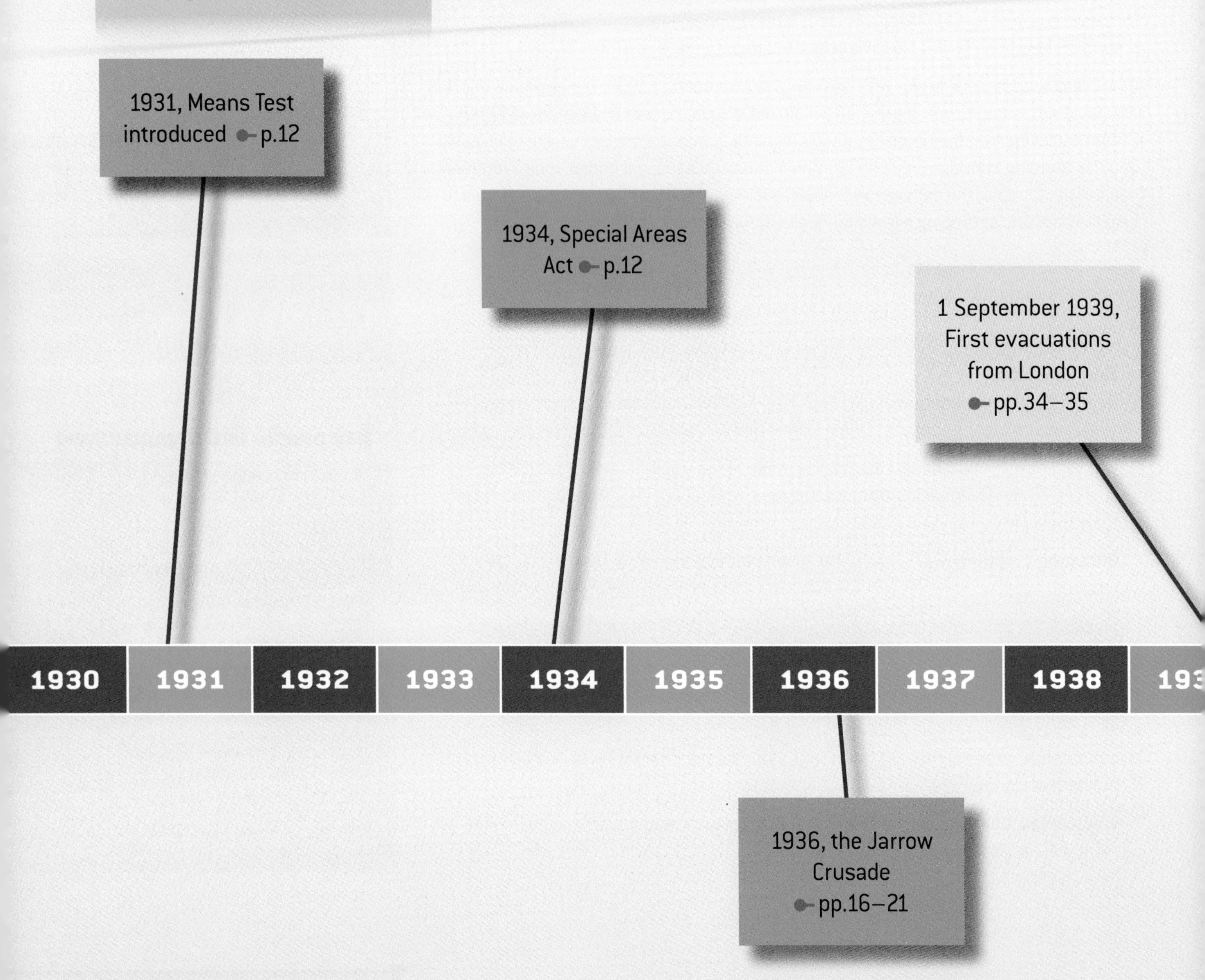

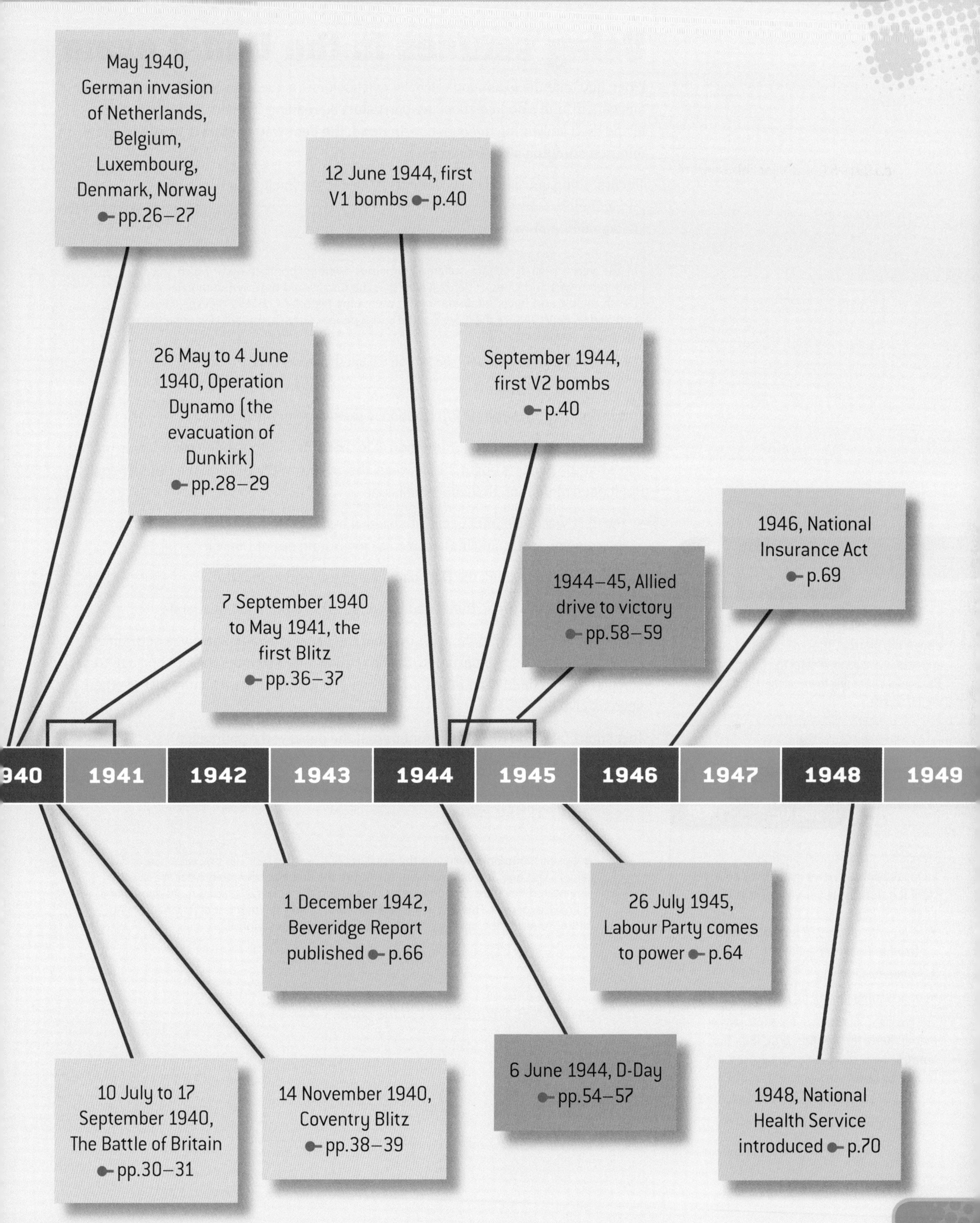
May 1940, German invasion of Netherlands, Belgium, Luxembourg, Denmark, Norway pp.26–27
12 June 1944, first V1 bombs p.40
26 May to 4 June 1940, Operation Dynamo (the evacuation of Dunkirk) pp.28–29
September 1944, first V2 bombs p.40
1946, National Insurance Act p.69
1944–45, Allied drive to victory pp.58–59
7 September 1940 to May 1941, the first Blitz pp.36–37
940
1941
1942
1943
1944
1945
1946
1947
1948
1949
1 December 1942, Beveridge Report published p.66
26 July 1945, Labour Party comes to power p.64
6 June 1944, D-Day pp.54–57
10 July to 17 September 1940, The Battle of Britain pp.30–31
14 November 1940, Coventry Blitz pp.38–39
1948, National Health Service introduced p.70

Using sources in the Unit 3 exam

When you take the exam you will have two booklets, a question booklet you write your answers in, and a sources booklet. Don't start by reading Question 1, looking at Source A, and then answering the question. **Instead, the best way to start is to spend a few minutes studying all the sources.**

The first thing you'll find isn't a source at all, it is the Background information.

> **Background information**
>
> In the years 1940-41 Britain suffered numerous German bomber raids which mainly targeted towns and cities. Hitler believed that the Blitz would destroy the morale of the British people and force Britain out of the war. Some historians believe that the German raids did seriously reduce the morale of the British people. Other historians claim that there were far worse effects.
>
> So, what was the worst effect of the Blitz on the British people?

This is how the Background information is presented in the paper.

Don't skip the Background information. It is there for a purpose. The examiner is telling you what the paper is about. In this case, the effects of the Blitz on the British people. But it does more than that. It also tells you:

- the Blitz was the bombing of British cities by the Germans 1940–41, with the intention of destroying morale and forcing Britain out of the war
- some historians think the Blitz badly damaged British morale
- other historians argue that it had far worse effects than just on morale.

The Background information tells you what the paper is about, and gives you some information. It is also, importantly, the only thing in the sources booklet you can trust completely. You need to be prepared to consider how accurate a picture all the other sources give.

This brings us to the most important part of the paper – the sources.

> **Source C:** The diary entry from 16 November 1940 by a woman who lived in Coventry during the bombings.
>
> It was not long after reaching the outskirts of Coventry that we saw evidence of the raider's visit and as we drew nearer the centre the damage became greater. We saw the devastated Rex Cinema, bombed twice over and the hospital seemed more damaged than we expected. This was deliberate bombing of non-military targets by the German brutes to terrify the ordinary citizen into fright and submission.

This is how sources are presented in the paper.

The source heading and caption are printed **above the source**. The next source heading and caption may follow directly underneath. Be careful not to mix them up, and look at the wrong source.

The caption tells you very important information about the source. **Make sure you read it carefully**. In this case, it tells you three important things:

- it is part of a **diary of a woman who lived in Coventry** during the bombings
- **when** it was made – 16 November 1940
- it was **about** the air raid on Coventry.

The caption comes before the source for a reason. **Read the caption first, then the source**. It will make more sense when you know who said it, and when.

Key skills for using sources

Inference

To make an inference is to work something out from a source that the source doesn't actually tell you or show you.

For example, read Source D on page 173:

Source D **tells** you the family's life was difficult before the Means Test and that the Means Test meant they had to reduce their living expenses even more.

You can **infer** from Source D that the man had been unemployed for well over a year (they had only just been getting by for over a year, so it has to be more than that).

Now you try with Source F on page 173.

(i) Give an example of something Source F tells you.

(ii) Give an example of something you can infer from Source F.

The sources

From now on, you will be using the sources for Britain 1931–51 on pages 172–73 of this book. Cut them out so you can have the pages in front of you while you work on the sources, without having to keep turning back and forth in the book. Be careful though – don't lose the pages, because you will need them for all the work on Unit 3.

Message and Purpose

Working out the message of a source is working out what the source shows you or tells you. Working out the purpose is going one step further. **Why** has the source shown or told you those things? What effect was the source intended to have?

For example, in Source C on page 172:
The **message** of Source C is that there were demonstrations against the Means Test.

The **purpose** of Source C could be to get support for the protesters: it shows several kinds of protester (the well-off students and the less well-off man hiding his face with his hand behind the banner) and they are marching peacefully and so on.

Now you try with Source E on page 173.

(iii) What is the message of Source E?

(iv) What is the purpose of Source E?

Using the sources in the paper
Questions 1 to 4 all use specific sources. Question 5 asks you to use 'all the sources'. Be careful to use the sources referred to in the question. You won't get any credit for writing about Source E in a question that asks you about Sources A, B and C.

When you refer to a source, make it clear which one you mean.
Say, 'in Source A', or 'Source D says...' If you want to quote from a source, to prove your point, put the bit of the source you are quoting in quotation marks.

So don't write:
The government was advised to extend the Means Test to everyone.

But do write:
The 1931 report for the government advised, 'all those claiming benefit should be means tested, not just the special groups suggested by the government' (Source A).

Cross-referencing

Cross-referencing is when you compare two or more sources. One question in the exam (Question 3) will ask you to use (or cross-refer between) three sources in the question. In Question 5, you won't be able to get a good mark without cross-referencing.

When you cross-refer you need to look for things that agree, or things that don't agree, between the sources.

For example: Do Sources B, E and F support the view that people thought the Means Test had made things worse?

They **do agree**

- because Source B tells you how the Means Test was very strict and that it broke up families and got people informing on each other
- because Source E shows so many people marching against it.

But they **don't agree** as well

- because Source F says he doesn't mind the Means Test, that the previous way was worse.

Now you try, with a different question and different sources. ***Do Sources C, D and E support the view that people from all sorts of social groups opposed the Means Test?***

(v) Ways they do support this view:

(vi) Ways they do not:

Cross-referencing won't give you the full answer to the question. It gives you the material to support your answer.

The answer

You can find suggested answers to the tasks numbered (i), (ii) etc. on page 166.

Utility (usefulness)

This is quite straightforward. The only thing to remember is, it depends on the question. So, starting with the question you want to answer, you just need to decide whether the source tells you anything useful or not.

For example:

Did the Means Test save the government money?

Source A – useful

Source B – useful (talks of docking family income)

Source C – not useful

Source D – useful

Source E – not useful

Source F – useful.

Now you try, in the boxes on the right.

Reliability

Testing a source for reliability is about thinking whether you can believe it or not. What are the clues to look for?

- **Provenance** – who created the source and why?
- **Language** is a useful clue – often a biased source shows up in its choice of language.
- **Selection** is a very powerful clue – sources don't tell us everything, and the person who created the source probably chose what to include and what to leave out. This can be just as true of a photograph as of a written source. A photographer decides which bit of what is happening to photograph, and a newspaper editor decides which photograph to use. For example, in a demonstration they could choose to show thousands of people protesting peacefully, or a few people starting a fight with the police. The two photographs would give very different impressions of what happened.

Reliability affects what a source is useful for. An unreliable source might not be useful for facts – but it tells you useful things about the opinions of the person who created it.

Repeat the exercise you did for utility, this time for reliability.

(vii) *Was there widespread opposition to the Means Test? Are the sources useful?*

(viii) *Did the Means Test penalise the unemployed? Are the sources useful?*

(ix) *Was there widespread opposition to the Means Test? Are the sources reliable? Give reasons for your answers.*

(x) *Did the Means Test penalise the unemployed? Are the sources reliable? Give reasons for your answers.*

ResultsPlus
Top tip

An **inference** is a judgement that can be made by studying the source, but is not directly stated by it.

A **supported inference** is one that uses detail from the source to prove the inference.

Consider this example:

Source A: 'The furious neighbour told Anna that her tennis ball had broken his window and he would tell her parents about her carelessness.'

Question: ***What can you learn from Source A about Anna?***

Information: Source A tells us that Anna broke a neighbour's window. [This is directly stated in the source, so it's not an inference.]

Inference: Source A tells me that Anna is likely to be in trouble with her parents. [The source does not directly tell us this, but we can infer that it is likely.]

A supported inference: Source A tells me that Anna is likely to be in trouble with her parents. She broke the neighbour's window and he was going to tell her parents. [This is an inference, with details quoted from the source to support it.]

Answering questions: Question 1

What you need to do

Question 1 will always ask '***What can you learn from Source A about ...* [something]**'.

The best answers:

- not only extract **information** from the source
- but will also make **inferences** from the source *[see Top tip box]*
- and **support** those inferences with detail from the source.

Note: make sure you answer the question – after **about** comes the **subject**. You can't just make *any* inference from the source, it has to be about the *something* in the question.

Let's practise. Study Source A (cut out from page 173).

What can you learn from Source A about the Means Test?

Inference	Supporting detail
I can learn from Source A that the burden of benefit payments on government finances had been getting worse for a long time.	I can infer this because Source A talks about the increased cost 'under the difficult economic conditions since the war' [i.e. 1918]. It also compares 1930 payments with 1911. If the problem had been sudden, it would have compared the 1930 situation with 1928 or 1929, a more recent date.

Now test yourself

(i) Here's another inference. You try writing the **supporting detail**.

I can learn from Source A that, though the cost of benefit payments had been getting worse gradually for a long time, it got suddenly much worse in about 1930 or 1931.	**[Supporting detail]**

(ii) Can you write out the **inference** that matches this supporting detail?

[Inference]	I can infer this because Source A says the government had already suggested means testing benefits and asked for a report on possible spending costs. It also says the cost of benefits was 7 times the 1911 figure which would also make them worried.

In the exam, one inference with support scores well. If you have time, find two or three.

The answer

You can find suggested answers to the tasks numbered (i), (ii), etc. on page 166–67.

Answering questions: Question 2

What you need to do

Question 2 will always ask you to explain the **purpose** of a source.

How you do it

The best way to approach these questions is a two-step approach.

- First, use details in the source to explain what **message** it is giving out.
- Second, say **why** the author or photographer is putting out this message. The reason why they are doing it is their **purpose**.

Let's practice. Use Source B (cut out from page 172).

What was the purpose of the book this extract comes from? Use detail from the source and your own knowledge to explain your answer.

Step 1 is to ask yourself what is the **message** in the extract. For example: • What impression does it give of the Means Test – and how does it do this? • What impression does it give about the effects of the Means Test – and how does it do this? • What impression does it give about people's lives at the time – and how does it do this? (i) Now write a couple of sentences saying what message the extract gives. Use details in the source to support your answer.	(i) *The message this book gives is that…*
Step 2 is to ask yourself why people may have wanted to spread this message. For example, could the message in the extract… • change views on the Means Test? • change views on society? • cast a new light on the place of the Means Test in society? (ii) Now explain why you think people published this book. Use details from the source to support your answer.	(ii) *The purpose of the book …*

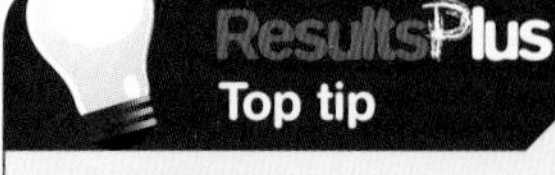

Message

The message of a source is:
- the impression it gives
- what it is trying to say.

For example, does Source B give the impression:
- it is for or against the Means Test?
- that means tests helped or harmed people?
- people lived happy or unhappy lives under the existing benefit rules?

Purpose

The purpose of a source is what the author/photographer, etc., was trying to achieve.

For Source B, for example, the people who took the photo or publicised it could have been trying to:
- change people's views about the Means Test
- change or abolish the Means Test
- change people's views about how society should be organised.

If you understand the **message** of a source, this gives you a clue to what its **purpose** may have been.

ResultsPlus
Top tip

Note that we have used the key words *message* and *purpose* as signposts for the examiner at the start of the answers to steps (i) and (ii).

The answer

Model answers to these questions are given on page 166.

Answering questions: Question 3

Question 3 will ask you to study three sources and then ask if they support a view **or** agree about [something].

What you need to do

There are two stages to answering these questions. The best answers will:

- firstly, **cross-refer** what the sources say – i.e. compare what they say, to find ways in which they **do** and **do not** support the view stated
- secondly, consider **how convincingly** the sources support the view stated.

Test yourself

Use Sources A, B and C (cut out from page 172). Consider the following question:

> ***Do these sources support the view that there was widespread opposition to the Means Test? Explain your answer, using the sources and your own knowledge.***

Firstly, let's practise **cross-referencing** between the sources.

We have done this below, showing ways in which the sources do support the view that there was widespread opposition to the Means Test.

> There are some parts of Sources A, B and C which do support the view that there was widespread opposition to the Means Test. For example, Source C shows us Lancashire marchers and Oxford University students joining together in a march against the Means Test. Added to this, Source B opposes the Means Test and this was promoted by a left-wing book club and written by a famous author. That's four very different types of people all opposing the Means Test. This strikes me as 'widespread opposition'. On the other hand, there's nothing in Source A which suggests widespread opposition to the Means Test – except perhaps when it says the Government favoured means testing for special groups only. This could be because they knew there was widespread opposition to means testing for all.

Now, you try. Write a paragraph saying how the sources **do not** support the view that there was widespread opposition to the Means Test.

> (i) There are some parts of Sources A, B and C which do not support the view that there was widespread opposition to the Means Test. For example ...

An answer like those we've produced so far, which:

- cross-references information in different sources
- to show parts of the sources which **do support** the view
- **AND** show parts of the sources which **do not support** the view

would get a good mark in the exam. However, the best answers go one step further.

ResultsPlus
Top tip

Cross-referencing

Cross-referencing between two or more sources means checking what different sources say about the same thing.

So, if one source says that there was widespread opposition to the Means Test, then we can cross-reference this in the other sources. This means we can look to see if they say the same thing – or something different.

Cross-referencing helps you to make judgements.

- If you cross-reference between lots of sources and they all agree about something, this encourages you to believe it.
- If you cross-reference between lots of sources and they disagree, then you may have to be more careful about the judgement you make.

The final step

So far, our answer says **how much** support the sources give.
But sources can only really support the view in question if they are reliable.

Read about **reliability** in the Top tip box on this page.

Now consider the **provenance** and **content** of Sources A, B and C.

We've written our conclusions about the reliability of **Source C** for this question.

Source A is an official report written for the government. We can trust what it says to be the real recommendations because it was made public. The report writers would have complained if it had been changed. I think we can trust that the report is the true view of the report writers too. They don't seem to be writing just what the government wanted to hear; they disagree with government views when they need to – e.g. about means testing all benefit claimers. I also trust it to be reliable because an official report would be well researched. Its content is very detailed, (comparing 1911 with 1930 and giving exact details of savings) so it seems authoritative. I think we can trust what it says.

Now you write your conclusions about the reliability of **Source B** for this question.

Don't forget to think about its **provenance** and **content**.

(ii) Source B is an extract from a book.

Now write your conclusions about the reliability of **Source C** for this question.

Again, remember to bear in mind its **provenance** and **content**.

(iii) Source C is a photograph of a march.

The best candidates will round off this part of their answer with a **conclusion**.

This should be a very short summary of the answer's main points. It could look like this.

Overall, Source A shows some people supported a Means Test, so the sources don't support the idea that EVERYONE opposed it. But what about WIDESPREAD opposition? Sources B and C give reliable support that there was SOME opposition and it was from a wide spread of different types of people. But there's not enough evidence in A, B and C to prove widespread opposition from lots of people.

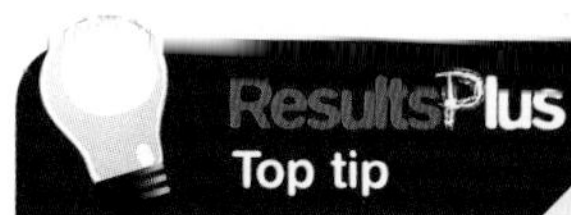

ResultsPlus
Top tip

Reliability
The reliability of a source is how far you can trust what it says about the thing you are studying.
You can test the reliability of a source by looking at its **provenance** and **content**.

Provenance means:
- who wrote or produced it
- where and when
- what kind of source it is
- why it was produced (its *purpose*)

Content includes:
- the language it uses
- signs of exaggeration
- things it includes or leaves out
- how *typical* it is.

Asking these questions about a source will give you ideas about how reliable it is.

Typicality
Typicality is one aspect of the content of a source that affects how much you trust it.
- If information in a source is much the same as the information in other similar sources, then your source is typical. This would encourage you to trust it.
- If information in a source is very different from information in other similar sources then your source is not typical. This might lead you not to trust it.

ResultsPlus
Top tip

Note that we have used key words and phrases such as *'I trust this source to show me'*, *'it is evidence of'*, *'it doesn't tell me'*, and *'in conclusion'* as signposts for the examiner at the start of the answers to steps (i) and (ii).

The answer
Model answers to these questions are given on page 167.

Answering questions: Question 4

What you need to do

Question 4 will always ask you how **useful** sources are as evidence of... [a specified thing] or how **reliable** sources are as evidence of... [a specified thing].

How you do it

The technique for answering this type of question is always the same.

There are two issues to consider.

- Firstly, how much **useful** information do these sources contain?
- Secondly, how **reliable** is that information; how much do you trust it?

Now test yourself

Let's practice. Use Sources D and E (cut out from page 173) to answer this question.

> ***How useful are Sources D and E as evidence of opposition to the Means Test? Explain your answer.***

Read the Top tip box about **utility** on this page.

Now write a paragraph to say how much useful and relevant information there is in Sources D and E.

(i) Sources D and E are useful, because they have relevant information about opposition to the Means Test. For example...

However, there is a limit to how useful the sources are. For example ...

Check your answer against the model answer on page 167 before you continue.

Utility

When you are asked about the utility of a source in the examination, you are always asked how useful two sources are as evidence of a particular thing. Always consider the usefulness of the sources in providing evidence of that particular thing.

Be careful to point out the evidence that the source provides **and** the things it doesn't tell us about that particular enquiry.

Notice how, in our answers, we use key phrases such as *'is useful because'*, *'we should be able to trust it because'*, or *'it is of limited use because'* as **signposts** for the examiner.

So far, our answer says **how much** useful information Sources D and E **do** and **don't** give. But this information is only useful if we can **trust** it.

So Step 2 of our answer involves saying whether the useful information is **reliable**.

Assessing their **provenance** and **content** will help you decide how much to trust them.

So, think about the **provenance** of Sources D and E. Write a paragraph saying if this makes you trust the information in these sources about opposition to the Means Test.

Remember, when we ask if the **provenance** of a source affects how much we *trust* it, we think about: • who wrote/produced it • where and when • what kind of source is it • why was it produced (its *purpose*).	(ii) The information in Sources D and E is only useful if we can trust it. In this case...

Now look at the **content** of sources D and E and then write a paragraph saying whether it makes you trust the information in the sources about opposition to the Means Test.

Remember, when we ask if the **content** of a source affects how much we can *trust* it, we look at: • the language it uses • signs of exaggeration • things it chooses to include and leave out • how *typical* is its content compared to other similar sources.	(iii) The information in Sources D and E is only useful if we can trust it. In this case...

Answers that assess how useful the sources are by setting out:

- how much **useful** and **relevant information** they have
- and how **reliable** this information is

should be rewarded with marks in the top level.

Sometimes Question 4 will ask you only about **reliability**. For example, the question in this spread could have been:
How reliable are Sources D and E as evidence of opposition to the Means Test? Explain your answer.

In this case, to answer the question you would only need to include those parts of your answer to the question on this page – i.e. parts (ii) and (iii).

The answer

Model answers to these questions are given on page 167.

Answering questions: Question 5

Question 5 will always:

- give you a **statement**
- then ask you ***'How far do the sources support this statement?'***

What you need to do

You should try to use **all the sources** in your answer.

The best answers to these kinds of questions will always look like this.

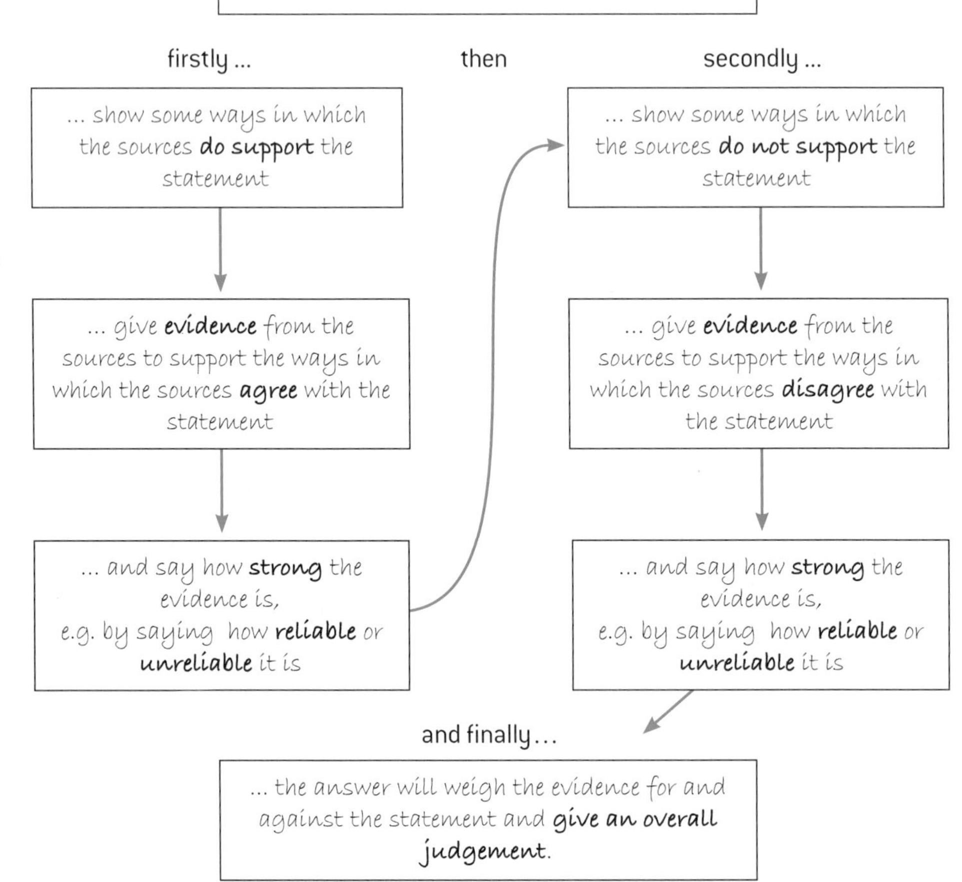

ResultsPlus
Watch out!

Quality of Written Communication

When your answer to Question 5 is marked, the quality of your written communication will always affect your mark.

To get to the top of each level of the mark scheme you have to:

- write effectively
- organise your thoughts coherently
- spell, punctuate and use grammar well.

Test yourself

Use all the sources (cut out from pages 172–73). Consider the following question:

'The Means Test was unpopular, unfair and unnecessary.'

How far do the sources in this paper support this statement?

Use details from the sources and your own knowledge to explain your answer.

On the following page, we have provided an answer to this question. Your task is:

a) to cut out the paragraphs provided and sort them into the correct order

b) to fill in the missing parts of the paragraphs, to show that you understand how each kind of paragraph should be constructed.

Paragraph 1

(i) ____________ both show the Means Test's unpopularity: they show protests. And Source B says it was unfair. For example it says (ii) ____________. Source D supports B because the person thought it was unfair that half his benefit had to be spent on rent. However, no source actually discusses the idea that the Means Test was unnecessary, but no one says 'we need a fair version of this' so maybe that implies they don't see it as necessary either.

Paragraph 2

The sources show, in some ways, the Means Test was unpopular, unfair and unnecessary.

Paragraph 3

However, there is also evidence in the sources that does NOT support this view.

Paragraph 4

So, looking at all the sources, they seem to show that the Means Test was unpopular with lots of people. They show that some people – but not everyone – thought that it was unfair and possibly unnecessary. However they also show that the government certainly, and probably other people, thought it was necessary because of the financial crisis.

Paragraph 5

I think I can trust Sources A and F for the reasons I have already explained.

Paragraph 6

For example, Source A shows the people who wrote the 1931 report for the government wanted a Means Test. They said (iii) ____________ And it shows the government thought there should be a Means Test. It says the government suggested one that just covered (iv) ____________. It was not totally unpopular with all benefit claimers either. Source F says the Means Test was not that bad. For example, he said (v) ____________.

Paragraph 7

Sources C and E work together as reliable support for the idea that the Means Test was unpopular, because they seem genuine photos from newspapers, and they show lots of very different types of protesters. I don't trust Source B to tell the whole truth. It was written to promote left-wing political views, so it is probably one-sided. I also think Source D is unreliable as evidence of the fairness of the Means Test, because (vi) ____________.

ResultsPlus
Top tip

Remember, when the question says:

'How far do the sources support this statement?'

Your answer looks like this:

Say that in some ways the sources **do support** the statement.
Give the **evidence** using as many sources as you can.
Assess **how strong** that evidence is.
Say that in some ways the sources **do not support** the statement.
Give the **evidence** using as many sources as you can.
Assess **how strong** that evidence is.
Give your **overall** judgement.

The answer

You can find suggested answers to the tasks numbered (i), (ii), etc. on page 167.

Unit 3 Exam A divided union? The USA 1945–70

The exam for Unit 3 is quite different from the other exam papers in Modern World History. This is because this paper tests your understanding of how historians use sources. There is less information for you to learn before you go into the exam. Instead you have to use the sources you are given in the exam to answer the questions. So, in Unit 3, it is not so much *how much you know, as what you know how to do*.

Sources are the raw material of history. Historians use them to work out what happened and why. But it isn't as simple as that. Historians need a range of skills to puzzle out the answers from lots of different sources, which may contradict one another, and even deliberately mislead. The exam tests that you have some of these skills.

There are five questions in the exam, and the good news is they will always test the same skills in the same order.

- **Question 1** tests your ability to understand a source and to make an **inference** from it.
- **Question 2** sees if you can understand the **purpose** of a source – why it was created or used.
- **Question 3** asks you to **cross-refer** between three sources.
- **Question 4** asks you to judge the utility or reliability of sources.
- **Question 5** gives you a hypothesis about what happened, and asks you to judge **how far the sources support or prove it**.

Because the exam is different, this section of the revision book is different too. There are no SuperFacts. Instead, the next three pages remind you of the general shape of the course you have studied. When you are given sources in the exam, it helps to be able to put them in context, and these three pages are designed to help you get the general overview you need.

Next, you have four pages to help you remember how to use sources. Finally, you practise answering questions.

ResultsPlus
Top tip

Context

To understand the context of a source is to see how it fits into the background of things that were happening when it was created.

For example, Source B on page 174 shows some black teenagers being taken to a car by a group of armed troops. Someone who was shown the photograph and did not understand the context would be puzzled by it. Have the teenagers been causing trouble? But why are they escorted by the army (not the police, as you might expect), why are they armed with rifles, and why are the teenagers being taken to an ordinary car not a police or army van?

Using the caption and the context provided by your revision, you will know the troops are an armed guard to protect the students because of the violent reaction in some places to the integration of schools in the 1950s.

Overview: A divided union? The USA 1945–70

When the Second World War ended in 1945, the USA entered a period of economic prosperity. During the 1950s and 60s, the USA grew to be a world superpower, confident and rich. But it also felt threatened by communism, a political system many people feared wanted the downfall of the American way of life. They saw this threat as coming from outside the USA (via its Cold War rival, the USSR) and from plots laid by American communists, working against their own country. This led to a 'Red Scare' and an increasingly hysterical campaign to 'root out' American communists as spies and traitors, led by Senator Joseph McCarthy.

As well as fears of communist groups, people were divided over the rights of black people. The civil rights movement grew in strength between 1945 and 1970, pressing for black people to be given the rights that, according to the Constitution, they already possessed. But the civil rights movement faced angry (often violent, even murderous) opposition from many people, especially in the South.

Women and young people formed various groups, especially in the 1960s, to campaign for their right to be heard, and for reform. They used similar tactics to the civil rights movement and, like that movement, faced a similarly escalating level of violence from the police sent to control their demonstrations.

key words

segregation (in the context of this book) Black and white people living separately and having to use different facilities.

desegregation Stopping segregation, having shared facilities and living areas.

integration Having shared facilities and living areas.

sit-in Sitting down in a place and refusing to move on as a protest.

Need more help?

You can find more about each key term, key word and key person in your Edexcel textbook, *A divided union? The USA 1945–70*. Look for this symbol, which will give you the page number ●–.

key terms

The Cold War ●– p.9
Truman Doctrine ●– p.9
Marshall Plan ●– p.9
Red Scare ●– p.12 & 13
HUAC ●– p.12

McCarthyism ●– pp.14–15, 18–19
Ku Klux Klan ●– p.36
Freedom rides ●– p.34 & 35

Black Power ●– pp.54–5

Student protest ●– pp.64–7
Women's liberation ●– pp.70–73

key people and organisations

Joseph McCarthy ●– pp.14–15, 18–19
The Hollywood Ten ●– p.12
The Rosenbergs ●– pp.16–17

NAACP (National Association for the Advancement of Colored People) ●– p.23
CORE (Congress of Racial Equality) ●– p.23
SNCC (Student Nonviolent Coordinating Committee, said 'snick') ●– p.34
Martin Luther King ●– p.26
Rosa Parkes ●– pp.28–9
Little Rock Nine ●– pp.32–3

President Kennedy ●– pp.48–9
Malcolm X ●– pp.46–7
Stokely Carmichael ●– p.54
Black Panthers ●– pp.54–5

Hippies ●– p.64
SDS ●– p.64 & 67
Eleanor Roosevelt ●– p.70
Betty Friedan ●– p.70
NOW ●– p.72

Colour coding

The information boxes on pages 149–51 use the same colour used to distinguish the Key Topics in your student textbook, so you know which key topic they come from.

Need more help?

You can find out about each key event in your Edexcel textbook, *A divided union? The USA 1945–70*. Look for this symbol, which will give you the page number.

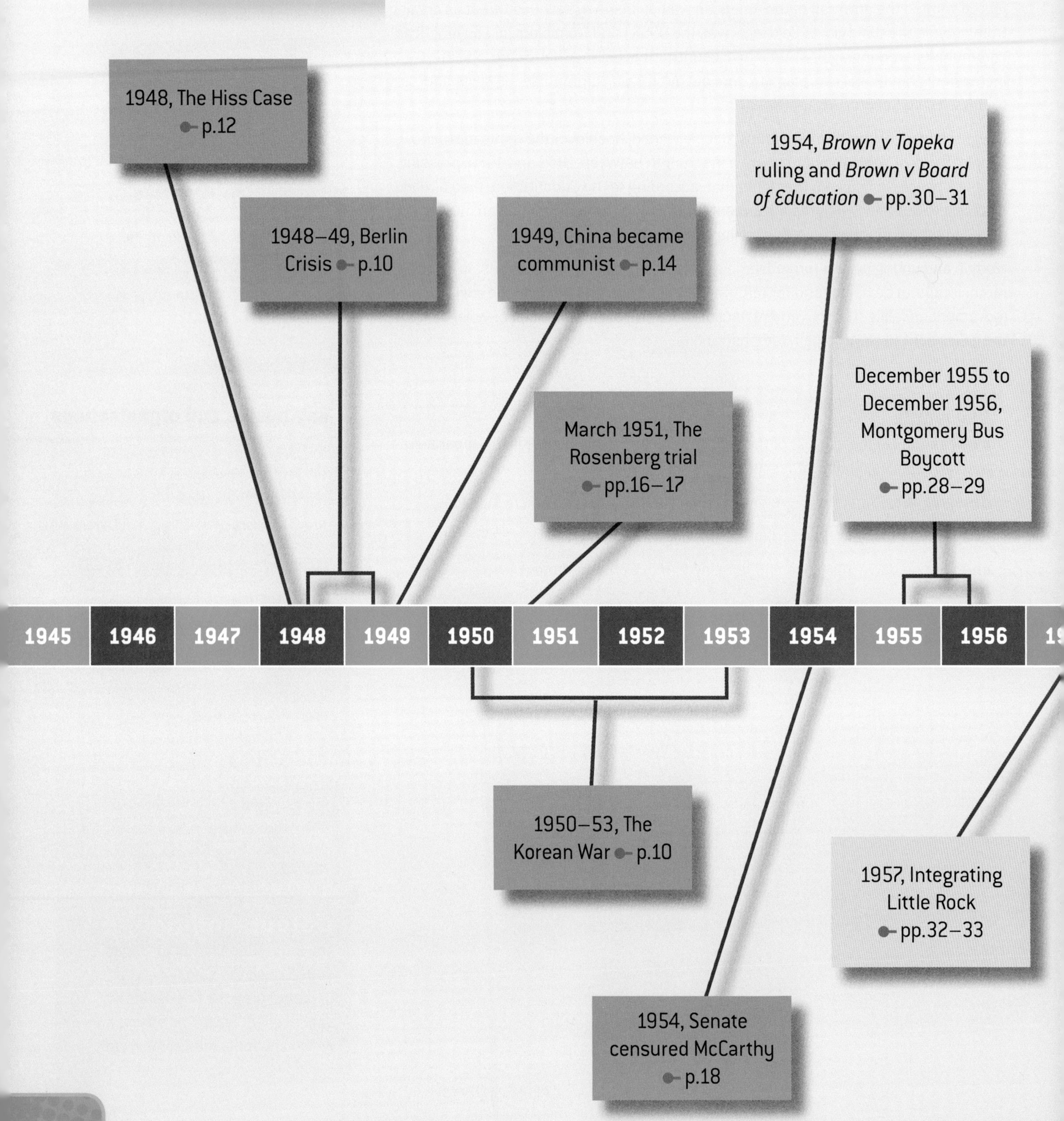

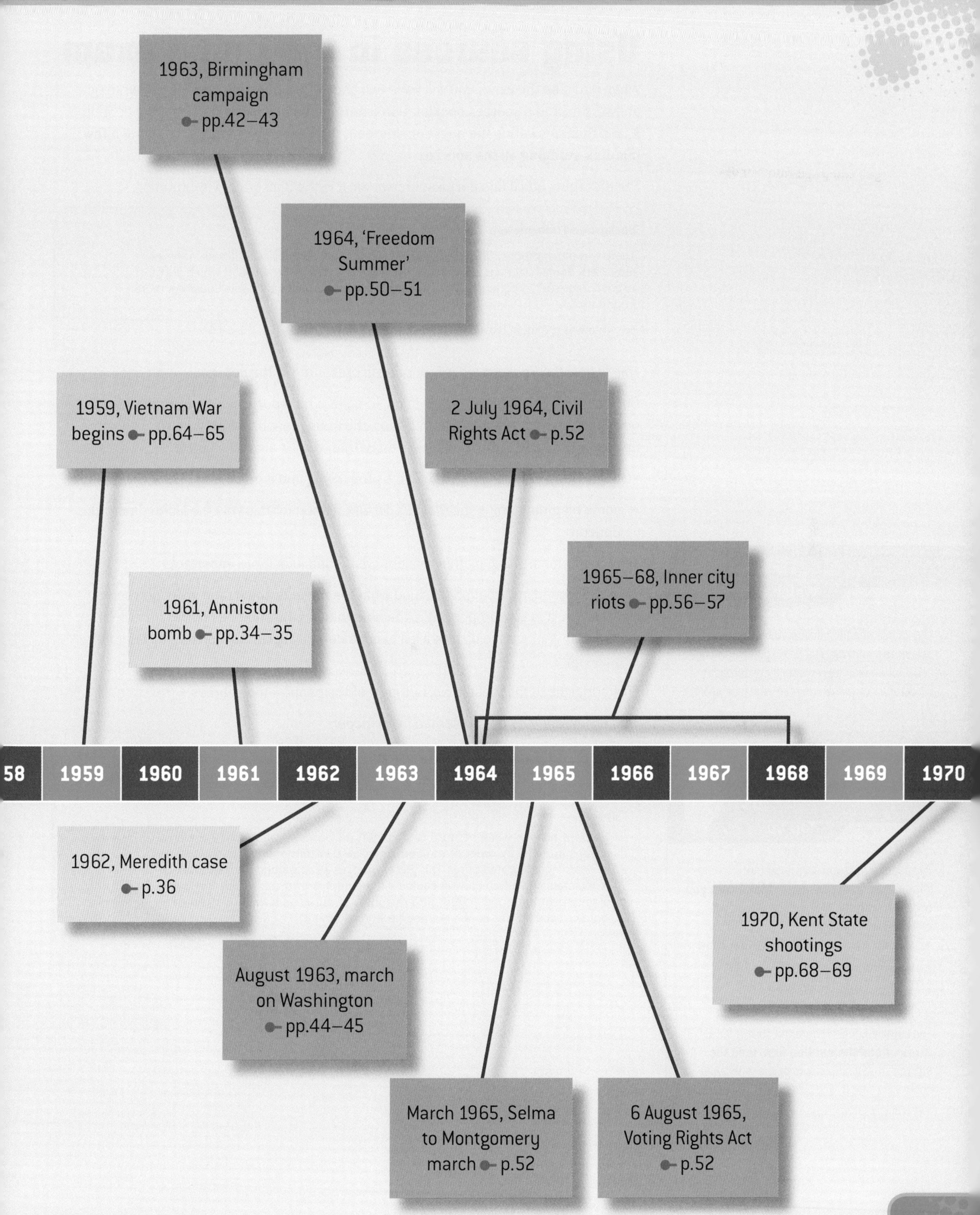
1963, Birmingham campaign pp.42–43
1964, 'Freedom Summer' pp.50–51
1959, Vietnam War begins pp.64–65
2 July 1964, Civil Rights Act p.52
1965–68, Inner city riots pp.56–57
1961, Anniston bomb pp.34–35
58
1959
1960
1961
1962
1963
1964
1965
1966
1967
1968
1969
1970
1962, Meredith case p.36
1970, Kent State shootings pp.68–69
August 1963, march on Washington pp.44–45
March 1965, Selma to Montgomery march p.52
6 August 1965, Voting Rights Act p.52

Using sources in the Unit 3 exam

When you take the exam you will have two booklets, a question booklet you write your answers in, and a sources booklet. Don't start by reading Question 1, looking at Source A, and then answering the question. **Instead, the best way to start is to spend a few minutes studying all the sources.**

The first thing you'll find isn't a source at all, it is the Background information.

Background information

There was much progress in the campaign for civil rights for black US citizens in the years after 1945. Some historians claim that it was the Montgomery Bus Boycott which did most to encourage such progress. Other historians argue that other factors were equally or more important.

So, what was the main reason for progress in civil rights in the years 1945-60?

This is how the Background information is presented in the paper.

Don't skip the Background information. It is there for a purpose. The examiner is telling you what the paper is about. In this case, the main reasons for progress in civil rights between 1945 and 1960. But it does more than that. It also tells you:

- there was a campaign for civil rights after 1945, and it made progress
- some historians think the most important reason for this was the Montgomery Bus Boycott
- other historians argue other reasons were equally or more important.

The Background information tells you what the paper is about, and gives you some information. It is also, importantly, the only thing in the sources booklet you can trust completely. You need to be prepared to consider how accurate a picture all the other sources give.

This brings us to the most important part of the paper – the sources.

This is how sources are presented in the paper.

Source D: A statement by Martin Luther King, on behalf of the Montgomery Improvement Association, December 1956.

This is a historic week because segregation on buses has now been declared unconstitutional by order of the Supreme Court. Within a few days you will be re-boarding integrated buses. This places upon us all a tremendous responsibility of maintaining, in face of what could be more unpleasantness, a calm and loving dignity befitting good citizens and members of our race. If there is violence in word or deed it must not be our people who commit it.

The source heading and caption are printed **above the source**. The next source heading and caption may follow directly underneath. Be careful not to mix them up, and look at the wrong source.

The caption tells you very important information about the source. **Make sure you read it carefully**. In this case, it tells you three important things:

- it is a statement by **Martin Luther King**
- **when** he made it – December 1956
- he made it **for** the Montgomery Improvement Association.

The caption comes before the source for a reason. **Read the caption first, then the source**. It will make more sense when you know who said it, and when.

Key skills for using sources

Inference

To make an inference is to work something out from a source that the source doesn't actually tell you or show you.

For example, look at Source B on page 174:

Source B **shows** you seven black teenagers. The caption says they are students leaving school with an armed guard arranged by the president.

You can **infer** from Source B that there is a possibility of violence of some kind breaking out because of the presence of armed troops in the picture. You can also infer that it was important to the president that the students got to and from school safely.

Now you try with Source E on page 175.

(i) Give an example of something Source E tells you.

(ii) Give an example of something you can infer from Source E.

Message and Purpose

Working out the message of a source is working out what the source shows you or tells you. Working out the purpose is going one step further. **Why** has the source shown or told you those things? What effect was the source intended to have?

For example:
The **message** of Source B is that these students are under threat and need protecting.

The **purpose** of Source B could be to show that resistance to integration was so strong at this school that an armed guard was needed to keep the students safe.

Now you try with Source E.

(iii) What is the message of Source E?

(iv) What is the purpose of Source E?

The sources

From now on, you will be using the sources for the USA 1945–70 on pages 174–75 of this book. Cut them out so you can have them pages in front of you while you work on the sources, without having to keep turning back and forth in the book. Be careful though – don't lose the pages, because you will need them for all the work on Unit 3.

Using the sources in the paper

Questions 1 to 4 all use specific sources. Question 5 asks you to use 'all the sources'. Be careful to use the sources referred to in the question. You won't get any credit for writing about Source E in a question that asks you about Sources A, B and C.

When you refer to a source, make it clear which one you mean.
Say, 'in Source A', or 'Source D says...' If you want to quote from a source, to prove your point, put the bit of the source you are quoting in quotation marks.

So don't write:
It was decided that separate educational facilities are inherently unequal.

But do write:
The Supreme Court ruled that, "Separate educational facilities are inherently unequal." (Source A)

Cross-referencing

Cross-referencing is when you compare two or more sources. One question in the exam (Question 3) will ask you to use (or cross-refer between) three sources in the question. In Question 5, you won't be able to get a good mark without cross-referencing.

When you cross-refer you need to look for things that agree, or things that don't agree, between the sources.

For example: ***Do Sources B, C and D support the view that there was tension between the races in the USA in the 1950s?***

They **do agree**

- because Source B shows that black students needed an armed guard, just to go to classes
- because there were rumours there would be violence when black students joined the school in Source C
- because in Source D the white president of the student body said it would affect him if he saw a white girl dating a negro boy, because of the way he was brought up.

But they **don't agree** as well

- because Source C says, 'the only black male student to enrol in classes on September 10, Preston Lackey, entered with the support of white students'.

Now you try, with a different question and different sources. ***Do Sources C, D and E support the view that white students and parents were against the desegregation of schools?***

(v) Ways they do agree:

(vi) Ways they do not agree:

Cross-referencing won't give you the full answer to the question. It gives you the material to support your answer.

The answer

You can find suggested answers to the tasks numbered (i), (ii) etc. on page 168.

Utility (usefulness)

This is quite straightforward. The only thing to remember is, it depends on the question. So, starting with the question you want to answer, you just need to decide whether the source tells you anything useful or not.

For example:

Was there a need to enforce segregation?

Source A – useful

Source B – useful

Source C – useful

Source D – useful (he says 'it's the law', suggesting it wouldn't happen otherwise)

Source E – not useful

Source F – useful (had to go to court).

Now you try, in the boxes on the right.

Reliability

Testing a source for reliability is about thinking whether you can believe it or not. What are the clues to look for?

- **Provenance** – who created the source and why?
- **Language** is a useful clue – often a biased source shows up in its choice of language.
- **Selection** is a very powerful clue – sources don't tell us everything, and the person who created the source probably chose what to include and what to leave out. This can be just as true of a photograph as of a written source. A photographer decides which bit of what is happening to photograph, and a newspaper editor decides which photograph to use. For example, in a demonstration they could choose to show thousands of people protesting peacefully, or a few people starting a fight with the police. The two photographs would give very different impressions of what happened.

Reliability affects what a source is useful for. An unreliable source might not be useful for facts – but it tells you useful things about the opinions of the person who created it.

Repeat the exercise you did for utility, this time for reliability.

(vii) How did black people feel about the segregation of schools? Are the sources useful?

(viii) Was there violence during the desegregation of schools? Are the sources useful?

(ix) How did black people feel about the segregation of schools? Are the sources reliable? Give reasons for your answers.

(x) Was there violence during the desegregation of schools? Are the sources reliable? Give reasons for your answers.

Answering questions: Question 1

ResultsPlus
Top tip

An **inference** is a judgement that can be made by studying the source, but is not directly stated by it.

A **supported inference** is one that uses detail from the source to prove the inference.

Consider this example:

Source A: 'The furious neighbour told Anna that her tennis ball had broken his window and he would tell her parents about her carelessness.'

Question: ***What can you learn from Source A about Anna?***

Information: *Source A tells us that Anna broke a neighbour's window.* [This is directly stated in the source, so it's not an inference.]

Inference: *Source A tells me that Anna is likely to be in trouble with her parents.* [The source does not directly tell us this, but we can infer that it is likely.]

A supported inference: *Source A tells me that Anna is likely to be in trouble with her parents. She broke the neighbour's window and he was going to tell her parents.* [This is an inference, with details quoted from the source to support it.]

What you need to do

Question 1 will always ask '***What can you learn from Source A about ...* [something]**'.

The best answers:

- not only extract **information** from the source
- but will also make **inferences** from the source *[see Top tip box]*
- and **support** those inferences with detail from the source.

Note: make sure you answer the question – after **about** comes the **subject**. You can't just make *any* inference from the source, it has to be about the *something* in the question.

Let's practise. Study Source A (cut out from page 175).

What can you learn from Source A about the impact of Brown v. the Board of Education on segregated schools?

Inference	Supporting detail
I can learn from Source A that segregated schools for whites only must have harmed the education of black kids.	*I can infer this because, though Source A doesn't actually say this, people wouldn't have complained about separate schools for whites unless it caused them harm in some way.*

Now test yourself

(i) Here's another inference. You try writing the **supporting detail**.

I can learn from Source A that the Brown ruling did not affect segregation in other facilities, e.g. hospitals and transport	**[Supporting detail]**

(ii) Can you write out the **inference** that matches this supporting detail?

[Inference]	*I can infer this because, even though Source A doesn't say the plaintiffs were black, I know from my own knowledge and the Background Information that the segregation they were complaining about was racial segregation.*

In the exam, one inference with support scores well. If you have time, find two or three.

The answer

You can find suggested answers to the tasks numbered (i), (ii), etc. on page 168.

Answering questions: Question 2

What you need to do

Question 2 will always ask you to explain the **purpose** of a source.

How you do it

The best way to approach these questions is a two-step approach.

- First, use details in the source to explain what **message** it is giving out.
- Second, say **why** the author or photographer is putting out this message. The reason why they are doing it is their **purpose**.

Let's practise. Study Source B (cut out from page 174).

What was the purpose of taking and publicising this photo? Use detail from the photograph and your own knowledge to explain your answer.

Step 1 is to ask yourself what is the **message** in the photograph. For example: • What impression of the students does it give – and how does it do this? • What impression of the soldiers does it give – and how does it do this? • What impression of integrated schooling does it give – and how does it do this? (i) Now write a couple of sentences saying what message the photograph gives. Use details in the source to support your answer.	(i) The message this photo gives is that...
Step 2 is to ask yourself why people may have wanted to spread this message. For example, could the message in the photo... • affect views on segregation? • change the policy of schools? • affect views on civil rights? (ii) Now explain why you think people published this photo widely. Use details from the source to support your answer.	(ii) The purpose of taking and publicising this photo could have been to...

ResultsPlus
Top tip

Message
The message of a source is:
- the impression it gives
- what it is trying to say.

For example, does Source B give the impression of:
- secure students or threatened ones?
- safe or unsafe surroundings?
- soldiers who are determined or uncommitted?

Purpose
The purpose of a source is what the author/photographer, etc., was trying to achieve.

For Source B, for example, the people who took the photo or publicised it could have been trying to:
- change people's view of segregation
- change white people's views about black people
- emphasise government commitment to ending segregation.

If you understand the **message** of a source, this gives you a clue to what its **purpose** may have been.

ResultsPlus
Top tip

Note that we have used the key words *message* and *purpose* as signposts for the examiner at the start of the answers to steps (i) and (ii).

The answer

Model answers to these questions are given on page 168.

Answering questions: Question 3

Question 3 will ask you to study three sources and then ask if they support a view **or** agree about [something].

What you need to do

There are two stages to answering these questions. The best answers will:

- firstly, **cross-refer** what the sources say – i.e. compare what they say, to find ways in which they **do** and **do not** support the view stated
- secondly, consider **how convincingly** the sources support the view stated.

Test yourself

Use Sources A, B and C (cut out from pages 174–75). Consider the following question:

> ***Do these sources support the view that integrated schools had to be forced on many areas of the US? Explain your answer, using the sources and your own knowledge.***

Firstly, let's practise **cross-referencing** between the sources.

We have done this below, showing ways in which the sources do not support the view that integration had to be forced on many areas.

> There are some parts of Sources A, B and C which do not support the view that integration had to be forced on many areas. For example, Source C says that at Fayetteville High School there was only one protester who turned up to oppose integration. So it infers that no enforcement was necessary. Indeed, it says that some white students actually supported the only black boy who joined lessons. This tells us that, in this area, integration didn't require force. Sources A and B clearly disagree with Source C on this though. Source A shows that the Supreme Court had to pass a ruling to force desegregation and Source B shows force was needed at Little Rock.

Now, you try. Write a paragraph saying how the sources do support the view that integration had to be forced on many areas of the US.

> (i) There are some parts of Sources A, B and C which do support the view that integration had to be forced on some areas. For example,

An answer like those we've produced so far, which cross-references information in different sources

- to show parts of the sources which **do support** the view
- **AND** show parts of the sources which **do not support** the view

would get a good mark in the exam. However, the best answers go one step further.

ResultsPlus
Top tip

Cross-referencing

Cross-referencing between two or more sources means checking what different sources say about the same thing.

So, if one source says that integration had to be imposed by force, then we can cross-reference this in the other sources. This means we can look to see if they say the same thing – or something different.

Cross-referencing helps you to make judgements.

- If you cross-reference between lots of sources and they all agree about something, this encourages you to believe it.
- If you cross-reference between lots of sources and they disagree, then you may have to be more careful about the judgement you make.

The final step

So far, our answer says **how much** support the sources give.
But sources can only really support the view in question if they are reliable.

Read about **reliability** in the Top tip box on this page.

Now consider the **provenance** and **content** of Sources A, B and C.

We've written our conclusions about the reliability of **Source C** for this question.

Source C is an extract from a web history. We don't know who wrote or published this web site, so we can't tell from its provenance if it might have been biased. However, we can see that the content is very detailed; it gives exact dates, numbers of students, the name of one student, etc. So the source seems well informed, which makes it more reliable. However, the main thing about the content of this source is that it only tells us about one school. This may not have been typical. So it is not a very reliable source of information about whether integration had to be forced on other areas of the US.

Source B is a similar source. So, now you write your conclusions about the reliability of **Source B** for this question. Don't forget to think about its **provenance** and **content**.

(ii) *Source B*

Now write your conclusions about the reliability of **Source A** for this question.

Again, remember to bear in mind its **provenance** and **content**.

(iii) *Source A*

The best candidates will round off this part of their answer with a **conclusion**.

This should be a very short summary of the answer's main points. It could look like this.

Overall, the sources give us very clear and reliable evidence that force had to be used to achieve integration in some areas. However, one source, Source C, shows that force was not needed in all areas. So we are left with the conclusion that integration needed to be enforced in some places but not in others. We can't tell whether force was needed in many areas.

ResultsPlus
Top tip

Reliability
The reliability of a source is how far you can trust what it says about the thing you are studying.
You can test the reliability of a source by looking at its **provenance** and **content**.

Provenance means:

- who wrote or produced it
- where and when
- what kind of source it is
- why it was produced (its *purpose*)

Content includes:

- the language it uses
- signs of exaggeration
- things it includes or leaves out
- how *typical* it is.

Asking these questions about a source will give you ideas about how reliable it is.

Typicality
Typicality is one aspect of the content of a source that affects how much you trust it.

- If information in a source is much the same as the information in other similar sources, then your source is typical. This would encourage you to trust it.
- If information in a source is very different from information in other similar sources then your source is not typical. This might lead you not to trust it.

ResultsPlus
Top tip

Note that we have used key words and phrases such as *'I trust this source to show me'*, *'it is evidence of'*, *'it doesn't tell me'*, and *'in conclusion'* as signposts for the examiner at the start of the answers to steps (i) and (ii).

The answer
Model answers to these questions are given on pages 168–169.

Answering questions: Question 4

What you need to do

Question 4 will always ask you how **useful** sources are as evidence of... [a specified thing] or how **reliable** sources are as evidence of... [a specified thing].

How you do it

The technique for answering this type of question is always the same.

There are two issues to consider.

- Firstly, how much **useful** information do these sources contain?
- Secondly, how **reliable** is that information; how much do you trust it?

Now test yourself

Let's practice. Use Sources D and E (cut out from page 175) to answer this question.

How useful are Sources D and E as evidence of opposition to integration of schools? Explain your answer.

Read the Top tip box about **utility** on this page.

Now write a paragraph to say how much useful and relevant information there is in Sources D and E.

(i) *Sources D and E are useful, because they have relevant information about opposition to integration in the South. For example,...*

However, there is a limit to how useful these sources are. For example, they are not able to tell us...

Check your answer against the model answer on page 169 before you continue.

ResultsPlus
Top tip

Utility
When you are asked about the utility of a source in the examination, you are always asked how useful two sources are as evidence of a particular thing. Always consider the usefulness of the sources in providing evidence of that particular thing.

Be careful to point out the evidence that the source provides **and** the things it doesn't tell us about that particular enquiry.

Notice how, in our answers, we use key phrases such as *'is useful because'*, *'we should be able to trust it because'*, or *'it is of limited use because'* as **signposts** for the examiner.

So far, our answer says **how much** useful information Sources D and E **do** and **don't** give. But this information is only useful if we can **trust** it.

So Step 2 of our answer involves saying whether the useful information is **reliable**.

Assessing their **provenance** and **content** will help you decide how much to trust them.

So, think about the **provenance** of Sources D and E. Write a paragraph saying if this makes you trust the information in these sources about opposition to the integration of schools.

Remember, when we ask if the **provenance** of a source affects how much we *trust* it, we think about: • who wrote/produced it • where and when • what kind of source is it • why was it produced (its *purpose*).	(ii) The information in Sources D and E is only useful if we can trust it. In this case...

Now look at the **content** of sources D and E and then write a paragraph saying whether it makes you trust the information in the sources about opposition to integration.

Remember, when we ask if the **content** of a source affects how much we can *trust* it, we look at: • the language it uses • signs of exaggeration • things it chooses to include and leave out • how *typical* is its content compared to other similar sources.	(iii) The information in Sources D and E is only useful if we can trust it. In this case...

Answers that assess how useful the sources are by setting out:

- how much **useful** and **relevant information** they have
- and how **reliable** this information is

should be rewarded with marks in the top level.

Sometimes Question 4 will ask you only about **reliability**. For example, the question in this spread could have been:
How reliable are Sources D and E as evidence of opposition to the integration of schools? Explain your answer.

In this case, to answer the question you would only need to include those parts of your answer to the question on this page – i.e. parts (ii) and (iii).

The answer

Model answers to these questions are given on page 169.

Answering questions: Question 5

Question 5 will always:

- give you a **statement**
- then ask you ***'How far do the sources support this statement?'***

What you need to do

You should try to use **all the sources** in your answer.

The best answers to these kinds of questions will always look like this.

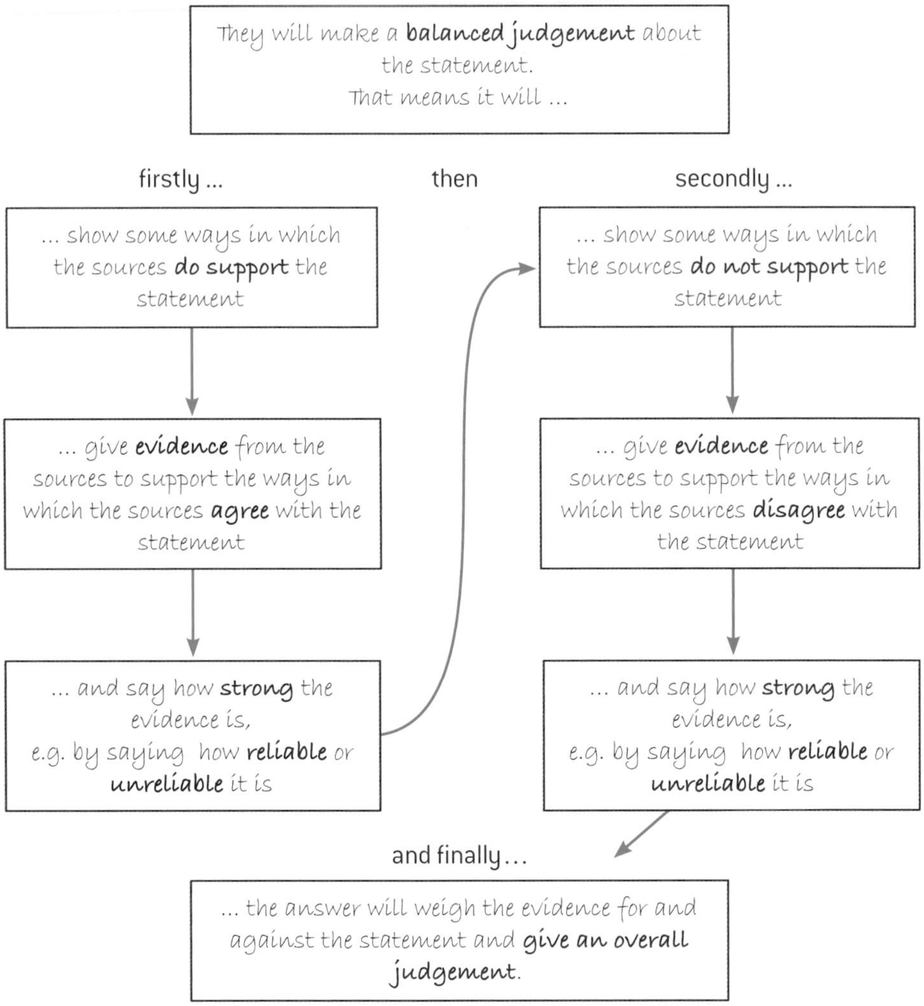

They will make a **balanced judgement** about the statement.
That means it will ...

firstly ...

... show some ways in which the sources **do support** the statement

... give **evidence** from the sources to support the ways in which the sources **agree** with the statement

... and say how **strong** the evidence is, e.g. by saying how **reliable** or **unreliable** it is

then

secondly ...

... show some ways in which the sources **do not support** the statement

... give **evidence** from the sources to support the ways in which the sources **disagree** with the statement

... and say how **strong** the evidence is, e.g. by saying how **reliable** or **unreliable** it is

and finally...

... the answer will weigh the evidence for and against the statement and **give an overall judgement**.

ResultsPlus
Watch out!

Quality of Written Communication
When your answer to Question 5 is marked, the quality of your written communication will always affect your mark.

To get to the top of each level of the mark scheme you have to:

- write effectively
- organise your thoughts coherently
- spell, punctuate and use grammar well.

Test yourself

Use all the sources (cut out from pages 174–75). Consider the following question:

> ***'The Brown v. the Board of Education case led to the successful integration of US schools.' How far do the sources in this paper support this statement?***

On the following page, we have provided an answer to this question. Your task is:

a) to cut out the paragraphs provided and sort them into the correct order
b) to fill in the missing parts of the paragraphs, to show that you understand how each kind of paragraph should be constructed.

Paragraph 1

For example, (i) ____________says that black students were admitted to Fayetteville High School with no trouble, apart from one white woman protester. Source D supports this too, it says (ii) ______________________

____

____

__________. So sometimes the Brown ruling led to integration.

Paragraph 2

In some ways, the sources do support the statement that the Brown v The Board of Education case led to the successful integration of US schools.

Paragraph 3

However, there is also evidence in the sources that shows that the Brown ruling did not integrate US schools.

Paragraph 4

When you look at all the sources, they give evidence both ways. They show the Brown case got things moving, but that Integration happened slowly and with difficulty.

Paragraph 5

I find Source B particularly reliable evidence because (iii) ______________

____

____

____

____.

Paragraph 6

For example, Source E shows integration was slow, because (iv) __________

____

____

____________________. Source B clearly shows us that the Brown ruling was not enough, because the students need an armed guard. The Brown ruling wasn't working on its own.

Paragraph 7

However, I don't find Source D reliable, because he contradicts himself. First, he tells us he would accept 'negro' students in schools; then he says it would 'affect' him if he saw a white girl with a 'negro'. So I think he is mixed up or telling lies. However, I believe Source C more because (v) ______

____

____

____

____

____.

ResultsPlus
Top tip

Remember, when the question says:

'How far do the sources support this statement?'

Your answer looks like this:

Say that in some ways the sources **do support** the statement.
Give the **evidence** using as many sources as you can.
Assess **how strong** that evidence is.

Say that in some ways the sources **do not support** the statement.
Give the **evidence** using as many sources as you can.
Assess **how strong** that evidence is.

Give your **overall** judgement.

The answer

Model answers to these questions are given on page 169.

Answers: War and the transformation of British society, c1903–28

KEY SKILLS FOR USING SOURCES

(i) *It is an aircraft workshop and the workers are all men.*

(ii) *Men went back into their old jobs (or into new ones) after the war. There isn't a single woman in the picture. At least some of these men must have been fighting, so women would have done their jobs.*

(iii) *Women are being trained for work (and will probably find jobs) in 'normal women's trades'.*

(iv) *To convince women the government doesn't want them all to stop working, but they ought to aim to work in the industries the government wants them to work in, not to protest and* demand to work in 'men's' jobs.

(v)
- *Source A says the general view of women was 'as a mother and a wife'.*
- *In Source C Mrs Pazzey is saying single women and widows should be able to carry on working.*
- *In Source F the government says women will be trained for 'normal women's work' and are likely to get jobs.*

(vi)
- *Mrs Pazzey (Source C) doesn't want all women to go on working. She thinks the married ones should stop.*
- *The government (Source D) says training will only be in certain jobs. And they don't say how many jobs are likely to be available.*

(vii) *Source A – not useful*
Source B – useful
Source C – useful
Source D – useful
Source E – not useful
Source F – useful

(viii) *Source A – useful*
Source B – useful
Source C – not useful
Source D – useful
Source E – useful because they are not there
Source F– useful

(ix) *Source A – not useful so not relevant*
Source B – reliable because it shows at least one woman wanted to vote. The women watching seem approving.
Source C – reliable ***only*** *for this woman's views on employment*
Source D – reliable for what happened in employment
Source E – not useful, so not relevant
Source F – reliable for government's attitude to work

(x) *Source A – reliable*
Source B – reliable, shows a change, a woman voting
Source C – not useful, so not relevant
Source D – reliable for what happened in employment
Source E – reliable for what this workshop was like at the time
Source F – reliable for government's attitude to work

QUESTION PAPER

Question 1

(i) *I can infer this because Source A says 'In 1921, women were allowed to work at all levels of the civil service [not just the lower ones]'.*

(ii) *I can learn from Source A that there must have been other successes for women apart from the examples it gives us about 1918, 1919 and 1921.*

Question 2

(i) *The message is of a woman happy to vote. The impression it gives us about her is that she is well-dressed and respectable. She looks like someone who should be trusted to vote. She has happy and well-behaved children. The people behind the ballot box seem happy that she is voting too.*

(ii) *The purpose of taking and publishing this photo could have been to change people's views about women. The photo makes the woman look trustworthy. Perhaps it was meant to persuade people to support votes for women. Perhaps people who used the photo wanted to change other views about women. Perhaps this photo was used to try to persuade people that women should be trusted by society to vote, have jobs and bring up their families at the same time.*

Question 3

(i) *... Source C is a letter saying that married women should give up their jobs and go back to 'clean their houses and look after the man they married and give a mother's care to their children'. Source A says this is what people thought too. It says 'the popular view of the women was still as a mother and wife'. Source A says that the government and trade unions saw women in the old way too. It says they pressed women to give up their jobs. Source B doesn't directly say anything about people's views on women.*

(ii) *Source B is a photo of a woman voting. I trust that what this photo shows is true. There are voting officials there. I don't think they would have let a photographer fake the photo. However, I think the woman was chosen carefully. She looks respectable and trustworthy and gives a good impression of women voting. It might not be typical. There must have been lots of other women who voted who didn't give this impression. And lots of women who didn't want to vote.*

(iii) *Source A is a published book. It should have been researched by the writer and checked by the publishers. This makes what the book says more trustworthy, but the author could have been trying to prove a point of view. The other thing that makes me trust this source is that it is balanced. It puts both points of view across, telling us about women's gains (the vote, MPs, jobs in the civil service) and their losses (being told to give up jobs and being seen again only as mother and wife). So I think this is a balanced, well informed source and I trust what it tells me about the view of women after the war.*

Question 4

(i) *... Source D shows that 35% of all women were working in 1911 but only 34% in 1921, so it shows that the percentage of women working had actually fallen slightly. It also shows us that this was the same situation for single women, married women and divorced or widowed women. Source E supports that view too. Although the Background information says that women worked in factories in the war, this picture of an aircraft factory in 1920 shows no women workers at all.*

However, there is a limit to how useful Sources D and E are. For example, they are not able to tell us what work women were doing. We know that about a third of all women worked in 1921, but Sources D and E can't tell us what jobs they did.

(ii) *... the employment figures in Source D come from the official census returns. This should make them quite accurate and reliable. We don't know who produced the photograph of the Vickers factory in Source E however or why it was produced. All the women in the picture could have been moved out of shot for some reason. Because we don't know its provenance, we can't be sure we can trust this photo.*

(iii) *... the content of Source D is very thorough. But, it only compares 1911 with 1921. These years may not be typical of what was happening before and after the war. We don't know the photo in Source E is typical . Lots of women could have worked in other factories – even other aircraft factories. So the photo may be useful for what was happening at Vickers, but not in all factories.*

Question 5

The correct order for the paragraphs is:
2, 1, 7, 3, 6, 5, 4

The missing words are:

(i) *Source A*

(ii) *put them out [of their jobs] and send them home to clean their house and look after the man they married*

(iii) *women gained the vote in 1918 and the first woman MP was elected in 1919*

(iv) *if there were no women staying in their jobs, there would have been no problem for this woman to write to the newspapers about*

(v) *a post-war factory with no women workers*

Answers: War and the transformation of British society, c1931–51

KEY SKILLS FOR USING SOURCES

(i) *This unemployed man's benefit stopped after the Means Test, but he appealed and now gets 10s. He doesn't mind the Means Test visits too much.*

(ii) *He might be feeling better about the Means Test because his appeal worked. Also, he only says the Means Tests visits aren't as bad as the interviews that went before – he's not saying they are a good thing.*

(iii) *It is a big protest, there are lots of people, but they are orderly, marching and not fighting with the police. Quite a few people are lining the street as they pass.*

(iv) *Its purpose is to show a lot of people are angry about the Means Test. The focus on the banner you can read (which calls the Means Test 'mass murder') suggests they want people to see the Means Test as unfair.*

(v)
- *In Sources C and E, there are all kinds of different people marching. And they are marching on a hunger march that was against the 10% cut in benefit and the Means Test so they both support this idea.*
- *In Source D, you can infer the man thought the Means Test made things worse, and it does show that there were unemployed people who didn't support the Means Test.*

(vi)
- *In Source D, you only get evidence about the unemployed.*
- *In Source C, you don't get to see many of the marchers and most of them are the better-off students.*

(vii) *Source A – not useful*

Source B –useful

Source C – useful

Source D – not useful

Source E – useful

Source F – not useful

(viii) *Source A – not useful*

Source B – useful

Source C – useful if you assume the opposition is because the Means Test penalises

Source D – useful

Source E – useful

Source F – useful

(ix) *Source A – not useful so not relevant*

Source B – not reliable, clearly biased against the Means Test

Source C – reliable for the fact there was opposition in Oxford and Lancashire

Source D – not useful, so not relevant

Source E – reliable for scale of opposition and people from Edinburgh

Source F – not useful, so not relevant.

(x) *Source A – not useful, so not relevant*

Source B – not reliable, clearly biased against the Means Test

Source C – reliable in that it shows these people thought so

Source D – reliable because he's unemployed and clearly feels penalised

Source E – reliable in that it shows these people thought so

Source F – reliable in that it shows there is some possibility of appeal and so on.

QUESTION PAPER

Question 1

(i) *I can infer this because Source A says 'the present crisis in government finances'. You only use the word 'crisis' when things get very bad.*

(ii) *I can learn from Source A that the government was very worried about the cost of benefit payments by 1931 and wanted to lower it to cut their spending.*

Question 2

(i) *The message this book gives is that the Means Test made people suffer. It does this by using language like 'strictly enforced' and 'the most cruel and evil effect'. It tells us about a man accused of having a job when he fed his neighbour's chickens and a person who had their dole cut because they had their old father live with them. The message is it's unfair.*

(ii) *The purpose of the book was to spread left wing political and social ideas. We know this because the source caption tells us. However, one particular purpose could have been to attack the Means Test. I think this because it calls it 'cruel and evil', which makes me think they wanted it abolished or changed.*

Question 3

(i) *... in Source A, the authors of the report for the government say 'We recommend all those claiming benefit should be means tested'. And the report goes on 'all should be means tested, not just the special groups suggested by the government'. So the government suggested limited means testing and the report said they needed to test everyone. The person who reported the chicken feeder (Source B) must have supported the Means Test to have reported him.*

(ii) *Its content is very detailed (e.g. the stories about the chicken feeder and the old age pensioner). So it was clearly well researched. However, looking at its provenance, a group called the Left Book Club (which supported left-wing ideas) asked for the book to be written. I think what the author wrote was probably true, but he chose the things he included to support his point of view. This makes it less reliable as a source for the whole picture.*

(iii) *The caption says it's a newspaper photograph, so this makes me believe it was a real march with real protesters, not a posed or fake photo. The caption says they were marching against the Means Test, which fits with the words on the banner. However, the views about the Means Test shown here may not have been typical of many people. There are only about a dozen marchers shown. So I think this source is reliable for proving there was opposition, but it can't show us how widespread it was.*

Question 4

(i) *Source E shows hundreds of protesters against the Means Test. It also shows us how varied opposition was, with men and women of different classes (from the clothes). It also shows that opposition came from all over the country (one banner says Edinburgh). And it shows strong opposition; one banner calls the Means Test 'mass murder'.*

However, there is a limit to how useful the sources are. For example, Source E can't tell us WHY people opposed the Means Test. Source D does this. The skilled worker has had his benefit cut. He says that because of the Means Test his family can't afford new clothes or shoes.

(ii) *Source E is a newspaper photograph. The paper may have opposed the Means Test, so it could have picked a photo that stressed how big the opposition was. But we know there were at least that many. Source D might be exaggerated, and may not be reliable for the Means Test generally, but it tells us clearly about this person's experience of (and feelings about) the Means Test.*

(iii) *The photographer could have focused on a bit of the march to make it look crowded; they chose a shot of a woman, arm raised, cheering on the marchers; they chose to show the emotive words 'mass murder – smash it'. All this makes me think they opposed the Means Test and used the photo to exaggerate public opposition to it. The content of Source D makes me think we should be careful about trusting it too. After all, Source D tells us about only one family. Their story may not have been typical.*

Question 5

The correct order for the paragraphs is:
2, 1, 7, 3, 6, 5, 4

The missing words are:

(i) *Sources C and E*

(ii) *one man lost his benefit for feeding his neighbours chickens and another family lost benefit for taking in an aged relative.*

(iii) *'we recommend all those claiming benefit should be means tested'*

(iv) *special groups*

(v) *when he appealed his benefit went up and he says 'I don't mind the visits from the Public Assistance Officer'.*

(vi) *it only tells us about one family; this may not be typical. And the person speaking seems to have a grudge, so I don't' trust him. The man in Source F has a more balanced view; I trust him more than Source D.*

Answers:
A divided union? The USA 1945–70

KEY SKILLS FOR USING SOURCES

(i) *They are protesting against school segregation because that is what their placards say.*

(ii) *This was a well organised protest because their placards have been printed – at least four of the placards the adults are carrying are exactly the same.*

(iii) *It is not a big protest, we can only see six adults and one child, and it is not a riot – they are all well-dressed and peaceful.*

(iv) *To show people that the civil rights protestors were respectable and peaceful people.*

(v)
- *In Source C there were rumours there would be trouble, and a reporter came along because he expected there would be violence.*
- *In Source D you can infer there was opposition otherwise there would be no point in having the interview and asking those questions.*

(vi)
- *In Source C white students supported the entry of Preston Lackey.*
- *In Source D the white president of the student body said he thought negro students should come to the school.*

(vii) *Source A – useful*

Source B – only useful if we infer they were so against segregation they would put up with the danger.

Source C – useful

Source D – not useful

Source E – useful

(viii) *Source A – not useful*

Source B – useful

Source C – useful

Source D – not useful

Source E – not useful

(ix) *Source A – reliable, black people took the cases to the court and this is the court record*

Source B – probably reliable, unless this photo was a set-up

Source C – it might be biased and trying to say there wasn't much trouble, with the bit about the white students helping and one 'lone' white woman protesting

Source D – not useful, so not relevant

Source E – reliable for the things we can see – probably reliable that this was a peaceful protest

(x) *Source A –not useful, so not relevant*

Source B – reliable because troops were sent in and we can infer this only happened because there was the possibility of violence

Source C – reliable, because it admits there was the expectation of violence even though it tries to play this down

Source D – not useful, so not relevant

Source E – not useful, so not relevant

QUESTION PAPER

Question 1

(i) *I can infer this because Source A only refers to schools. It says 'separate but equal has no place in state education' and 'separate educational facilities are unequal'.*

(ii) *I can learn from Source A that the plaintiffs in the Brown v Board of Education case were black people.*

Question 2

(i) *The message this photo gives is that the protection given to the students is very strong, because the source shows about a dozen soldiers armed with rifles for just seven students. It also gives the message that the students are well-dressed, normal looking kids, who shouldn't have to be guarded just to go to school.*

(ii) *The purpose of taking and publicising this photo could have been to support integration. The photographer has shown the students as respectable; perhaps he wanted to persuade people that integration was fair and safe. He has also shown the soldiers as very determined. So perhaps he wanted to convince people that integration was going to happen no matter what opposition there was.*

Question 3

(i) *... Source A is a Supreme Court ruling forcing segregated schools to desegregate. Source B shows seven black students with about a dozen armed soldiers protecting them. Source C gives a different impression though. It shows an area where integration went smoothly. Even then, it says the press turned up expecting trouble.*

(ii) *Source B is a photo used in the press. It supports the view that integration had to be forced on some areas, because it shows soldiers escorting black students to their car. The contents of the photo could be selected for their impact though. So the source could be biased. For example the photo emphasises the use of force by showing stern soldiers, with metal helmets and rifles.*

However, the biggest problem with this source as support for the view that integration was forced is that it only shows one school. We don't know if this was typical. So we don't know whether integration had to be forced in many areas.

(iii) *Source A is part of the Supreme Court summing up at the end of the Brown case. It's provenances is clear. It is an official record showing the courts using a legal ruling to force segregated schools to integrate. Its content is clear too. It is a very reliable source for showing that integration had to be forced on some schools.*

Question 4

(i) *... Source D shows us that some white people were allowing integration. The student said he wouldn't oppose integration because 'If it's a court order we have to follow it'. But Source E suggests that there was still opposition. It is from 1963, long after the Brown ruling. But the protesters want the end of segregation, so there must have been places where opposition stopped integration.*

However, there is a limit to how useful these sources are. For example, they are not able to tell us how much opposition there was, or how many schools integrated and how many didn't.

(ii) *Source D is an interview with a white student at Little Rock High. Considering all the controversy about integration at that school, he might not want to say that he's against integration. So the provenance of this source makes me suspicious about how useful this information is. Source E is a photo which was used in the press. This means it was unlikely to have been a fake photo – the protest must really have happened. This makes it more reliable evidence that there was still segregation for them to protest about.*

(iii) *... the content of Source D makes me suspicious about how reliable it is as evidence of opposition to integration in general. At one point, he says he has no black friends and would feel funny about seeing a white girl with a 'negro'. But he also says he wouldn't oppose integration. I'm not sure I believe him. So it isn't reliable, but it shows how that student feels about integration. Source E shows people protesting about segregation in 1963. So there were some areas holding out against integration. However, we don't know how typical Missouri was, so can't use Source E to generalise.*

Question 5

The correct order for the paragraphs is:
2, 1, 7, 3, 6, 5, 4

The missing words are:

(i) *Source C*

(ii) *the white student president at Little Rock said about integration, 'If it's a court order, we have to follow it'.*

(iii) *they would not have needed so many heavily armed guards unless there was serious opposition to the Brown ruling. Also Sources E and F support Source B.*

(iv) *people are protesting against segregation in Missouri in 1963, ten years after the Brown ruling.*

(v) *it gives exact dates and numbers of students. And when it says there was little opposition, this fits with the caption of the source which says that the state supported integration. So I think this is reliable evidence.*

Background information

Before the First World War, women could not vote. They were expected to marry and have children, then to stay at home and care for the family and home. Many jobs, such as mining, were seen as unsuitable for women. In some jobs, such as teaching, women had to leave if they married. Most working women were household servants. The First World War meant women had to do all the jobs men had done before they went to war and make ammunition, etc., for the war. Between 1914 and 1918, an estimated two million women took over men's jobs. They showed they could do these jobs.

So did the position of women change after the First Word War?

Source A: *From The Women's Suffrage Movement in Britain, 1866–1928, by Sophie A van Wingerden in 1999.*

> The early 1920s seemed to give women a string of successes. In 1918, they got the vote. In 1919, the first woman took her seat in the House of Commons. In 1921, women were allowed to work at all levels of the civil service [not just the lower ones]. ... But women's war work had not brought down the barriers. No sooner was the war won than the government and trades unions were pressing women to give up their jobs to returning soldiers. The popular view of the woman was still as a mother and wife.

Source B: *A photograph of a young mother (she must have been over 30) voting in the 1918 election. It was widely published in news reports on women voting in their first election.*

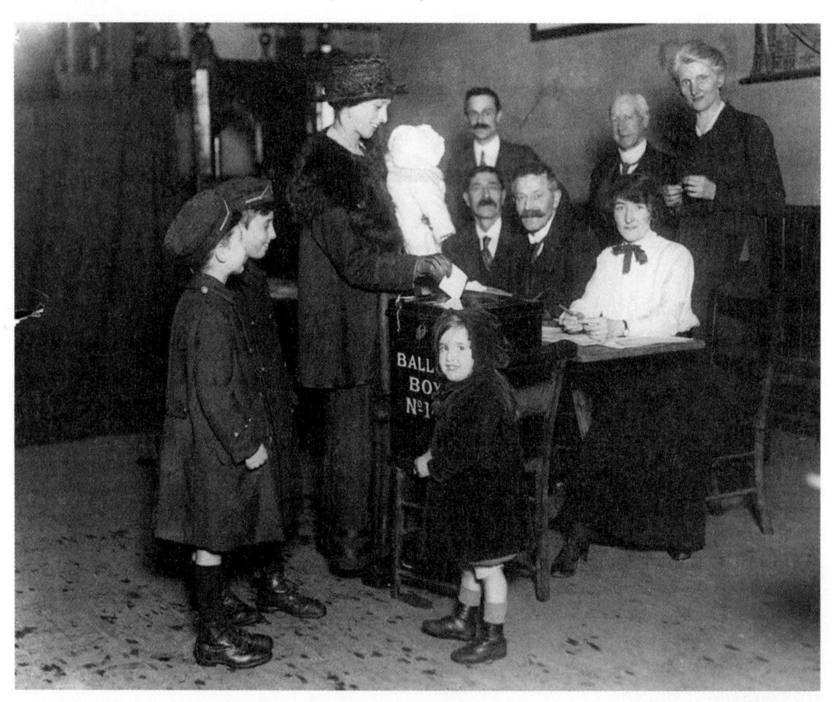

Source C: *From a letter written to the* Daily Herald *newspaper by Isobel Pazzey in October 1919. It was one of a series of letters about married women continuing to work after the war.*

> No decent man would allow his wife to work, and no decent woman would do it if she knew the harm she was doing to the widows and single girls who are looking for work. Put the married women out [of their jobs], send them home to clean their houses and look after the man they married and give a mother's care to their children. Give the single women and widows the work.

Source D: *Employment statistics for 1911 and 1921, taken from the census returns for those years.*

Year	% of single women working	% of married women working	% of divorced and widowed women working	% of all women working
1911	69	10	29	35
1921	68	9	26	34

Source E: *A photograph of one of the workshops in the Vickers aircraft factory, Crayford, in 1920.*

Source F: *From a statement by the government Ministry of Labour about the training it would provide for women in industry, issued March 1919.*

Industrial training will for the present be limited to normal women's trades, for example clothing manufacture, in work know as 'women's processes' before the war. There is a need for skilled workers in these industries and a good prospect of employment.

Background information

Unemployment in Britain rose from 1.5 million in 1929 to 3.3 million in 1931. The cost of basic government unemployment benefit payments ('the dole') rose sharply. But the government was desperate to save money and make spending cuts, not spend more money. So, in November 1931, it cut the dole by 10% and introduced a household Means Test. Officials visited the home of anyone wanting to claim benefit. They used the income and savings of **everyone** in the home to work out if the person claiming really was 'in need'. They were expected to use their savings and sell everything of value (even their home if they owned it) before getting benefit.

So what were reactions to the Means Test?

Source A: *From a report made for the government on how to make spending cuts, published in May 1931.*

> Benefit payments in 1930 cost the government about seven times what they cost in 1911. Under the difficult economic conditions since the war, this increased cost has been the main cause of the present crisis in government finances. The Transitional Benefits Scheme [cutting the dole, introducing a 'means test'] would reduce payments from the expected £44 million to £34 million. We recommend all those claiming benefit should be means tested, not just the special groups suggested by the government.

Source B: *From* The Road to Wigan Pier, *by George Orwell, published in 1937. Orwell was asked to write the book by the Left Book Club, set up to spread left-wing ideas (for a more equal society, social reform, etc).*

> The Means Test is very strictly enforced. One man I knew was seen feeding his neighbour's chickens while the neighbour was away. It was reported to the authorities that he 'had a job feeding chickens'. He had great difficulty disproving this. The most cruel and evil effect of the Means Test is the way in which it breaks up families. An old age pensioner, if a widower, would normally live with one of his children. Under the Means Test, however, he counts as a 'lodger' and his child's dole will be docked by the 10s of his pension.

Source C: *A newspaper photograph of Oxford University students walking through Oxford with Lancashire marchers taking part in a national hunger march to London in 1932, protesting against the Means Test and the 10% cut in benefits.*

Source D: *From a 1934 interview with an unemployed skilled worker for* The Listener, *a magazine published by the BBC. Those interviewed were sent a list of questions, including what benefits they were receiving and how they felt about the future. There were not asked specifically about the Means Test.*

It was very difficult for us to manage after the Means Test. It was bad enough before, but 17s. a week, when we pay 8s. 6d for rent, is precious little for three people who have only just been getting by for over a year. It means reducing your living still more when you are already at your wit's end to know how to mend your shirts any more or get a new pair of shoes. We have none of us had new shoes since I lost my job.

Source E: *A newspaper photograph of some of the marchers on the national hunger march to London in 1932. The marchers were protesting against the Means Test and the 10% cut in benefits.*

Source F: *From a 1934 interview with an unemployed skilled worker for* The Listener, *a magazine published by the BBC. Those interviewed were sent a list of questions, including what benefits they were receiving and how they felt about the future. There were not asked specifically about the Means Test.*

At first, after the Means Test came in, my benefit stopped. I have appealed and now get 10s. a week, because my wife works. I don't mind the visits from the Public Assistance Officer. The Means Test is just one of the many evils of unemployment. Previously, you were questioned at the local Labour Exchange and by the end of it everyone in the room knew as much about me as the official. At least now the investigation takes place in my own home and takes only half an hour, against three or four in a crowded waiting room.

Background information

Under the 14th Amendment of the US Constitution, black people were full US citizens with the same rights as white people. In fact, they were often discriminated against. Many Southern states passed laws enforcing segregation. Black civil rights groups, such as the NAACP, opposed segregation laws, including going to court to get them overturned. The 1896 case of *Plessy v. Ferguson* said states could segregate schools and other facilities, such as transport and hospitals, as long as the provision was 'separate but equal'. This made it harder to win a court case against segregation. The NAACP kept trying. In 1954, they won the case of *Brown v. the Board of Education*. The Supreme Court ruled school segregation illegal.

So did winning the court case lead to the successful integration of schools?

Source A: *Part of the Supreme Court summing up in the case of* Brown v. the Board of Education, *17 May 1954.*

> We conclude that the idea of 'separate but equal' has no place in state education. Separate educational facilities are inherently unequal. Therefore, we hold that the plaintiffs [the people who brought the court case to desegregate] are, by reason of the segregation complained of, deprived of the equal protection of the law guaranteed by the Fourteenth Amendment.

Source B: *A photograph, widely used in the press of black students at Central High School, Little Rock, Arkansas, leaving school in 1957. The US president had to send in a federal army division to replace the state troops to give them an armed escort to and from classes.*

Source C: *From an article on school integration in a web history of Arkansas, a southern state that had anti-segregation laws before* Brown v. the Board of Education. *Four days after the* Brown *ruling, the state began making plans for integration.*

On September 10 1954, five black students entered Fayetteville High School. A few days later, two more black students entered the school, bringing the total to seven. The only male black student to enrol in classes on September 10, Preston Lackey, entered with the support of white students who had heard rumours of planned violence. Similarly, an Associated Press reporter came prepared to report on violent protests. The only opposition was a lone white woman with a placard.

Source D: *From an interview with the president of the student body at Central High School Little Rock, 17 September 1957. He was white.*

Q: Speaking personally, would you let the Negro students come to school?
A: Sir, it's the law. We are going to have to face it sometime.
Q: Are you opposed to integration?
A: If it's a court order we have to follow it.
Q: Do you have any Negro friends?
A: No, sir.
Q: Would it affect you if you saw a white girl dating a Negro?
A: I believe it would.
Q: Why?
A: I don't know. I was just brought up that way.

Source E: *A newspaper photograph showing a civil rights protest in St. Louis, Missouri, 1963.*

Source F: *From an interview in 1992 with Spottswood Thomas Bolling Jr, one of the students in the* Brown *case. He was one of over 3,000 black students who started attending 165 previously 'white only' schools in Washington D.C. on September 14 1954.*

Of course we knew, even as children, the importance of the court cases [brought by the NAACP and other groups against segregation laws]. Every case brought to court was reviewed by the NAACP to see if there was a chance that the case would be successful. There was a lot of pressure on the families and especially on the students. I was expected to be perfect, and there's no such thing as a perfect child. I had to always be on my best behaviour.

Published by Pearson Education Limited, a company incorporated in England and Wales, having its registered office at Edinburgh Gate, Harlow, Essex, CM20 2JE. Registered company number: 872828

www.pearsonschoolsandfecolleges.co.uk

Edexcel is a registered trademark of Edexcel Limited

First published 2010

14 13 12
10 9 8 7 6 5 4 3 2

British Library Cataloguing in Publication Data

A catalogue record for this book is available from the British Library.

ISBN 978 1 84690 587 2

Produced by Paul & Jane Shuter Ltd for Pearson Education Limited

Edited by Jane Anson and Ag MacKeith

Typeset by AMR Design Ltd (www.amrdesign.com)

Illustrated by AMR Design Ltd

Picture research by Thelma Gilbert

Printed in Malaysia, KHL-CTP

Acknowledgements
We would like to thank Nigel Kelly for his invaluable help in the development of this book.

Exam paper excerpts are reproduced by kind permission of Edexcel.

The author and publisher would like to thank the following individuals and organisations for permission to reproduce photographs:

Corbis pp 170, 171, 175; Getty Images/Hulton Archive p173; Topfoto pp 172, 174

Details of written sources:
p64, John Child, *History A: The Making of the Modern World: Germany 1918-39*, Edexcel, 2009; p.84: Jane Shuter, *The Making of the Modern World, Russia 1917–39*, Edexcel, Pearson Education Limited, 2009; p.104: Jane Shuter, *The USA 1919–41,* Edexcel, Pearson Education Limited, 2009; p.170: A – Sophie A van Wingerden, *The Women's Suffrage Movement in Britain, 1866-1928*, Palgrave McMillan; C – www.bbc.co.uk/history/british/britain_wwone/women_employment_01.shtmlWeb history 1.3.2003; D – A H Halsey, *British Social Trends since 1900*, A H Halsey, McMillan Press, 1988; p.171: F – Deborah Thom, *Nice Girls and Rude Girls: women workers in World War I*, I B Taurus, 1998; p.172: A – Rex Pope, Alan Pratt and Bernard Hoyle, *Social Welfare in Britain, 1885-1985*, by. Routledge & Keegan Paul, London, 1986; George Orwell, *The Road to Wigan Pier*, Victor Gollancz, 1937; p.173: D and F – R S Lambert & H L Beales, *Memoirs of the Unemployed*, Victor Gollancz, London, 1934; p.174: A – www.archives.gov/education/lessons/brown-v-board/; p.175: C – www.encyclopediaofarkansas.net/encyclopedia/entry-detail.aspx?entryID=5278; D – http://mediarichlearning.com/pg/pw/tg/down/1957-0915_arkansas_gazette_interview.pdf; F – Belinda Rochelle, *Witnesses to Freedom*, Puffin, New York, 1997

Every effort has been made to contact copyright holders of material reproduced in this book. Any omissions will be rectified in subsequent printings if notice is given to the publishers.